William Henry Giles Kingston

Captain Cook

His Life, Voyages, and Discoveries

William Henry Giles Kingston

Captain Cook
His Life, Voyages, and Discoveries

ISBN/EAN: 9783744793247

Printed in Europe, USA, Canada, Australia, Japan

Cover: Foto ©Andreas Hilbeck / pixelio.de

More available books at **www.hansebooks.com**

THE DEATH OF CAPTAIN COOK.
From the picture published in 1785, by J. Bartolozzi, R.A.

HIS

LIFE, VOYAGES, AND DISCOVERIES.

BY

WILLIAM H. G. KINGSTON,

AUTHOR OF
"LITTLE BEN HADDEN," "THE STORY OF A SUPERCARGO," ETC.

THE RELIGIOUS TRACT SOCIETY;
56, PATERNOSTER ROW; 65, ST. PAUL'S CHURCHYARD;
AND 164, PICCADILLY.

CONTENTS.

CHAPTER I.

EARLY TRAINING. 13

Parentage—Birth—School-days and Apprenticeship—Friendship of Captain Palliser—Appointment to the *Mercury*—Siege of Quebec—Narrow escape from Indians—Becomes Master on board the *Northumberland*—Marriage.

CHAPTER II.

FIRST VOYAGE OF DISCOVERY, 1768—1771. . . . 21

Voyages of Wallis and Carteret—Expedition to observe the Transit of Venus—Cook becomes Commander of the *Endeavour*—Madeira—Rio de Janeiro—Dangers at Cape Horn—Society Islands—Arrival at Otaheite—Rules to be observed in intercourse with Natives—Thieves in Tahiti—The astronomical instruments set up—Fresh Difficulties—Character of the Tahitians—Tupia—Etuas—Temples and Burial-places—Natural Productions—Houses and mode of cooking—Canoes—Fishing—Leave Tahiti—Huaheine, Ulietea, and Oheteroa—Arrival at New Zealand—Attempts to open up intercourse at Poverty Bay—Botanizing—Food of Natives—Pahs—Productions of New Zealand—Bay of Islands—Cannibalism—Middle Island—Mount Egmont—Discovery of New South Wales—First Landing-place, Botany Bay—The *Endeavour* in danger—The Kangaroo and Opossum—Plants, Trees, and Turtle—A Dangerous Reef—New Guinea—Results of the Voyage—Hard Terms at Savu—Java—Deaths at Batavia—St. Helena—Return, and Arrival in London.

CHAPTER III.

SECOND VOYAGE OF DISCOVERY, 1772—1775 131

Search for the great Southern continent—Cook appointed—Sailing of the *Resolution* and *Adventure*—Loss of Live Stock through Cold—Among the Icebergs—Auroral Lights—New Zealand again—Waterspouts—More Thieves and Quarrels—Omai taken on board—Arrival at Ulietea again—Plays—Human Sacrifices—The Tonga or Friendly Islands—Visit and Offerings to the Etuas—A great Chief—Canoe-building—Leave Tongatabu—Separation of the *Adventure* and *Resolution*—Animals put ashore for stocking—New Zealanders—Among the Ice again—Easter Island—Wonderful Statues—Marquesas Islands—Return to Tahiti—Warriors and War Canoes—Huaheine—Ulietea—Tonga Group—Mallicollo—Sandwich Islands—Fight with the Natives—Erromanga—John Williams—Tanna—New Caledonia and its Natives—Terra del Fuego—Among the Sea-Lions and Seals—Sandwich Land—Health of the Crew—Home again.

CHAPTER IV.

THIRD VOYAGE OF DISCOVERY, 1776—1778 234

Honours conferred on Cook—Omai's Reception in England—"The Northwest Passage"—Cook offers to head the Expedition—The *Resolution* and *Discovery* fitted out—Delays—Van Diemen's Land—New Zealand revisited—Native Ferocity and Ignorance—Mangaia—Feenou—Native Entertainments—The King of the Friendly Isles—Plots against the Expedition—Toobouai—Tahiti revisited—Misconduct and End of Omai—What may be made of an old Anchor—Cannibalism—Captain Vancouver—Nootka Sound—Behring's Straits—The North-west Passage attempted—Return to the Sandwich Islands—Legend of Rono—Difficulties with the Natives—Death of Captain Cook—His Character and Achievements—Captain Clerke succeeds to the Command—Sail northward again—Russian Hospitality—Arctic Exploration resumed—Death of Captain Clerke—Return.

CHAPTER V.

SUBSEQUENT HISTORY OF POLYNESIA 311

Missionary Work in the Pacific—The good ship *Duff*—Tahiti—Failure of the Marquesan Mission—Pomare—Dark clouds in Tahiti—The Huaheine Mission—Borabora—Raiatea—Aitutaki—Rarotonga—Savage Island—Missions in the Fiji Islands—Death of John Williams—Samoa—Loyalty Group—Sandwich Islands—Tabular Statement.

LIST OF ILLUSTRATIONS.

	PAGE
Map of Polynesia	10
Quebec	16
Bay of Funchal, Madeira	25
Rio Janeiro	28
Cook's arrival at Otaheite, or Tahiti	32
Bread-fruit	33
Coral Island in the South Seas	39
A Mystery Man's Hut	45
The Cacao, or Cocoa	49
Cocoa-nut Palm	50
Huaheine, Society Islands	59
Patoo-patoo	73
New Zealand Pah	81
War Clubs and Adze made by New Zealanders	83
A Carved Coffer in New Zealand Work	83
Bay of Islands	87
First Landing-Place in Australia at Botany Bay	95
The Endeavour laid up on Shore for Repairs	100
The Kangaroo	102
Chlamydosaurus, or Frilled Lizard of New Holland	107
Driving on to a Coral Reef	111
Ornithorhynchus Paradoxus of Australia	116
Batavia from the Sea	121
St. Helena, showing the Ladder up to the Fort	125

List of Illustrations.

	PAGE
HARBOUR OF PANGO PANGO, TUTUILA	139
HIGH-PROWED DOUBLE CANOE OF TAHITI	131
GREAT PATAGONIAN PENGUIN	137
ICE-BOUND	138
AURORAL LIGHTS	140
WATERSPOUT	145
NATIVE DRUM—MODE OF PLAYING	156
DOUBLE CANOE	165
CANOE BUILDING	167
NEW ZEALANDERS	173
MARQUESAS ISLANDER	181
VALLEY OF AKAOUI, MARQUESAS ISLANDS	185
CORAL ISLAND, NAMED WHITSUNDAY ISLAND, IN THE PACIFIC OCEAN	189
POLYNESIAN SCENE	196
CRATER OF KILANEA, SANDWICH ISLANDS	199
ATTACKED BY THE SAVAGES	204
NATIVE HUT, EXTERIOR	214
NATIVE HUT, INTERIOR	214
CABBAGE PALM	216
NATIVES OF TERRA DEL FUEGO	220
CAPE TOWN, TABLE BAY, AND MOUNTAIN	227
ISLAND OF ASCENSION	231
AUSTRALIAN BOWER BIRD	233
NEW ZEALAND IDOL	249
AXE LEFT BY COOK AT MANGAIA	251
A STORM IN THE FOREST	262
TROPICAL VEGETATION	268
THE ALBATROSS	280
KARAKAKOOA BAY, OWHYHEE	289
DIAMOND HEAD CRATER, HONOLULU, OWHYHEE	291
PORTRAIT OF CAPTAIN COOK	299
AMONG THE ICEBERGS	307
TITIKAUEKA CHAPEL, RARATONGA	329
MISSIONARY CHURCH IN THE FIJI ISLANDS	333
HOUSE AT RAROTONGA OCCUPIED BY THE MISSIONARY WILLIAMS	344

b

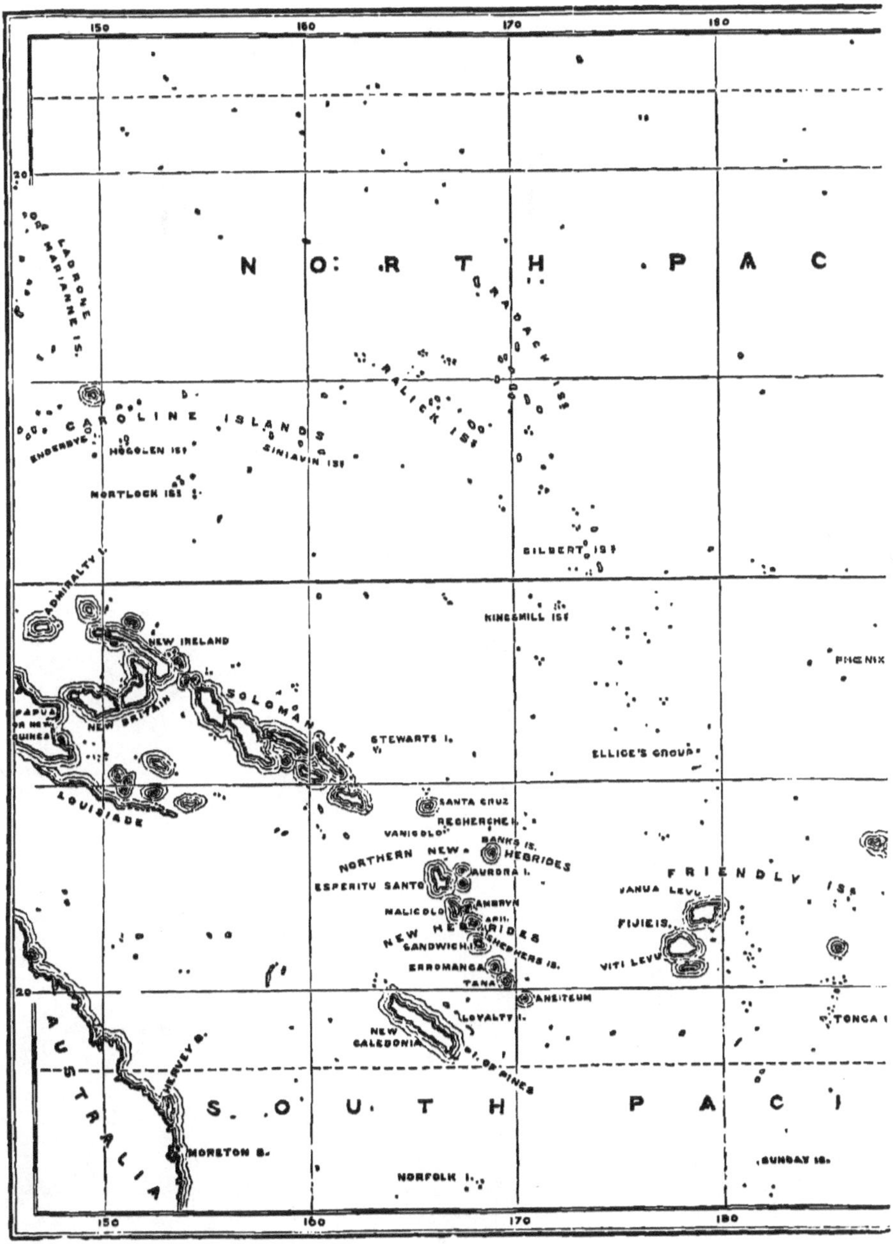
150
160
170
180
20
N O R T H P A C
LADRONE
MARIANNE IS.
RADACK ISS
RALICK ISS
CAROLINE ISLANDS
ENDERBYE
HOGOLEN ISS
SINIAVIN ISS
NORTLOCK ISS
GILBERT ISS
ADMIRALTY I.
NEW IRELAND
KINGSMILL ISS
PHŒNIX
PAPUA OR NEW GUINEA
NEW BRITAIN
SOLOMAN ISS
STEWARTS I.
ELLICE'S GROUP
LOUISIADE
SANTA CRUZ
RECHERCHE I.
VANICOLO
BANKS IS.
NORTHERN NEW HEBRIDES
AURORA I.
ESPERITU SANTO
FRIENDLY ISS
VANUA LEVU
MALICOLO
AMBRYN
FIJI IS.
NEW HEBRIDES
SANDWICH I.
SHEPHERS IS.
VITI LEVU
ERROMANGA
TANA
ANEITEUM
TONGA I
LOYALTY I.
NEW CALEDONIA
I. OF PINES
AUSTRALIA
HERVEY B.
S. O U T H P A C I
MORETON B.
SUNDAY IS.
NORFOLK I.

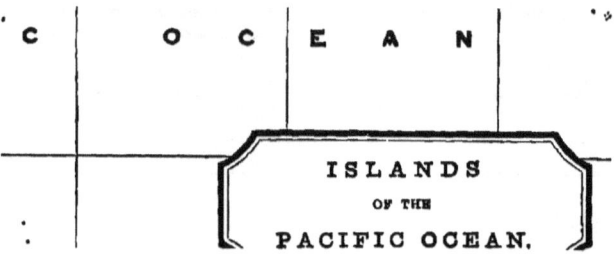

ISLANDS
OF THE
PACIFIC OCEAN.

Life and Voyages of Captain Cook.

CHAPTER I.

EARLY TRAINING.

AMONG all those Englishmen who, from a humble origin, have risen to an honourable position, Captain James Cook is especially worthy of record. His parents were of the peasant class—his father having commenced life as a farm-labourer, and his mother being a cottager's daughter. Probably, however, they were both superior to others of the same station, as the husband, in process of time, became farm-bailiff to his employer—a Mr. Thomas Skottowe. This was about the year 1730, and the farm of which he had the management was called Airy-Holme, near Ayton, in Yorkshire. Not far from this place, at the village of Marton, near Stockton-upon-Tees, his son James was born, on the 27th of October, 1728. James was one of nine children, all of whom he survived, with the exception of a sister who married a fisherman at Redcar.

The father of this family spent the latter years of his life with his daughter at Redcar, and was supposed to have been about eighty-five years old at the time of his death, so that he must have had the satisfaction of seeing his son rising in his profession; though probably he little thought of that son as establishing a fame which would be handed down in history.

James Cook does not appear to have enjoyed any peculiar educational advantages: but owed his subsequent advancement chiefly to his own intelligence, perseverance, and diligence. He first went to a village school, and was afterwards sent, at the expense of Mr. Skottowe to an ordinary commercial school kept by a Mr. Pullen. He continued there four years, and was then apprenticed to Mr. William Sanderson, a grocer and haberdasher at the fishing town of Straiths, ten miles from Whitby. It may be supposed that the occupation in which he was engaged was not suited to his taste. The sea was constantly before his eyes, and the desire to seek his fortune on it sprang up within him, and grew stronger and stronger till in about a year after he went to Straiths he obtained a release from his engagement with Mr. Sanderson, and apprenticed himself to Messrs. Walker and Co., shipowners of Whitby. He went to sea for the first time when he was about eighteen, on board one of their vessels—the *Truelove** collier, of 450 tons burden, trading between Newcastle and London. The lad soon showed that he was well fitted for his new profession, and in 1748, not two years after he had commenced it, we find him especially directed to assist in fitting for sea the *Three Brothers*, a new ship of six hundred tons. While he served on board this ship she was hired by Government as a transport; and on her being paid off she was employed in the Norway trade.

After making several voyages in the *Three Brothers* up the Baltic, young Cook was promoted to the rank of mate on board the *Friendship*. He had by this time gained the good will of

* In the biographies of Cook the name of the vessel in which he first went to sea is given as the *Freelove*—evidently a misprint. I have never known a vessel of that name, whereas the *Truelove* is a favourite name.

his employers and had made several other friends on shore, who, before long, were enabled to render him essential service. He was now known as a thorough seaman; indeed, from the moment he went on board ship, he had steadily applied his mind to acquiring a knowledge of his profession. Still he served on as mate of the *Friendship* till the breaking out of the war between England and France in 1756, when he made up his mind to push his fortunes in the Royal Navy. He knew that at all events there was a great probability of his being pressed into the service, and he had good reason to hope that he might be placed ere long on the quarter deck, since many young men at that time had been who went to sea, as he had done, before the mast. He accordingly volunteered, and entered as an able seaman on board the *Eagle*, of 60 guns, then commanded by Captain Hamer, but shortly afterwards by Captain Palliser, who became the well known Sir Hugh Palliser—Cook's warm and constant friend.

As soon as the young sailor's Yorkshire friends heard that he had entered on board a man-of-war, they exerted themselves in his behalf, and a letter of introduction was procured from Mr. Osbaldeston, member for the county, to his captain, who, having already remarked the intelligence and assiduity Cook exhibited in all his professional duties, was the more ready to give him a helping hand.

Considering how best he could assist the young man, who had served too short a time in the navy to obtain a commission, Captain Palliser advised that a master's warrant should be procured for him—this being a position for which, both from age and experience, he was well fitted.* This was done; and on the 10th of May, 1759, James Cook was appointed to the *Grampus*,

---

* Masters in the navy were in those days appointed by warrant, and were very generally taken direct from the merchant service without going through any preparatory grade, as at present. They are now also commissioned officers, and on retiring receive commanders' rank.

Early Training.

sloop of war; and was now in a fair way of gaining the object of his ambition. He had, however, to undergo a trial of patience at the first outset of his career; for the former master returning, his appointment was cancelled. His friends were not idle, and four days after this he was made master of the *Garland*; but on going to join her he found that she had already sailed for her destination. On the following day, the 15th of May, he was

QUEBEC.

appointed to the *Mercury*, on the point of sailing for the North American station to join the fleet under Sir Charles Saunders, which, in conjunction with the army under General Wolfe, was engaged in the siege of Quebec. The termination of that contest gained for Great Britain one of her finest provinces. To this success Cook contributed in his particular department; and it is remarkable that he should have been in various ways instrumental in giving to his country the three finest provinces she possesses—Canada, the Australian settlements, and New Zealand.

James Cook was now about thirty-two years of age, and although the position in life he had filled for the previous twelve years was not one (especially in those days) conducive to refinement of manners, he appears from the first to have conducted himself with propriety and credit. He had already shown his superiority as a seaman. He was now to exhibit his talents in the more scientific part of his profession in which officers in the navy were in those days greatly deficient.

It was necessary to take the soundings in the channel of the St. Lawrence, between the island of Orleans and the north shore, directly in front of the French fortified camp of Montmorency and Beauport, in order to enable the admiral to place his ships so as to oppose the enemy's batteries, and to cover the projected landing of the British army under Wolfe, and a general attack on their camp. Captain Palliser, who now commanded the *Shrewsbury*, a seventy-four gun ship, recommended Cook for this difficult and dangerous service. He was engaged on it for many consecutive nights, it being a work which could not be performed in the daytime. At length his proceedings were discovered by the French, who laid a plan to catch him. They concealed in a wood near the water a number of Indians and their canoes. As the *Mercury's* barge in which Cook was making the survey passed, the canoes darted out on him and gave chase. His only chance of escape was to run for it. He pushed for the isle of Orleans with a whole host of yelling savages paddling at full speed after him. On they came, every moment gaining on his boat. The English hospital where there was a guard was before him; towards this he steered, the bows of the Indian canoes almost touching the barge's stern; a few strokes more, and the Indians would have grappled him. He sprang from his seat over the bow of his boat, followed by his crew, just as the enemy leaped in overwhelming numbers over the quarters. They carried off the barge in triumph, but Cook and his comrades escaped; and he succeeded, in spite of all difficulties, in furnishing the admiral with a correct and complete draft of the channel and soundings. This was the more extraordinary, as Sir Hugh Palliser afterwards expressed his belief that before this time Cook had scarcely ever used a pencil, and knew nothing of drawing; and it is one of many proofs that the ardent seaman not only threw his soul into the duties of his profession, but that this determination enabled him quickly to master every subject to which he applied his mind.

While his ship remained in the St. Lawrence, Cook, at the desire of the admiral, made an accurate survey of the more difficult parts of that river below Quebec. So complete and perfect was the chart which he executed, and which, with his sailing directions, was afterwards published, that until a late period no other was thought necessary. So little were the English acquainted with the navigation of the river before this, that when, early in the season, the fleet under Rear-Admiral Darell arrived at its mouth, some difficulty was expected in getting up it. Fortunately when off the island of Caudec, the inhabitants, mistaking the English ships for their own fleet, sent off their best pilots. These were of course detained, and proved of great use in taking the English fleet up the river.

After the conquest of Canada had been accomplished, Admiral Saunders despatched the larger ships to England, following himself in the *Somerset*, and leaving the command of the fleet in North America to Captain Lord Colvill, who had his commodore's flag flying on board the *Northumberland*. To this ship Cook was appointed as master by warrant from his lordship on the 22nd of September, 1759. The squadron wintered at

Halifax. Cook employed the leisure which the winter afforded him in acquiring that knowledge which especially fitted him for the service in which he was thereafter to be engaged. At Halifax he first read Euclid, and began to study astronomy, and other branches of science, in which, considering the few books to which he had access, and the want of assistance from others, he made wonderful progress. In the following year, 1760, a lieutenant's commission was presented to him as a reward for his services.

In 1762 the *Northumberland* was engaged in the recapture of Newfoundland. The activity which Cook displayed in surveying its harbour and heights attracted the attention of Captain Graves, the acting governor, and commander of the *Antelope*. Captain Graves, on becoming further acquainted with Cook, formed a high opinion of his abilities, while he admired the energy and perseverance he exhibited in surveying the neighbouring coasts and harbours.

At the end of the year Cook went to England, and on the 21st of December he married, at Barking, in Essex, Miss Elizabeth Batts, a young lady of respectable family, to whom he had some time before been engaged. As she died in 1835 at the age of ninety-three, she must at the time of her marriage have been twenty years old. Her husband was tenderly attached to her, but his married life, like that of most sailors, had long and frequent interruptions. She bore him six children, three of whom died in their infancy.

Soon after Cook's marriage, peace with France and Spain was concluded. On this Captain Graves, was again appointed governor of Newfoundland. As the island was of great importance to England, he obtained from the Government, with some difficulty, an establishment for the survey of its coasts, and offered the direction of it to Cook, who, notwithstanding his recent marriage, accepted the offer. In the following year, 1764,

Sir Hugh Palliser, being appointed governor of Newfoundland and Labrador, Cook was made marine surveyor of the province; the *Grenville* schooner, being placed under his command. The charts made by Cook enlightened the Government as to the value of Newfoundland, and induced them, when drawing up articles of peace with France, to insist on arrangements which secured to Great Britain the advantages which its coasts afford. Not content, however, with merely surveying the shore, Cook penetrated into the interior of the country, and discovered several lakes hitherto unknown.

On the 5th of August an eclipse of the sun occurred, an observation of which was taken by Cook from one of the Burgeo islands, near the south-west end of Newfoundland. The paper he wrote on it was published in the Philosophical Transactions of the Royal Society. This fact alone proves that he must already have become a good mathematician and astronomer. The last time he went to Newfoundland as marine surveyor was in 1767.

We have now briefly traced the career of James Cook from his childhood to the period when he had established his character as an able seaman, a scientific navigator, and a good officer. He was soon to have an opportunity of proving to his country and to the world in general the very high degree in which he possessed these qualities, and which enabled him to accomplish an undertaking which has proved of inestimable benefit to millions of the human race. By his means, discovery was made of fertile lands of vast extent, previously trodden only by the feet of wandering savages; and numberless tribes, sunk in the grossest idolatry and human degradation, were made known to the Christian world. And Christians, roused at length to a sense of their responsibility, began to devise means, under the blessing of God, for teaching these, their ignorant brethren of the human family, the knowledge of the only true God, and the way of eternal life.

CHAPTER II.

FIRST VOYAGE OF DISCOVERY.

August 1768 to July 1771.

IN the year 1763, on the restoration of peace, the desire to explore unknown seas and to discover new countries revived among the English, and was warmly encouraged by King George the Third. Two expeditions were at once fitted out to circumnavigate the globe, one under Lord Byron, and another under Captains Wallis and Carteret, the former commanding the *Dolphin* in which Lord Byron had just returned, the latter the *Swallow*. As, however, Captains Wallis and Carteret accidentally parted company at an early period of their voyage and kept different routes, they are generally considered as having led two separate expeditions.

Before the return of these ships, another expedition was determined on, the immediate object of which was to observe a transit of Venus, which it had been calculated by astronomers would occur in 1769. It was believed that one of the Marquesas, or one of the Friendly Islands, called by Tasman, Amsterdam, Rotterdam, and Middleburg, would be an advantageous spot for making the proposed observation.

The king was memorialized by the Royal Society, and through his Majesty's intervention the Lords Commissioners of the Admiralty undertook to furnish a suitable vessel and crew to convey the astronomers and other scientific persons who might be selected to carry out the proposed objects. The Royal Society had fixed on Mr. Alexander Dalrymple to take the direction of the expedition, but as he was not in the royal navy, Sir Edward Hawke, then at the head of the Admiralty, would not hear of his being appointed. Mr. Dalrymple, on the other hand, would not consent to go unless he received a brevet commission as captain. It was necessary, therefore, to find some one else, and Mr. Stephens, the Secretary of the Admiralty, a warm supporter of the expedition, mentioned Cook to the Board, and suggested that Sir Hugh Palliser's opinion should be asked respecting him. This, as may be supposed, was in every respect favourable; and consequently Lieutenant Cook was directed to hold himself in readiness to take command of the proposed expedition. Sir Hugh Palliser was requested to select a fit ship for the purpose, and with Cook's assistance he fixed on a barque of three hundred and seventy tons, to which the name of the *Endeavour* was given. She mounted ten carriage and ten swivel guns; her crew, besides the commander, consisted of eighty-four persons, and she was provisioned for eighteen months.

The well known Sir Joseph Banks, then Mr. Banks, one of the chief promoters of the expedition, volunteered to accompany it. On leaving Oxford he had visited the coasts of Newfoundland and Labrador to obtain information on scientific subjects. Although he suffered no small amount of hardship on that occasion he returned home with unabated zeal in the cause he had adopted, and ready again to leave all the advantages which his position afforded him, for the discomforts and dangers of a long voyage in unknown seas. Mr. Banks was however more than a philosopher—he was a large-hearted philanthropist—and he was animated with the hope of diffusing some of the advantages of civilization and Christianity among the people who might be discovered. He engaged as naturalist to the expedition the services of Dr. Solander, a Swede by birth, educated under Linnæus, from whom he had brought letters of introduction to England. Mr. Banks also, at his own charge, took out a secretary and two artists, one to make drawings from subjects of natural history, the other to take sketches of scenery and the portraits of the natives who might be met with. He had likewise four personal attendants, two of whom were negroes.

The Government, on its part, appointed Mr. Charles Green, who had long been assistant to Dr. Bradley at the Royal Observatory Greenwich, to assist Lieutenant Cook in the astronomical department of the expedition; and in every respect the persons engaged in this celebrated expedition were well fitted to attain the objects contemplated.

While these preparations were going forward, Captain Wallis returned from his voyage round the world. He expressed his opinion that a harbour in an island he had discovered, and called King George's Island, since well known as Otaheite or Tahiti, was a fit spot for observing the transit of Venus. That island was accordingly to be the first destination of the *Endeavour*. After having accomplished the primary object of the voyage, the commander was directed to proceed in making discoveries through the wide extent of the Great Southern Ocean.

Lieutenant Cook received his commission as commander of the *Endeavour* (which was then in the basin in Deptford Yard), on the 25th of May, 1768. On the 27th he went on board, and immediately began fitting her for sea. The work in dock-yards was not executed so rapidly in those days as it is now; and it was upwards of two months before the vessel was ready. On the 30th of July she dropped down the river; but it was not till the 15th of August that she reached Plymouth. On Friday, the 26th of August, the wind becoming fair, the *Endeavour* finally put to sea, and commenced the first of one of the most memorable series of voyages which have ever been performed by a single vessel. Next to Commander Cook in authority in the *Endeavour*, were her two lieutenants—Zachary Hicks and John Gore: her senior mate was Charles Clerke, who accompanied Cook in each of his subsequent voyages, and succeeded to the command of the third expedition on the death of his beloved captain. He had previously served as midshipman under Lord Byron in his first voyage round the world.

A long sea voyage is almost always felt to be extremely tedious and dull to landsmen; but every change in the atmosphere; the varied appearance presented by the sea; the numberless creatures found in it; the birds which hovered about the ship, or pitched on the rigging; all afforded matter of interest to the enlightened persons on board the *Endeavour*.

At Madeira the naturalists of the expedition set to work collecting specimens. The social condition of the people has probably altered little since those days, though the monasteries, which then existed, have long since been abolished. The nuns of the convent of Santa Clara especially amused Mr. Banks and his companions by the simplicity of the questions they put on hearing that they were philosophers. Among others they requested them to ascertain by their art whether a spring of pure water existed within the walls of their convent and also when the next thunderstorm would occur.

BAY OF FUNCHAL, MADEIRA.

On leaving Madeira the course was shaped for Rio de Janeiro, which was reached on the 13th of November. The voyagers were not treated by the viceroy with the courtesy which might have been expected. The object of the voyage was utterly beyond the comprehension of that functionary, who could form no other conception of the matter than that it had something to do with the passing of the North Star through the South Pole. This ignorance and suspicion caused the voyagers a great deal of annoyance during the whole of their stay; though the viceroy could not refuse them water and other necessaries. When at length these were procured and the *Endeavour* was going out of the harbour she was fired at from the forts of Santa Cruz. Cook immediately sent on shore to demand the cause of this act. The excuse offered by the commandant of the port was that he had received no orders from the viceroy to allow the ship to pass. It appeared that the letter had been written, but that through neglect it had not been forwarded. Through the whole of the contest with the viceroy, Cook behaved with equal spirit and discretion. Among the remarks which Cook makes in his journal on the Brazils, is one on the fearful expense of life at which the royal gold mines in that country were worked. No less than forty thousand negroes were annually imported to labour in the royal mines. In the year 1766, through an epidemic, the number required falling short, twenty thousand more were drafted from the town of Rio. A very similar account may be given of the silver and other mines on the other side of the continent; while the treacherous system which was organized to supply the demand for labour from among the inhabitants of the Pacific Islands must be looked on with even greater horror and indignation than that which existed for supplying the Brazils with slave labour. So strictly were the Brazilian gold mines guarded that no stranger was allowed to visit them, and any person found on the roads leading to them was immediately hanged by the guards stationed there. Altogether Cook formed a very unfavourable opinion of the inhabitants of the Brazils, though few parts of the tropics surpass it in beauty of climate, fertility of soil, and power of production.

After a stay of three weeks in the harbour of Rio, the *Endeavour*

RIO JANEIRO.

put to sea on the 7th of December, and stood down the coast of South America. On approaching the latitudes of the Falkland Islands, the crew complaining of cold, received what was called a Magellanic jacket, and pair of trousers made of a thick woollen stuff called Fearnought. Instead of going through the straits of Magellan, as was the custom in those times, the *Endeavour* was steered from the strait of Le Maire between Helen Island and

Terra del Fuego. On her anchoring in the Bay of Good Success several of the party went on shore. Thirty or forty Indians soon made their appearance, but distrustful of the stranger quickly retreated to a distance. On this, Mr. Banks and Dr. Solander advanced, when two of the Indians approached them and sat down. As the Englishmen drew near, the savages rose and each threw away from him a stick which he had in his hand, returning immediately to their companions and making signs to the white men to follow. This they did, and friendly relations were at once established between the two parties. Three of them were induced to go on board and were chiefly remarkable for the entire want of interest with which they regarded all the novelties by which they were surrounded. One of them, who was conjectured to be a priest, did little else than shout all the time he was on board. He was supposed, by this, to be engaged in the performance of some heathenish incantation. When these three men were landed, their fellow-savages showed great eagerness to learn what they had seen in the strange big canoe, as they would probably have termed the English ship.

On the 16th of December, Mr. Banks and Dr. Solander, with Mr. Green, Mr. Monkhouse the surgeon, and several attendants, landed with the intention of ascending a mountain seen in the distance, and penetrating as far as they could into the country. The atmosphere when they set out was like that of a warm spring day in England. It being the middle of summer the day was one of the longest in the year. Nothing could have been more favourable for their expedition. They had gone through a wood, and were about to pass over what at a distance they had taken to be a plain, but which proved to be a swamp covered thickly with tangled bushes three feet high. Still they pushed across it and reached the mountain, on which Mr. Banks and Dr. Solander commenced collecting specimens. Most of the party were greatly fatigued, and Mr. Buchan, the draughtsman, was seized with a fit.

He was therefore left with some of the party while the rest went forward. The weather however changed—the cold became intense, and snow fell very thickly. Dr. Solander had warned his companions not to give way to the sensation of sleepiness which intense cold produces, yet he was one of the first to propose to lie down and rest. Mr. Banks however, not without the greatest difficulty, urged him on, but the two black servants lay down and were frozen to death, and a seaman who remained with them nearly shared the same fate. The survivors collected together at night, but their provisions were exhausted; one or two were very ill, and they were a long day's journey from the ship. There appeared indeed a great probability that the chief objects of the voyage would be frustrated by the death of the principal scientific persons engaged in it. After a night of great anxiety, a vulture they had shot being their only food, the snow partially cleared off and they made their way to the beach which was not so far distant as they had supposed.

After this disastrous adventure the party again went on shore, and found a tribe of savages, numbering fifty persons, living in a collection of conical huts, rudely formed of boughs, and open on the lee side. The people, who were stoutly and clumsily formed, had their faces painted, and were very imperfectly covered with seal skins. Their chief article of clothing indeed was a small cloak which they wore on the side from which the wind comes when walking or sitting. They lived chiefly on shell-fish, and in search of them wandered from place to place. They were considered as among the most dull and stupid of the human race. No wonder, indeed, considering the few objects on which their minds could be expanded. A further acquaintance with these tribes has shown that they have minds as capable of receiving good impressions as other human beings, and that they are not destitute of a considerable amount of intelligence.

COOK'S ARRIVAL AT OTAHEITE OR TAHITI

The *Endeavour* took her departure from Cape Horn on the 26th of January, 1769. She ran for seven hundred leagues without land being seen. After that she passed several coral islands, the appearance of which is now familiar to most people, but in those days was but little known. To three of them the names of Lagoon Island, Bow Island, and Chain Island, were given; several of them were inhabited.

On the 11th of April she sighted Otaheite,* called King George's Island by Captain Wallis, which appeared high and mountainous, and on the 13th came to an anchor in Matavia Bay. As she approached the land numerous canoes came off, their crews carrying young plantains and other green branches as a sign of friendship. Several of the boughs were handed on board, and it was intimated that they should be placed in different parts of the ship, to shew that the voyagers also wished for peace. The natives exhibited great satisfaction on this being done. They gladly exchanged cocoa-nuts, fruit resembling apples, bread-fruit, and small fish, for beads and other trifles. They had a pig, which they would not part with for anything but a hatchet; this Cook would not allow to be given, considering that if a hatchet was given them it would be considered from that time forward to be the proper price of a pig.

The bread-fruit, with which the voyagers now first became acquainted, grows on a tree about the height of an ordinary oak. Its leaves are about a foot and a half long, of an oblong shape, deeply sinuated like those of the fig-tree, which they resemble in consistency and colour; they also on being broken exude a white milky juice. The fruit is about the size and shape of a child's head, and the surface is re-

BREAD-FRUIT.

* Now known as Tahiti.

D

ticulated. It is covered with a thin skin, and has an oblong core four inches long. The eatable part, which lies between the skin and the core, is as white as snow, and of the consistency of new bread. It must be roasted before it is eaten, being first divided into three or four parts. Its taste is insipid, with a slight sweetness somewhat resembling the crumb of wheaten bread mixed with a Jerusalem artichoke.

The first person who came off was Owhaw. He was well known to Mr. Gore, and to others who had been there with Captain Wallis. It was hoped that he would prove useful, and he was therefore taken on board and every attention shewn him. Captain Cook at once issued a set of rules to govern the ship's company in all their intercourse with the natives. They were as follows:—

"1. To endeavour by every fair means to cultivate a friendship with the natives; and to treat them with all imaginable humanity.

"2. A proper person or persons will be appointed to trade with the natives for all manner of provisions, fruit and other productions of the earth; and no officer or seaman, or other person belonging to the ship, excepting such as are so appointed, shall trade or offer to trade for any sort of provision, fruit or other productions of the earth, unless they have leave so to do.

"3. Every person employed on shore, on any duty whatsoever, is strictly to attend to the same; and if by any neglect he loses any of his arms or working tools, or suffers them to be stolen, the full value thereof will be charged against his pay, according to the custom of the navy in such cases; and he shall receive such further punishment as the nature of the case may deserve.

"4. The same penalty will be inflicted on every person who is found to embezzle, trade, or offer to trade with any part of the ship's stores of what nature soever.

"5. No sort of iron, or anything that is made of iron, or any sort of cloth, or other useful or necessary articles, are to be given in exchange for anything but provisions."

Though there can be no doubt as to Captain Cook's own feelings and wishes, his subordinates did not always act in accordance with them; and his judicious and benevolent designs with regard to the natives were thus frequently frustrated. As soon as the ship was secured, he, with Mr. Banks, Dr. Solander, and a party of men under arms, went on shore, where they were received by hundreds of the natives, whose countenances exhibited their friendly feelings. At first, however, the simple people were so struck with awe that they approached their visitors crouching down almost on their hands and feet, while they carried in their hands the green boughs as emblems of peace. The leader presented Captain Cook with a bough, which he and his companions received with looks and gestures of kindness and satisfaction. Each of the Englishmen also immediately gathered a bough, and carried it in the same way the natives did theirs. The party then proceeded about a mile and a half towards the place where Captain Wallis' ship, the *Dolphin*, had watered. Here a halt was called, and the natives having cleared away all the plants that grew on the ground, the principal persons among them threw their green branches on the bare spot, and made signs that their visitors should do the same. Captain Cook at once yielded to this request. The marines being drawn up, each as he passed dropped his bough on those of the Indians, the officers then doing the same. The natives now intimated to Captain Cook that he might make use of the ground for any purpose he desired; but as it was not suitable for the purpose of the expedition, the offer was declined.

The party now took a circuitous route of four or five miles through groves of trees which were loaded with cocoa-nuts and bread-fruit, and afforded the most grateful shade. Under these trees were the habitations of the people, most of them in the daytime presenting the appearance of a roof without walls. Mats at night were let down to afford such privacy and shelter as the habits of the people and the genial climate required. The whole scene seemed to realize to the voyagers the poetical fables of Arcadia.

The reception Captain Wallis met with from these people was in the first instance very different from that which Captain Cook and his companions now received. No sooner did the *Dolphin*, which the savages called a huge canoe without an outrigger, appear, than several thousand people in canoes laden with stones came off and attacked her. Not until they had been repeatedly fired on, and many of their number had been killed, did they retire. Several shots were fired at the crowds on shore before they would disperse. The people then saw that it would be hopeless to contend with the strangers, and with green boughs in their hands sued for peace. After this, Captain Wallis was treated with great attention, especially by a female chief, whom he called a queen or princess, and who lived in a house much larger than any others in the neighbourhood. On Captain Cook's arrival, no trace of her house was to be found; and the princess herself had disappeared. Indeed the voyagers were convinced that as yet they had seen none of the leading chiefs of the island. The next day however two persons of greater consequence than any who had yet appeared came off, called Matahah and Tootahah; the first fixing on Mr. Banks as his friend, and the latter on Captain Cook. The ceremony consisted in the natives taking off a great part of their clothing and putting on that of their white friends. A similar ceremony exists among some of the tribes of North America. The dress of the natives was formed from cloth made of the bark of the paper mulberry tree.

Captain Cook, Mr. Banks and others, accompanied their chiefs on shore, where they met another chief, Tubourai Tamaide, and formed a treaty of friendship with him. He invited them to his house, and gave them a feast of fish, bread-fruit, cocoa-nuts and plantains, dressed after the native fashion. The natives ate some of the fish raw, a feat the Englishmen could not accomplish. The general harmony was interrupted by Dr. Solander and Mr. Monkhouse finding that their pockets had been picked, the one of an opera glass, the other of his snuff-box. Mr. Banks on this started up and struck the butt end of his musket violently on the ground. On this, most of the people ran away, but the chief remained. To show his concern, and that he had nothing to do with the theft, he offered Mr. Banks several pieces of native cloth as a compensation. When Mr. Banks refused it and let him understand that he required only what had been taken away, the chief went out, and in half an hour returned with the snuff-box and the case of the opera glass. His countenance fell when he found the case empty, and taking Mr. Banks by the hand led him out towards the shore at a rapid rate. On the way, followed by Dr. Solander and Mr. Monkhouse, he passed a woman, who handed him a piece of cloth which he took, and went on till he reached another house, where a woman received them. He intimated that they should give her some beads. These with the cloth were placed on the floor, when the woman went out, and in half an hour returned with the glass. The beads were now returned, and the cloth was forced on Dr. Solander, who could not well refuse it, though he insisted on giving a present in return. This, among many other instances, shows that the people had a sense of justice, and were raised above the savage state in which the inhabitants of many of the surrounding islands were plunged.

A spot was at last fixed on, away from habitations, where the astronomical instruments could be set up, protected by a fort; and on the 15th, Captain Cook accompanied by Mr. Banks, Dr. Solander, and Mr. Green, went on shore with a party of men to commence operations. A number of natives on seeing them, collected to watch their proceedings; though they had no weapons, it was intimated to them that they must not cross a line which the captain drew in front of the ground it was proposed to occupy. Having taken all the precautions he considered necessary, he left a midshipman and a party of marines to guard the tent, and with Mr. Banks, and the other gentlemen, set off on an excursion through the woods, accompanied by Owhaw, who however seemed very unwilling that they should go far from the shore. One of their objects was to obtain poultry and pigs. Owhaw's unwillingness to proceed arose, they believed, from the fact that their live stock had been driven into the interior by the natives lest their white visitors should lay violent hands on them.

As fresh meat or poultry was much wanted, Mr. Banks, seeing some ducks, fired and killed three at one shot, which so astonished the natives that most of them fell flat on the ground as if knocked down by the same discharge. They soon recovered, however, and proceeded with the white men. The Englishmen were walking somewhat apart when, shortly after the above-mentioned incident, two shots were heard. Owhaw, on this, seemed to think, as the visitors did, that something was wrong, and signing to them to keep together sent most of the natives away. Three chiefs, however, remained, who instantly broke off green boughs from the nearest trees, and extended them towards the English, to show that they wished to be on terms of friendship, whatever had happened. The Englishmen, of course full of anxiety, hurried back to the tent. On their arrival, they found that the natives had fled, and that one of them had been killed. It appeared that a native had suddenly seized the sentry's musket and made off with it, when the midshipman, most improperly, ordered the marines to fire. This they did, into the very middle of the flying crowd; but finding that the thief did not fall, they pursued and shot him

Difficulty with Natives.

dead. It is easy to fancy Captain Cook's grief and annoyance at this incident. In spite of his humane desire to treat the natives justly and kindly, and to cultivate their good will, and notwithstanding all his precautions against violence, blood had been shed. Though the native had acted wrongly, death was too severe a punishment for his fault. The chiefs who had remained with Cook, behaved very well. Calling the people around they enabled him to explain to them that though the English would allow no liberties to be taken, yet their desire was to treat them with kindness.

Notwithstanding these assurances the next morning very few natives came near the ship, and she was consequently warped closer in, more effectually to protect the intended fort. Before long however the natives got over their alarm, and the two chiefs, Tubourai Tamaide and Tootahah, returned, bringing in their canoes, not branches only, but two young trees, and would not venture on board till these had been received as emblems of peace.

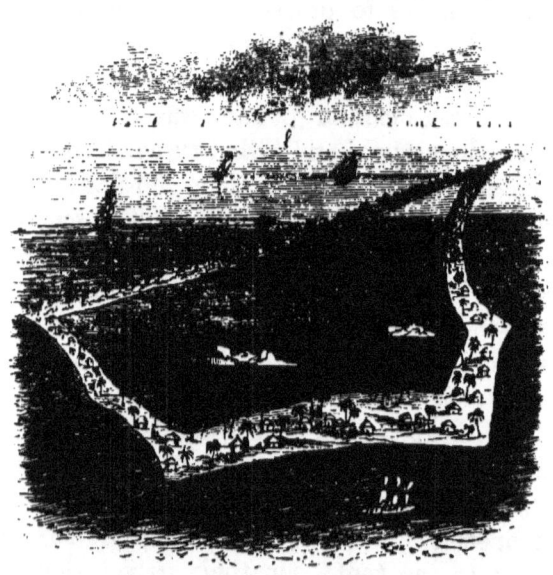

CORAL ISLAND IN THE SOUTH SEAS.

They each also brought as propitiatory gifts, a hog and bread-fruit ready dressed; both very acceptable articles at that time. In return, a hatchet and a nail were given to each of them.

At this time the expedition had the misfortune to lose Mr. Beechan, the landscape painter brought out by Mr. Banks.

Rapid progress was made with the forts, and on the 18th of April, Mr. Banks' tent being set up, he slept on shore for the first time. The natives had by this time, completely recovered from their alarm, and an abundance of provisions was offered for sale. Their friend, Tubourai Tamaide, even brought his wife and family to the fort, and did not hesitate to throw himself down and sleep on Mr. Banks's bed. The voyagers were gradually gaining an insight into the manners and customs of the people. Mr. Monkhouse, in one of his walks, learned their mode of treating their dead. He found the body of the poor man who had been shot. It was wrapped in cloth and placed on a high platform supported by stakes, with a roof over it; near it were some instruments of war and other articles. Two other bodies were seen near in a similar position, the bones of which were perfectly dry. The first was near the hut in which the man had lived. On the approach of the white man to the bodies the natives showed great uneasiness, and seemed greatly relieved when the examination was over.

A few days afterwards Tootahah amused them by a concert. There were four performers on flutes having two stops, which were sounded by the application to the end of the nose, instead of the mouth; one nostril being stopped by the hand.

Longer excursions from the shore than they had at first ventured to take, gave the explorers a good notion of the fertility and resources of the country. After passing a belt of fertile land, about two miles wide, they came to a range of barren hills. These being crossed, they descended into a wide plain watered by a river issuing from a fertile valley, which was nearly a hundred yards wide, and at a considerable distance from the sea.

This plain was thickly studded over with houses, the inhabitants of which seemed to live in the full enjoyment of the ample productions of their country. As they became better acquainted with the people, it was discovered that amiable as the people appeared, they had many vicious habits. They were generally expert and pertinacious thieves, although some of the chiefs appear to have been exempt from this vice, or to have been ashamed of practising it on their liberal visitors.

The fort was completed on the 26th of April, and six swivel guns were mounted on it. This seemed very naturally to excite the apprehensions of the people, and some fishermen who lived near wisely moved farther off. Owhaw, indeed, intimated by signs that the English would begin to fire their guns in four days. Notwithstanding this, Tubourai Tamaide and other chiefs, with their wives, came into the fort and ate without showing any signs of fear. Again the commander's patience was tried by the misconduct of one of his own people. The butcher had taken a fancy to a stone hatchet in the hands of the wife of the above-named chief, and because she refused to give it to him for a nail he threatened to kill her. Being proved guilty of this crime, as well as of an infraction of the rules drawn up by the commander, he received a severe flogging, in the presence of a number of the natives. It speaks well for their kind feelings that when they saw the first strokes given they begged that the rest of his punishment might be remitted, and when Captain Cook would not consent to this they burst into tears. Indeed, numberless instances proved that these people were mere children of impulse. They had never been taught to disguise or suppress their feelings; easily affected by all the changes of the passing hour their sorrows were transient, and their joy and pleasure speedily excited. Unaccustomed to dwell on the past, or to allow themselves to be troubled with thoughts of the future, all they desired was to gratify the desire of the moment.

About this time, the beginning of May, an event occurred which threatened disappointment to the object of the expedition. This was the disappearance, from the middle of the fort, of the quadrant, a large instrument in a case, on which the possibility of making the proposed observations entirely depended. Search was instantly made in every direction, and at length, through the intervention of the friendly chiefs, portions were discovered in the possession of the natives. It had been carried off by different people, but fortunately not broken, and finally all the parts were collected and the instrument set up. At the suggestion of the Earl of Morton before leaving home, Captain Cook sent out two parties to observe the transit of Venus from different situations— one to the east, the other to the westward. The anxiety for such weather as would be favourable to the success of the experiment was powerfully felt by all parties concerned. They could not sleep the preceding night, but their apprehensions were removed by the sun's rising without a cloud on the eventful morning of the 3rd of June. The weather continued with equal clearness throughout the day, so that the observations at each post were successfully made. At the fort, Captain Cook, Mr. Green, and Dr. Solander were stationed. The passage of the planet Venus over the sun's disk was observed with great advantage.

The explorers had been from the first anxious to see the person who had been looked upon by Captain Wallis as the queen of the island, and at length a number of people being collected at the tents, Mr. Mollineux, the master, declared that one of the females who was sitting quietly among the rest, was the lady herself. She, at the same time, acknowledged him to be one of the strangers she had before seen. Her name they soon learned was Oberea. She was tall and stout, and must have been handsome in her youth. Her countenance indicated much intelligence, and she was also unusually fair. She was thenceforth treated with great attention, and many presents were offered her. It was curious that among them all she seemed to value most a child's doll. On this Tootahah, who was apparently at that time the principal chief on the island, jealous of the favours shown to Oberea, was not content till he also had a doll given to him. For the moment he valued it more than a hatchet, probably supposing that its possession conferred some mark of dignity, or perhaps he took it for one of the gods of the white men. Whatever the position really held by Oberea, her moral conduct was not superior to that of most of her countrywomen. She seems to have been the repudiated wife of Oamo, one of the principal chiefs of the island. There appeared to have been three brothers, chiefs—Whappai the eldest, Oamo, and Tootahah. As soon as a son is born to a head chief he succeeds as king, and generally the father becomes regent. Whappai had a son who was thus king, but Tootahah, having distinguished himself as a leader in battle was chosen as regent, instead of Whappai, and a son of Oamo and Oberea was the heir apparent. It was thus manifest to our voyagers that even among those simple savages,—"the children of nature" as they were sometimes called,—ambition for greatness and jealousy of power were passions not unknown nor unfelt, any more than they are among civilized and highly-cultivated nations and races of men.

Among the attendants of Oberea was Tupia, who had been her minister in the days of her power, and was now a priest, and possessed of considerable influence. He from the first attached himself to the English, and soon expressed a strong desire to accompany them whenever they should leave the country. As it was very important to have an intelligent native of a South Sea island attached to the expedition, Captain Cook gladly availed himself of this desire, and Tupia was subsequently received on board the *Endeavour* as interpreter.

During his first visit to the island, Captain Cook learned very little about the religion of the people. He came to the conclusion that they believed in one God or creator of the universe, and in a number of subordinate deities called Etuas, as also in a separate state of existence with different degrees of happiness. They did not seem to fancy that their deities took any notice of their actions. Their religion, such as it was, had, therefore, no restraining influence over them. Their priests were called Tahowas. The office was hereditary. All ranks belonged to it. The chief priest was generally the younger brother of a good family, and was respected in a degree next to the king. Of the little knowledge existing in the country the priests possessed the greatest share, especially with regard to navigation and astronomy. The name Tahowa signifies, indeed, a man of knowledge. Like all heathen superstitions, their system was one of imposture; and the priests supported their authority by cunning, and by working on the credulity of the people. Captain Cook was not aware at that time that it was their custom to offer up human sacrifices, and that they exercised a fearful influence over the people by selecting for victims those who had in any way offended them. The persons fixed on, often young men or girls in the pride and strength of youth, were followed, unsuspicious of the fate awaiting them, and were struck down by the clubs of the assistant priests without warning. They were then offered up at their morais to the Etuas, whose anger they desired to propitiate. The priests professed also to cure diseases by incantations very similar to those practised by the medicine men, or mystery men among the Indians of North America. In the engraving is represented the interior of the hut of one of the mystery men. A society existed, called the Arreoy, the object of which was to set at defiance all the laws of morality, which the rest of the people acknowledged. Many of the principal people of the island belonged to it. By its rules any woman becoming a mother was compelled instantly to strangle her infant. Both Captain Cook and Mr. Banks spoke to some who

Religion of Tahiti. 45

acknowledged that they had thus destroyed several children, and, far from considering it as a disgrace, declared that it was a privilege to belong to the association. For a long period this

dissolute society existed, and opposed all the efforts of the Christian missionaries to get it abolished. From the lowest to the highest, the people were addicted to thieving; for even the principal chiefs could not resist temptation when it came in their way. On one of their expeditions, Mr. Banks and his companions had the greater part of their clothes stolen from them while they were asleep. They had no doubt that Oberea was concerned in the robbery.

Still the people possessed qualities which won the regard of their visitors. In all their habits they were scrupulously clean. They regularly bathed three times in the day, washed their mouths before and after eating, and their hands frequently during each meal. It was the custom for the chiefs to take their meals alone, seated on the ground, with leaves instead of a cloth spread before them, and their food ready cooked in a basket by their side. Their chief animal food consisted of pigs and dogs, the latter being carefully kept for the purpose, and fed entirely on vegetable diet. It was agreed that South Sea dog was but little inferior to English lamb. The meat was either broiled or baked in earth ovens. A hole was dug in the ground and a fire lighted in it, small stones being mixed with the wood. When the hole was sufficiently hot, the fire was raked out, and a layer of hot stones placed at the bottom; on this leaves were put. The animal to be cooked was laid on the top of them, and covered first with more leaves, and then with the remainder of the hot stones, the whole being then covered up with earth. All the fish and flesh eaten by the natives was baked in the same way.

An excursion in the pinnace, made by Captain Cook and Mr. Banks, round the island, gave them a perfect knowledge of its shape and size. It consists of two peninsulas joined by a narrow neck of land, and was found to be about thirty leagues in circumference. Though they were received in a very friendly way, the natives stole their clothes, or whatever they could lay hands on. On this excursion they met with a representation of one of their

Etuas or deities. It was the figure of a man constructed of basket work, rudely made, and rather more than seven feet high. The wicker skeleton was completely covered with feathers, which were white where the skin was to appear, and black in the parts which it is their custom to paint or stain. On the head was a representation of hair; there were also four protuberances, three in front and one behind, which the English would have called horns, but which were called by the natives Tate Ete (little men).

In the northern peninsula they visited a burying place, the pavement of which was extremely neat; upon it was raised a pyramid five feet high, covered with the fruit of two plants peculiar to the country. Near the pyramid, under a shed, was a small image of stone of very rude workmanship,—the first specimen of stone carving which had been seen among the people. Continuing their voyage, they came to a district belonging to Oberea, and were entertained at her house, which, though small, was very neat. Not far from it they saw an enormous pile, which they were told was the morai of Oamo and Oberea, literally their burying place and temple. It was a pile of stone-work, raised pyramidically, upon an oblong base or square two hundred and sixty-seven feet long and eighty-seven wide. It was like the small mounds erected for sun-dials, with steps leading on all sides to the summit. The steps at the sides were broader than those at the ends, and it terminated in a ridge like the roof of a house. There were eleven steps, each four feet high, so that the height of the pile was forty-four feet; each course was formed of white coral stone, neatly squared and polished; the rest of the mass, for there was no hollow within, consisted of round pebbles. Some of the coral stones were measured and found to be three feet and a half by two feet and a half. The foundation was of stones squared, and one of them measured four feet seven inches by two feet four inches. It was surprising that such a structure should have been raised without iron tools to shape the stones, or mortar to join them. The quarried stones must have been brought from a considerable distance by hand, and the coral must have been raised from under the water, where, though there is an abundance, it is at a depth of never less than three feet. To square these stones must have been a work of incredible labour, though the polishing might have been more easily effected by means of the sharp coral sand from the sea-shore. The whole pyramid was not straight but formed a slight curve, and made one side of a spacious area or square of three hundred and sixty feet by three hundred and fifty-four feet, enclosed by a stone wall and paved throughout its whole extent with flat stones. Several trees called *etoa*, and plantains, were growing through the pavement. On the top of the pyramid stood the figure of a bird carved in wood, and near it lay the broken figure of a fish carved in stone. About a hundred yards to the west of this building was another paved court, in which were several small stages raised on wooden pillars seven feet high. These were altars called Ewattas, and upon them were placed provisions of all sorts as offerings to their gods. In the neighbourhood of the morai were found large numbers of human bones. These were said to have been the remains of the inhabitants killed a few months before by the people of Tirrabou in the southeast peninsula, who had made a sudden descent on the coast. The jaw bones had been carried away as trophies, as the Indians of North America carry off the scalps of their enemies. The natives conjectured probably that the English would not approve of human sacrifices, and therefore refrained from offering up any, or did so only when they knew that their visitors would not interrupt them in their horrible proceedings.

The inhabitants of Otaheite were remarkably intelligent, and their minds were capable of a high state of cultivation. The climate was considered healthy, and the natural productions of the island abundant. The bread-fruit was perhaps the most valuable. They had also cocoa-nuts, thirteen sorts of bananas, plantains, a fruit not unlike an apple, sweet potatoes, yams, cacao, a kind of *arum*, the *yambu*, the sugar-cane, a fruit growing in a pod, like a large kidney bean, the pandana tree, which produces fruit like the pine-apple, and numerous edible roots of nutritious quality. Among other trees must be mentioned the Chinese paper-mulberry, from which their cloth was, and is still, manufactured, and two species of fig-trees. There were no serpents, and no wild quadrupeds on the island, except rats. Their tame animals were hogs, dogs, and poultry, and there were wild ducks, pigeons, parroquets, and a few other birds. The complexion of the people was olive or light brown, that of the women of the upper classes being very clear, with well-formed faces and expressive eyes—the nose only being flatter than is admired in Europe. In their persons, as already observed, they were remarkably cleanly; and they certainly showed that they were neither treacherous nor revengeful. Mr. Banks, and Dr. Solander, and Captain Cook himself, were constantly in their power, often in their villages, sleeping in separate huts without any watch or guard.

THE CACAO, OR COCOA.

Contrary to the usual custom, the men wore their hair long or tied up in a bunch, while the women wore it cropped short round their ears. The bodies of both sexes were tattooed, but not their faces. They manufactured three sorts of cloth for dress.

The finest and whitest was made from the paper-mulberry tree, and was used for the dresses of the chief people. The second, used by the common people, was made from the bread-fruit tree; and the third from a tree resembling a fig-tree. The latter was coarse and harsh, and of the colour of the darkest brown paper; but it was valuable because it resisted the wet, while the others did not. The women of the upper class wore three pieces of cloth; one, eleven yards long and two wide, was wrapped round the waist, and hung down like a petticoat; while the two others were formed like the South American poncho, the head being put through a hole in the middle, so as to leave the arms at liberty. The men dressed in much the same way, except that instead of allowing the cloth to hang down like a petticoat, they brought it between their legs so as to have some resemblance to breeches. The higher a person's rank, the more clothes he wore; some throwing a large piece loosely over the shoulders. They shaded their eyes from the sun with hats made at the moment required, of cocoa-nut leaves or matting, and the women sometimes wore small turbans, or a

COCOA-NUT PALM.

head-dress which consisted of long plaited threads of human hair, wound round and round with flowers of various kinds stuck between the folds, especially the Cape jessamine, which was always planted near their houses. The chiefs sometimes wore the tail feathers of birds stuck upright in their hair. Their personal ornaments besides flowers were few; but both sexes wore ear-rings of shells, stones, berries, or small pearls.

Their houses were always built in woods, sufficient space only being cleared to prevent the droppings from the boughs from rotting the roof. They were simply formed of three rows of parallel stakes for the support of the roof, the highest part of which was only nine feet from the ground, while the eaves reached to within three feet and a half. The houses were thatched with palm-leaves, and the floor was covered some inches deep with soft hay. They were indeed scarcely used for any other purpose than as dormitories, the people living almost constantly in the open air. The great chiefs, however, had houses in which privacy could be enjoyed; and there were guest houses for the reception of visitors, or for the accommodation of the people of a whole district. Some were two hundred feet long, thirty broad, and twenty high under the ridge; on one side of them was an area inclosed with low palings. They were maintained at the public expense.

The style of cookery among these islanders has already been described. They baked in their earth-ovens hogs and large fish, as also the bread-fruit. The baked pork and fish were considered more juicy and more equally done than by any mode of cooking known at home. Of the bread-fruit they made various dishes, by putting to it either water, or the milk of the cocoa-nut, and then beating it to a paste with a stone pestle, and afterwards mixing it with ripe plantains and bananas. They made an intoxicating beverage from a plant which they called *Ava*. The chiefs only indulged in the vice of drinking to excess, and even they consider it a disgrace to be seen intoxicated. They sometimes drank together, and vied with each other in taking the greatest number of draughts, each draught being about a pint. They ate a prodigious quantity of food at each meal, and would finish off by swallowing a quart of pounded bread-fruit of the consistency of custard.

They had various amusements, and were especially fond of dancing, in which they kept admirable time, their movements being often graceful; but their gestures too generally showed the very debased condition of their morals. Their musical instruments were flutes and drums. The flutes were made of hollow bamboo about a foot long. The drums were blocks of wood of cylindrical form, solid at one end, but scooped out and covered at the other with shark's skin. They were beaten by the hands instead of sticks. The natives sang to these instruments, and often made extempore verses.

The men delighted especially in wrestling. They also practised archery and spear-throwing. They shot, not at a mark, but to try how far they could send an arrow; their spears, however, they threw at a mark, generally the bole of a plantain, at the distance of twenty yards. These spears were about nine feet long. They also, in war, used clubs of hard wood, often well carved, and six or seven feet long; pikes headed with the stings of sting-rays; and slings which they wielded with great dexterity. Thus armed they fought with obstinacy and fury, and gave no quarter to man, woman, or child who, while their passion lasted, fell into their hands. Although they could not be said to live under a regular form of government, there was a certain subordination established among them, not unlike that of European nations under the feudal system.

Their tools were few and rude: an adze of stone, a chisel or gouge of bone, generally that of a man's arm between the wrist and elbow, a rasp of coral, and the sting of a sting-ray; with coral sand as a file or polisher. With these tools they built their houses and canoes, hewed stone, and felled, clove, carved, and polished timber. Their axes were of different sizes, but even with the largest it took them several days to cut down a tree.

The canoes were often large, and constructed with great labour and ingenuity. They were of two builds: one, the *Ivaha*, for short excursions, was wall-sided, with a flat bottom; the other, the *Pahie*, for longer voyages, was bow-sided, with a sharp bottom. There was the fighting Ivaha, the fishing Ivaha, and the travelling Ivaha. The fighting Ivaha was the largest; the head and stern were raised sometimes seventeen feet or more above the sides, which were only three out of the water. Two of these vessels were always secured together by strong poles about three feet apart. Towards the head a platform was raised, about twelve feet long, wider than the boats, and on this platform stood the fighting-men, armed with slings and spears, for they did not use their bows and arrows except for amusement. Below the stage the rowers sat with reserved men, who supplied the place of those that were wounded. Some of their war canoes had stages or decks from one end to the other. The fighting Pahie was often sixty feet long, and two were also joined together with a large platform above them. One measured by Captain Cook was, though sixty feet long, only one foot and a half at the gunwale, with flat sides; then it abruptly widened out to three feet, and narrowed again to the keel. The double canoes were sometimes out a month together, going from island to island. Some carried one, some two masts, with sails of matting, of shoulder of mutton shape. The bottom of a large Pahie was formed of three or more trunks of trees secured together and hollowed out; above this flooring were the sides of plank, two inches thick, and about fifteen inches broad; and then there were the upper works, hollowed out of trunks of trees like the bottom. Sometimes these canoes were used singly, but then they were fitted with outriggers like the flying Proa of the Ladrone Islands. The outrigger is a log of wood fixed at the end of two poles, which lie across the vessel, projecting eight or ten feet, according to her size. The length and high sterns of these canoes gave them great advantage in putting off from the shore through the surf; they also sailed and paddled very fast. The amount of time and labour expended in the construction of one of these canoes must have been very great, and speaks well for the intelligence as well as for the industry and perseverance of the islanders.

Before quitting the island, Mr. Banks planted a quantity of the seeds of water-melons, oranges, lemons, limes, and other plants and trees which he had collected at Rio de Janeiro. He had prepared the ground for them in the neighbourhood of the fort in as many varieties of soil as he could select. He also gave away seeds liberally to the natives, and planted others in the woods. The plants from some melon seeds which were sown on their first arrival were flourishing, and the natives eagerly begged for more.

Many articles manufactured by the natives have not yet been described. The mode of making cloth from the bark of the paper-mulberry was curious. When the trees were of a fit size, they were pulled up, and the tops and roots being cut off, the bark was slit longitudinally, and was thus easily removed. It was then placed under stones in running water. When sufficiently softened the coarser parts were scraped away with a shell, the fine fibres of the inner coat only remaining. They were then placed on plantain leaves, in lengths of about twelve yards, one by the side of the other, for about a foot in width. Two or three layers were also placed one on the other, care being taken that the thickness should be equal throughout. In this state it remained till the following morning, when all the water it contained being drained off or evaporated, the fibres were found to adhere so closely together that the whole piece could be lifted up and carried home. There it was placed on a long smooth board, to be beaten by the women. The instrument they used was a four-sided piece of wood, with a long handle. This mallet was scored with grooves of different finenesses; those on one side being wide enough to receive a small pack-thread, the size of the grooves diminishing by degrees till those on the last side were fine as the finest silk. The fabric was beaten with the coarser side first, the women keeping time, and it spread rapidly under their strokes. The finest side was the last used, and the groove marked the cloth so as to give it the appearance of having been made of fine thread. It was then almost as thin as an English muslin, and became very white on being bleached in the air. The scarlet dye used was very brilliant, and was extracted from the juice of a species of fig; a duller red was from the leaves of another tree. A yellow pigment was extracted from the root of the *Morinda citrifolia*. A brown and a black dye was also used.

The natives, when visited by Cook, manufactured mats of various descriptions, some of them exceedingly fine and beautiful. One sort served them for clothing in wet weather. They made also coarse mats of rushes and grass, to sit or sleep on, platting them with great rapidity and facility. They produced every variety of basket-work of great beauty; they also made ropes and string of all sorts; their fishing-line made from the bark of a species of nettle was far stronger than any English line of the same thickness. Their fishing-nets, though coarse, answered their purpose. They were often eighty fathoms in length. Harpoons made of cane were used to catch fish, and fish-hooks of mother-of-pearl. One used for trawling had a white tuft of dog's or hog's hair attached to it, to look like the tail of a fish. The fishermen watched for the birds which always follow a shoal of bonetas, and seldom returned without a prize. Both sexes were expert swimmers, and would dash out through the fiercest foam, diving under the breaking seas as they rolled in, and coming up on the other side. One of their amusements was to tow out a small raft on which they would sit, and allow themselves to be carried in on the top of a high foaming sea amid which no boat could live for an instant. They were not without the comfort of artificial light. Their candles were made of the kernels of a kind of oily nut, which were stuck one over another on a skewer running through the middle. The upper one being lighted burnt down to the second, which took fire, the part of the skewer which went through the first being consumed, and so on to the last. These candles burnt a considerable time, and gave a very tolerable light.

From the brief description which has been given of their manufactures it will be seen that the islanders of Otaheite possessed a considerable number of the conveniences of life. Had they but been blessed with true religion and a good government, they would already have had most of the elements of a happy existence, without further intercourse with the rest of the world.

That a life such as was apparently led by these South Sea islanders,—a life of comparative ease, and in a luxurious and enervating, but inviting climate,—should have presented charms to such men as chiefly composed the crew of the *Endeavour* can excite no surprise. Rude, ignorant, and, for the most part, vicious themselves, in spite of the boasted civilization of their country, they saw nothing repulsive in the rudeness, ignorance and vices of the dusky natives. On the other hand, they were attracted by visions of indolence and savage freedom from care. Some of them also had formed attachments not easy to be broken; and they were willing to barter their distant homes, and connections, and prospects, for the licentious pleasures so near at hand. It was very difficult for them to resist these enticements; and notwitnstanding the vigilance of the commander of the expedition, two marines managed to desert from the ship. In order to recover these deserters, Captain Cook thought himself under the necessity of detaining several of the principal people of the island on board the *Endeavour*. This led to reprisals; for on a party being sent on shore to bring off the deserters, they were, in turn, seized by the natives, who made it understood that they should not be restored till their chiefs were set at liberty. A stronger party was consequently sent from the ship, with a message from Tootahah (one of the captives), desiring that the Englishmen should be released. This happily had the desired effect, and the deserters, as well as the other men, were immediately sent back. Thus, in this, as in previous transactions, the prudence and mildness of the islanders averted a quarrel, which, had it proceeded to extremities, would have left the civilized visitors little to boast of, beyond the superior power they possessed. And it must be a source of deep regret to every Christian reader, that in the protracted intercourse which had been carried on between these professed Christians on the one hand, and the poor heathens on the other, not one attempt, so far as is known, had been made to impart a knowledge of that glorious Being who is the "Light of the World" and "the Saviour of men," nor of God the Holy Spirit, who is the Giver of the only true and eternal life. The scientific objects of the voyage had, indeed, thus far been successful, and, to a great extent, had been rendered so by the good will of the islanders; but to the silent appeal for religious teaching and spiritual aid made to the philosophers of that party by the ignorance of their hosts, there was no reply.

The fort was now completely dismantled, and preparations were made for sailing. At a last interview with the chiefs, all differences were settled, and the voyagers parted from the islanders on the most friendly terms. The latter, indeed, were loud in their demonstrations of grief. Tupia who still adhered to his determination of sailing in the *Endeavour*, though he shed tears, bade farewell to his countrymen in a dignified manner, and as far as he was able, concealed the sorrow he evidently felt. The *Endeavour* had remained exactly three months at the island. It was high time for her to leave; for the season for cocoa-nuts and bread-fruit being over, the natives could no longer spare any of their provisions for the strangers. Tupia who had gone on shore returned again on board with his servant, a lad of thirteen, called Tayeto, and on the 13th of July, 1769, the *Endeavour* sailed from Otaheite to continue her voyage towards the west.

Tupia informed Captain Cook that four islands called Huaheine, Ulietea, Otaha and Bolabola, lay at the distance of between one and two days' sail of Otaheite; and that refreshments in abundance might be procured at them. In consequence, however, of light winds, the *Endeavour* did not get off Huaheine till the morning of the 16th. Tupia probably fancied that he could impose on the white men as he did on his own people, for in his character of priest he began to offer prayers, or rather to perform incantations, as soon as he saw the prospect of a breeze springing up.

Upon the ship's getting close in with the land several canoes came off, but kept at a distance till they discovered Tupia. In one of them were Oree, king of the island, and his wife. On receiving reiterated assurances that they would be treated as friends they ventured on board. Though at first struck with astonishment at what they saw, they soon became familiar with their visitors, and the king expressed his wish to change names with the captain, who was henceforth called Captain Oree, while the chief took the name of King Cookee. The ship having anchored in a

HUAHEINE, SOCIETY ISLANDS.

small excellent harbour called Owharee, the captain, Mr. Banks, Dr. Solander, and Mr. Monkhouse, with Tupia and King Cookee, went on shore. On landing, Tupia stripped himself to the waist and desired Mr. Monkhouse, whom he seems to have looked on as a brother priest, to do the same; and sitting down in a large guest house, full of people, opposite the king, began a sort of incantation, the king answering in what appeared to be set responses. During it he made presents of some handkerchiefs, beads, two bunches of feathers, and plantains to the Etua or god of the island, and received in return a hog, two bunches of feathers, and some young plantains as presents to the white man's God.*

These he ordered to be carried on board. On the treaty, as the ceremony was supposed to be, being concluded, every one went his way, and Tupia repaired to worship at a morai. The next day, as Tupia was much engaged with his friends in the island, the captain and Mr. Banks took Tayeto as their companion in their rambles. The most interesting object they met with was a chest or cask, the lid of which was nicely sewed on, and neatly thatched with palm leaves. It was fixed on two horizontal poles and supported on arches of wood neatly carved. The object of the poles seemed to be to remove it from place to place. There was a circular hole at one end, stopped, when it was first seen, with cloth. The chest was, on a second visit, found to be empty. The general resemblance between it and the ark of the Lord among the Jews, was remarkable. The boy called it, *Ewharre no Etua* (the house of the god). He, however, could give no account of its use.

Some hogs were exchanged for axes, and some medals bestowed on the king, and no accident having happened to mar their friendly intercourse with the natives, the voyagers took their

* If this were so understood at the time, we must lament that our countrymen should have consented to take part in what must be considered as a profane farce.

departure. The people were superior in size and appearance to the general run of the natives of Otaheite, and the women fairer and better looking. Not having experienced the effects of the guns of the *Dolphin*, they were less timid than the people of Otaheite, and did not fall down on hearing a musket fired. On one of them being detected in thieving, his companions prescribed a good beating, which was at once administered.

The next island visited was Ulietea, where, within the coral reef, the ship anchored in a good harbour. Two canoes at once came off, each bringing a woman and a pig—the one as a mark of confidence, the other as a present. The ladies each received a spike nail and some beads, greatly to their delight. On landing, the union-jack was hoisted, and the three islands in sight taken possession of in the name of his Britannic Majesty. Here was a large morai, called Tapodeboatea, which was visited, and found to be different from those of Otaheite. It consisted only of four walls, eight feet high, built of coral stones, some of immense size, enclosing an area of five and twenty yards square, filled up with smaller stones. On the top of it many carved planks were set on end, and at a little distance was an altar, on which lay a hog of about eighty pounds weight, roasted whole, supposed to have been a sacrifice. Round it were four or five arks resting on poles like those seen at Huaheine. In the interior of one of them Mr. Banks found a package done up tightly in mats. He had opened several folds, but the last resisted all his attempts, and as he saw that his proceeding gave great offence he was compelled to desist. Not far off was a long house, where, among rolls of cloth, was the model of a canoe, about three feet long, to which were tied eight human jaw-bones. Other jaw-bones were seen near the ark, and Tupia affirmed that they were those of the natives of the island.

Bad weather detained the ship in the harbour of Oopoa for two more days, and when at length she got out, she was in imminent danger of striking on a reef, having got unexpectedly close to the edge of one, which was discovered from the water being shallow on one side, though deep enough under the keel to float her. Some time was expended in endeavouring to beat up to an anchorage off Bolabola, and several smaller islands were visited.

A leak having been discovered, and some more ballast being required, Captain Cook put into a harbour in Ulietea, at the opposite side of the island to that he had before visited. While the ship's company were taking in ballast and water, Mr. Banks and Dr. Solander went on shore, and were everywhere received with the greatest respect by the natives, who seemed conscious that their white visitors had the power though not the desire to do them every possible harm. Men, women, and children crowded round them, and followed them wherever they went; but no one was guilty of the least incivility. On the contrary, the men vied with each other in lifting them over any dirt or water in the way.

On approaching the first house they saw the people arrange themselves on either side of a long mat spread on the ground, at the farther end of which sat some young girls and very pretty children, dressed with the greatest neatness and taste, who kept their position, evidently expecting the strangers to come up and make them presents. At one house, at the end of a mat thirty feet long, sat a girl about six years old; her dress was red, and a large quantity of platted hair was wound round her head. She was leaning on the arm of a good-looking woman, supposed to be her nurse. The gentlemen walked up to her, and as soon as they approached she stretched out her hands for the beads which they offered, and received them with a grace which no princess in Europe could have surpassed. The people, in consequence of these gifts, seemed to be so pleased with their visitors that they employed every means in their power to amuse them. The master of one of the houses where they stopped ordered a dance to be performed before them, different from any they had yet witnessed. It was executed by one man, who put on a high head-dress of feathers, edged round with sharks' teeth. As he moved slowly round he made it describe a circle, bringing it often close to the faces of the spectators so as to make them start back, always to the great amusement of the rest.

In the course of their walk the next day they met a company of dancers, two women and six men, with three drums, who were making a tour of the island for their own amusement, for they received no pay, and were said by Tupia to be among the principal people of the country. The women wore graceful head-dresses of long braids of hair and flowers. The upper parts of their bodies were without clothing, but they were amply clothed from the breast downwards in black, and they wore pearls in their ears. The dances were of the immoral kind general in the islands. Regular dramas were also represented before the strangers.

It appeared that the island had lately been conquered by the subjects of Opoony, king of Bolabola, whose acquaintance Captain Cook wished to make. Instead of seeing a fine looking warrior as he had expected, he found a withered decrepid wretch, half blind with age: yet it seemed that he was the terror of all the surrounding islands.

A good supply of hogs, poultry, and other provisions having been obtained at Ulietea, and her leak being stopped, the *Endeavour* sailed on the 9th of August. As Bolabola was difficult of access, Captain Cook gave up his intention of touching there. To gratify Tupia, however, he fired a shot towards the island, though it was seven leagues distant. The object of Tupia appeared to be that of showing his resentment against the king of that island, as well as of exhibiting the power of his new allies.

To the six islands which had been visited, or seen, namely, Ulietea, Otaha, Bolabola, Huaheine, Tubai, and Maurua, Captain Cook gave the name of the Society Islands. Otaheite was not included in the group, but continued to be known as King George's Island.*

The voyagers were much disappointed in finding that they could not keep their live-stock. The hogs would not eat European grain of any sort, nor bread-dust; and the fowls were seized with a disease which made them hold their heads between their legs till they died.

Nothing worthy of notice occurred till the 13th, when an island, called by Tupia, Oheteroa, was seen. The next morning Mr. Gore was sent in the pinnace to attempt a landing, accompanied by Mr. Banks, Dr. Solander, and Tupia. As the boat approached the land a number of natives, armed with long lances, appeared. The main body sat down, while two walked abreast of the boat as she pulled along the shore. At length they leaped into the water and swam towards the boat, but were left behind. Two others followed but were soon distanced. At last one man, running on, got up to the boat. Mr. Banks, wishing to gain the goodwill of the natives by kind treatment, urged Mr. Gore to take him in; but he declined doing so. On the English attempting to land, soon after this, several natives came off in a canoe and boarded the boat, evidently with the intention of capturing her; indeed, it was not till muskets were fired over their heads that the savages leaped out and swam ashore. As no harbour or good landing-place was discovered in the circuit of the island, and as the natives were everywhere hostile, the attempt to land was abandoned. The clothing of the inhabitants was considered

* The names of several places visited by Captain Cook have, in course of time, been varied or altered. In this work, however, it has been thought proper generally to adhere to the original nomenclature.

superior to that of the natives of the islands before visited. The cloth of which their dresses were made was richly coloured. One piece of red or yellow was crossed on the breast, and sewed round the waist as a sash. They had also head-dresses, of white or lead-coloured cloth, shaped like a small turban; and some wore the feathers of the native birds round their heads. They had well-finished lances in their hands twenty feet long, and highly carved and polished clubs and pikes. The canoe also, though small, was richly carved; and her head and stern were ornamented with white feathers. Tupia stated that there were numerous islands between the south and north-west at different distances from Oheteroa; and that there was one, three days' sail to the north-east, called Manua, or Bird Island. The most distant island with which he was acquainted to the south was Mouton, but his father had told him of islands to the south of that. But considering the uncertainty of this information, Captain Cook determined not to lose time in looking for islands, but to steer to the south in search of a continent.

In leaving these islands, we cannot help expressing regret that the voyagers were so forgetful as they appear to have been of their obligations to the religion they professed, and of the eternal welfare of those among whom they sojourned. They found a people sunk in idolatry and superstition; and should have endeavoured to do as the apostle Paul did at Athens, where finding an altar inscribed "To the unknown God," he said to the assembled multitude,—" Whom ye ignorantly worship, Him I declare unto you," and then began to preach Jesus Christ and his great salvation. But so far from imitating this example, they, in many instances took part in their idolatrous and superstitious ceremonies. It is vain to attempt an excuse of these Englishmen by saying either that it was the fashion of the times to pass by the heathen without a thought for their wretched lost condition;

or that the party of philosophers, and scientific men, and discoverers, were not Christian missionaries. Every Christian ought to look upon himself as a missionary, when work for his Lord can be done by him: and it was a bad fashion to follow, surely,—that of suffering heathens to perish without one effort made for their salvation. No doubt there were great physical and natural impediments in the way of Cook and his associates in making anything known to the natives of those islands. But these impediments were overcome in relation to other matters.

The *Endeavour* sailed from Oheteroa on the 15th of August 1769. The 25th was the first anniversary of the day she had quitted the shores of England. To celebrate it a Cheshire cheese was cut, and a cask of porter broached, and both were found excellent. Those who have been long at sea and away from home best can understand the importance attached to such trifles, and the pleasure they afford.

On the morning of the 30th, a comet was seen in the east, a little above the horizon. Tupia, who observed it with others, instantly cried out that as soon as the people of Bolabola should perceive it they would attack the inhabitants of Ulietea, who would have to fly to the mountains to save their lives. Meeting with a heavy sea and strong gales from the westward, on the 1st of September Captain Cook wore and stood to the northward. On the weather moderating he continued his course to the westward during the whole of September. Several seals were seen asleep on the surface of the water, and various birds were perceived, a sure indication that the ship was approaching land. On October the 6th, land was seen from the masthead, bearing west by north. In the evening it could be seen from the deck. It was not till the evening of the next day that the voyagers got near enough to observe the nature of the country, when it appeared of great extent, with four or five ranges of hills rising one over the other, and beyond them a lofty chain of mountains. The general opinion was that they had found the *Terra Australis incognita*. A bay was seen, and smoke rising from the shore, but night coming on, they were obliged to stand off till day-light. The next day, on standing in again, some small but neat houses were seen, and a considerable number of people seated on the beach. Farther on was discovered a tolerably high and regular paling inclosing the whole of the top of a hill. Some on board supposed it to be a park for deer, others an inclosure for oxen or sheep. In the afternoon the ship came to an anchor in a bay off the mouth of a river. The sides of the bay were white cliffs of great height, the middle was low land with hills rising behind and terminating in a chain of lofty mountains.

Captain Cook with Mr. Banks, Dr. Solander, and a party of men in the yawl and pinnace, landed on the east side of the river; but some people being perceived on the west side, the yawl crossed over, and while the gentlemen landed, four boys were left in charge of her. On the approach of the Englishmen the natives ran away, and the former advanced towards some huts two or three hundred yards from the water's edge. When, however, they had got some distance from the yawl, four men with long lances rushed out of the woods towards her, and would have cut her off had not the people in the pinnace covered them, and called to the boys to drop down the stream. This they did, but the natives pursued in spite of two musket shots fired at them. At length one of the natives was poising his spear to dart it at the boys, when the coxswain of the pinnace fired a third time and shot the native dead. The other three at first attempted to drag off the dead body, but fear soon made them drop it and take to flight.

On the captain and his companions returning to the boat they stopped to examine the body, which had been shot through the heart. It was that of a man of middle stature, of a brown but not very dark complexion. One side of his face was tattooed in spiral lines of regular figure, and his hair tied in a knot on the top of his head, but no feathers in it. He wore a garment of a fine cloth, of a manufacture new to the English. When the voyagers returned on board, they could hear the natives talking very loudly. The next day the captain and the same party landed with Tupia, and the marines were afterwards sent for. A large body of natives had collected on the opposite side of the river, apparently unarmed, but on the approach of the English they started up, each man holding a spear or dart, and made signs to the strangers to depart. The marines being drawn up, the visitors again approached the natives, when Tupia addressed them in the language of Otaheite, which they perfectly understood. He told them that their visitors wanted provisions and water, and would pay them with iron, the properties of which he explained as well as he could. They replied that they were willing to trade if the English would cross over to them. Captain Cook consented to do this, provided they would put aside their arms. This they would not consent to do. Tupia warned the English during the conversation, that the natives were not friendly. Captain Cook then invited the natives to come across to them. At last, one of them stripped himself and swam over without his arms. He was soon after followed by others to the number of twenty, most of whom came armed, and though iron and beads were offered them, they set no value apparently on either, for a few feathers were offered in return, and they at once showed their hostile disposition, by endeavouring to snatch the weapons from the hands of their visitors. They were told, through Tupia, that if they continued to proceed in that manner they would be killed; notwithstanding this, one of them seized Mr. Green's hanger from his side, and ran off with it. Mr. Banks on this fired at him with small shot; but though hit, he still continued to wave the hanger round his head. Mr. Monkhouse, seeing this, fired at him with ball, when he instantly dropped. Upon this, the main body, who had retired to a rock in the middle of the river, began to return. Two that were near the man who had been killed tried to drag off the body. One seized his weapon of green talc; and the other tried to secure the hanger, which Mr. Monkhouse had but just time to prevent. As the whole body were now returning with threatening gestures, those who had their guns loaded with small shot, fired. The effect was to make the natives turn back, and to retreat up the country, several of them being wounded. Such was the first unhappy attempt of the English to open up an intercourse with the inhabitants of New Zealand, for such was the magnificent country Captain Cook and his companions had now reached. Painful as it is to reflect on the sacrifice of human life which often in those days attended the first intercourse of civilized Europeans with the savage inhabitants of newly discovered countries, and the cruelties and injuries inflicted, we must not judge our countrymen too harshly. Much less value was set on human life a century ago than is the case at present, and dark-skinned savages were scarcely regarded as beings of the same nature as white men. Captain Cook was, however, undoubtedly a kind and humane man, and was sincere in his expressions of regret at the blood his followers so frequently shed whenever they met with opposition from the natives of the lands they visited.

Having no longer any hope of establishing a friendly intercourse with the inhabitants of this place, and finding that the water in the river was salt, Captain Cook proceeded with the boats round the head of the bay, in search of fresh water; intending also, if possible, to surprise some of the natives, and, by kind treatment and presents, to obtain their friendship. Everywhere, however, a dangerous surf beat on the coast, and he was unable to land. But, seeing two canoes coming in towards the shore, one under sail and the other moved by paddles, he judged it necessary for the object he had in view to intercept them. Supposing that they were fishermen without arms he hoped to do this without bloodshed. Notwithstanding the way in which he had placed the boats, one of the canoes managed to escape; but the other, under sail, came directly into the middle of the English boats without perceiving what they were. On discovering the strangers, the natives lowered their sail and took to their paddles. Tupia called out to them that those in the boats wished to be friends; but the natives preferred trusting to their paddles, and continued their flight. On this, a musket was fired over their heads, when they ceased paddling and began to strip, not to swim to the shore but to fight to the last.

When the boat came up they attacked the English with paddles, stones, and other weapons, and showed a determination not to be taken alive. The English, in their own defence, fired, when four out of the seven people in the canoe were killed. The other three were lads—the eldest of whom, about nineteen years old, leaped into the sea, swimming vigorously, and resisting every effort made to capture him. At last he was seized and taken into the boat, as were the two younger lads, without further attempt to escape. As soon as they were in the boat, the lads squatted down, evidently expecting instant death. Every effort was made to win their confidence, and with so much success that by the time the ship was reached they appeared not only reconciled to their fate but in high spirits. On food being offered them they ate it voraciously, and asked and answered questions with every appearance of pleasure. At night, however, they sighed, and seemed to be mourning for the friends they had lost; but, encouraged by Tupia, they quickly regained their cheerfulness, and, in the morning ate another enormous meal. On being told that they would be put on shore where the English had landed the previous day, they expressed great alarm, and said that the inhabitants were their enemies and would eat them. At last, on landing on the other side of the bay, after hesitating for some time, the lads cried out that they saw, among a large body of natives who were approaching, one of their relations. Still they seemed doubtful about joining them, and evidently regretted leaving their new friends. The body of the native who had been killed the previous day still lay on the shore. The boys seeing it went and covered it with some of the clothes they had received on board the *Endeavour*. Soon after, a man, who proved to be the uncle of one of the boys, swam over with a green bough in his hand, which was here, as at Otaheite, an emblem of peace. Tupia received the branch, and several presents were made to the native. Notwithstanding this, he refused to go on board the strange ship. Breaking off another bough, he then approached the dead body, before which he performed numerous ceremonies. When this was done, he returned to his companions and held with them a long consultation. The boys refused to go back to their countrymen, and begged again to be taken on board. The natives after this were observed from the ship to cross the river, and to carry off the dead body on a kind of bier.

Later in the day, the captain directed Tupia to ask the boys if they had any longer a fear of landing, the body having been carried off, which was supposed to be a ratification of peace. They replied that they were perfectly ready to go, and stepped with alacrity into the boat which was prepared to carry them on shore.

On the boat reaching the shore they landed willingly, but soon after, when she put off, waded back into the water, and entreated to be taken on board. As the midshipman in charge of the boat had received strict orders not to receive them, their request was not granted. After a time a man came and took them across the river on a raft to where a large number of people were assembled. They appeared to be well received, and shortly after were seen standing on the beach, when they waved their hands three times and stepped nimbly back to their companions.

Captain Cook gave the name of Poverty Bay to the place where these events occurred; and in his journal he strongly expresses his regret at the destruction of the four unfortunate fishermen, saying, that had he supposed they would have resisted, he would not have attempted to stop them; but that, as it was, he could not allow his people to be knocked on the head by the savages. It may be asked why were the savages not permitted to escape? The reply of Captain Cook is, that he considered it his duty, in prosecution of his enterprise, to open a communication with the natives by force if he could not succeed by gentle means. In pursuance of that object, and in accordance with this supposed duty, our countrymen had little scruple in shedding the blood, and taking the lives of their fellow men, even when violence was not necessary for their own safety.

The next morning the *Endeavour* sailed from Poverty Bay, but, being becalmed, several canoes came off to her. The natives in one canoe setting the example, the rest were easily persuaded to come on board to the number of fifty men. Only two weapons were seen among them; these were made of green talc, and called *patoo-patoo*, being shaped somewhat like a pointed battle-dore, with a short handle and sharp edges. They were well contrived for close fighting, and would certainly split the thickest skull at a single blow. The sad truth of this some of our countrymen were afterwards to experience, when not far from this spot the

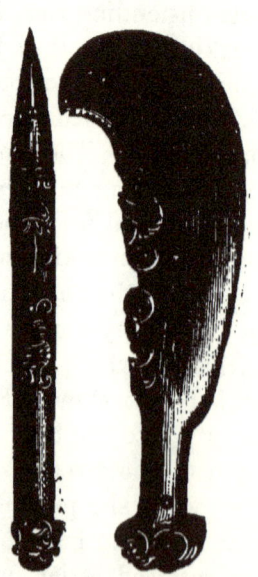

PATOO-PATOO.

greater part of a ship's company were destroyed, each savage producing one of these weapons from under his cloak, and singling out a victim for instant destruction. Presents were made by the officers of the *Endeavour* to the natives, who were all so eager for the white men's goods that they afterwards exchanged everything they had with them, even to the paddles of their canoes. Enquiries were made for the poor boys, and the captain was assured that no harm had happened to them, and that it was in consequence of the account they had given of their reception on board that the present party had come off to the ship.

An hour before sunset the natives paddled off, leaving three of their number below. As soon as this was discovered they were hailed, but would not return, nor did the deserted natives seem to be alarmed. The next morning, however, when they discovered that the ship was at a distance from the land, their consternation was excessive, and Tupia had great difficulty in pacifying them. On standing in again, a canoe with an old chief came off, but he and his followers would not venture on board till Tupia had used numerous arguments to persuade them;—among others, an assurance that the strangers did not eat men. This remark, coupled with those of the boys, gave the English their first suspicions of the horrible propensity of the people with whom they were now attempting to open up an intercourse. The old chief, after remaining a short time on board, returned with the three men to the shore.

The point of land first made to the north of Poverty Bay, proved to be the most eastern part of New Zealand, and was called East Cape. The *Endeavour* was now steered to the south. An island close to the main was passed, which, from its similarity to Portland in Dorsetshire, received the same name. A number of natives were here seen seated on the cliffs watching the ship's movements. When she suddenly got close to a reef, and there was some sign of confusion on board, they showed a disposition to attack her. Canoes at different times came off, and in one the people performed certain ceremonies, sometimes offering peace, and then threatening war. Five large canoes full of armed men soon after came off. As the boat's crew were sounding, it was necessary to drive them away. A musket fired over their heads had no effect, but a four-pounder charged with grape shot, though fired wide, put them to flight.

Farther along the coast, the next morning, nine or ten large canoes, which must have contained little short of two hundred men, came off. When the first five were within a hundred yards of the ship, the natives began to sing their war songs, and to brandish their weapons. Tupia, on this, was ordered to inform them of the power and effects of the English thunder-making arms, and a four-pounder loaded with grape was fired wide of them. The result was satisfactory, and the natives went peaceably away. The following day, another fleet of canoes came alongside, and though they had only stale fish to sell, Captain Cook accepted it for the sake of encouraging traffic. The natives, however, showed every disposition to take advantage of the strangers, and one of them having agreed to exchange a black cloak for a piece of red cloth, on receiving the cloth, packed it in a basket with the cloak, which he refused to give up, and made off with both cloth and cloak. Among those who were leaning over the ship's side to hand up the articles purchased from the natives, was Tupia's boy Tayeto. One of the natives, watching his opportunity, suddenly seized the boy, and, dragging him over, held him down in the canoe, which made off. The marines on deck were ordered to fire, and to aim at the end of the canoe farthest from the boy. One of the natives was seen to fall, when the other let go his hold of Tayeto, who leaped overboard and swam to the ship. A boat was lowered, and he was taken up unhurt, but dreadfully frightened. The canoes made towards the shore, and it was observed that three men were lifted out of them, either killed or badly wounded.

In this instance, the natives actually deserved the punishment they received. Captain Cook called the headland off which this circumstance occurred Cape Kidnappers. When Tayeto recovered from his fright he took a fish to Tupia that he might offer it to his Etua. Tupia praised him, and ordered him to throw it into the sea.

Captain Cook having now stood to the southward for a considerable distance without finding a harbour, tacked and stood to the northward, in hope of being more successful in that direction. The ship was off a high bluff headland with yellowish cliffs, which was accordingly called Cape Turnagain. Soon afterwards two chiefs and their three attendants paddled off, and willingly came on board. One of the chiefs had a very pleasing and honest expression of countenance. Though they would not eat, they seemed disposed to be very friendly, so much so, that they insisted on remaining on board all night. The next morning they were somewhat surprised at finding themselves so far from the shore, but went away without hesitation. As the ship sailed along, several canoes came off to her, a few at a time. In one were two old chiefs, who, with many expressions of good will, invited the strangers on shore. The surf prevented their going, but in the evening the wind moderating, Captain Cook, with Mr. Banks and Dr. Solander, landed, and were received in the most friendly manner. The natives took care not to appear in large bodies,—the members of two or three families only keeping together. These little companies sat on the ground, and by signs invited their visitors to draw near. These indications of a friendly disposition determined the commander to fill his casks with water at this place.

The next morning, while this operation was going forward, Mr. Banks and Dr. Solander walked along the shores of the bay by themselves without anxiety, and collected numerous plants. They visited several huts, and found the inhabitants at dinner, their food consisting at this time of the year of fish, and the root of a large fern. The roots were prepared by scorching them over a fire, and then beating them till the charred bark fell off. The remainder was a clammy soft substance, not unpleasant to the taste, but mixed with three times its bulk of fibres, which could not be swallowed. This part was spit out into baskets ready at hand for its reception. No animals were seen except some ugly little dogs. Carefully cultivated and closely fenced plantations of sweet potatoes and other vegetables were seen. The women were plain, and had their faces painted with red ochre and oil; the men generally did not follow the latter custom, but one man was observed who had a piece of yellow ochre in his hand, with which he renewed the coloured decorations on his person whenever he supposed them to be deficient. Mr. Banks and others, having remained on shore after the boats had gone off with the casks, were brought on board by the natives in one of their canoes. Indeed all the intercourse with the people in this place was carried on in the most friendly manner.

At the watering-place the natives entertained their visitors with a war song; in which the women joined with horrid distortions of countenance,—rolling their eyes, thrusting out their tongues and heaving deep sighs, all keeping perfect time. A canoe was seen here sixty-eight feet and a half long, five broad, and three feet and a half deep; she had a sharp bottom, consisting of three trunks of trees hollowed; the side planks were sixty-two feet long in one piece, carved in bas-relief; the head being still more richly carved. A large unfinished house was also visited; the side ports were carved in a masterly style, though with whimsical taste. The bay was called by the natives Tolaga.

Wood and water and an abundance of wild celery, which proved an excellent anti-scorbutic, having been got on board, the *Endeavour* weighed and stood to the north. The wood they had cut was like the English maple; and a cabbage-tree was met with and cut down for the sake of the cabbage, or the succulent soft stem, so called by the voyagers from its taste when boiled. The country abounded with plants, and the woods with birds in an endless variety, and exquisitely beautiful. After rounding each cape numerous villages were seen, and much cultivated ground. Some way on, an immense canoe with sixteen paddles on each side, and carrying sixty armed men, gave chase to the ship. To prevent an attack, a round shot was fired near them, when they paddled off; the headland near at hand was therefore called Cape Runaway. After this, a large number of canoes came off to trade; but the natives were disposed to cheat. At length some linen hanging over the bows to dry, was carried off by a man, who, though fired at, deliberately packed it up and made off with it. As the natives continued to insult the English, a shot was fired close to them, which went bounding over the water far ahead, and made them paddle away at great speed.

Several villages were seen larger than any before observed, built on eminences near the sea, and fortified on the land side by a bank and ditch, with a high paling within it, carried all round; some of them had also outworks. They were supposed to be the fortified villages, called by the natives Pahs or Hippahs. There seems to have been much doubt in the minds of the officers of the *Endeavour* as to whether the land on which they were now coasting was an island, or part of a vast continent. The captain seems to have held to the former opinion, his officers to the latter.

The ship was now near a cluster of islands to which the names of the Mayor and the Court of Aldermen was given. Farther on, more villages were in sight, with some hundreds of large canoes drawn up on the beach under them. The whole country from Cape Turnagain, thus far, was said to be under the rule of a single chief called Teratu. A large inlet was next entered, and here the ship anchored. Several canoes of a less ornamental description came alongside, and tried to steal the buoy of the anchor. Three times during the night they repeated the attempt, hoping, it seemed, to catch the crew asleep. Again they came at daylight, and sung a war song, preparatory to an attack. Tupia, however, expostulated with them, and explained so successfully that they would certainly be the sufferers in case of a skirmish, that instead of fighting they began to trade. Here, again, a native made off with two pieces of cloth, both of which he had got for one weapon, which he refused to deliver up. A musket ball was fired through his canoe; but he would not return. It was curious that the people in the other canoes paid no attention to him, though he was bleeding, but continued to trade as if nothing had happened. Soon afterwards, indeed, the same trick was played by others. Two muskets were fired, the bullets going through the sides of the canoe between wind and water. This only made the savages pull off more rapidly. As the commander intended to remain in this place for some days to observe the transit of Mercury, it was necessary to make the natives understand the superiority of the English; and a round shot was therefore fired over their heads.

All the natives, however, were not alike dishonest. One chief, in particular, had behaved with great propriety during the day, neither attempting to cheat, nor showing any fear of the English. He came off the next morning, and soon established friendly relations with them. He said that the people were generally convinced of their power, and would, he hoped, behave properly in future. His name was Toiava.

An officer with the marines and a party of men were sent on shore to cut wood. No houses were seen; but there were a number of people, who seemed to have slept under the bushes. The state of warfare in which the people existed, was shown by Toiava when on board one day. Two canoes were perceived coming in from the opposite side of the bay, when, saying that they were enemies, he hastened off to the shore with all his canoes. He soon returned, however, they not being the people he supposed. A large number of mackerel were obtained here from the natives, the sailors salting enough to last for a month.

Fortunately, a fine day enabled the commander and Mr. Green to obtain a satisfactory observation of Mercury; and the name of Mercury Bay was therefore given to the harbour on the shore of which it was taken. While they were on shore, another case of cheating by a native occurred. The thief and his companions having pulled off in their canoe, sang their war song, and shook their paddles in defiance. This so provoked Mr. Gore, the officer in charge, that he fired and killed the man, a circumstance for which Captain Cook expressed his deep regret. Though at first alarmed, the natives on shore on inquiring into the matter, seemed to think that the man had received his deserts; and the friendly intercourse begun between them and the English was not further interrupted.

A little before sunset, the natives retired to eat their supper, consisting of birds, fish, and lobsters. Some were roasted, stuck on sticks inclined towards the fire; others were baked in ovens on the ground, in the way practised by the people of Otaheite. Among the natives was a woman mourning for the death of a relative. She sat on the ground by herself, and cut herself all over with pieces of shell till she was covered with blood, singing in a mournful voice, at the same time, a song, the meaning of which Tupia could not understand.

The shore abounded with clams, cockles, and, in some places, rock-oysters. Numerous wild fowl also were seen, and several were shot. The boats rowed up a river at the head of the bay, for four or five miles, and near it a deserted fort of considerable strength was visited. Several beds of oysters were also discovered, dry at half ebb, and a boat being sent to fetch some, returned completely laden, so that the ship's company had a regular feast of them. Fish also in abundance were brought off by the natives. On the north side of the bay, a pah, small, but very strong and beautifully situated, was visited. It stood on the top of a rock detached

NEW ZEALAND PAH.

from the mainland, surrounded at high water. The centre part was perforated by an arch sixty feet in height, and of considerable width. The only way of reaching the top was by a very narrow winding path. Here there was room only for four or five huts. Farther on was a much larger fortified village, the inhabitants of which, to the number of a hundred, came out and invited the strangers to visit them, and seemed highly pleased when their invitation was accepted.

G

This pah, or fort, was examined with much interest, and afterwards minutely described by the English visitors. It seemed, indeed, a place which, if resolutely defended, was capable of holding out against any number of assailants furnished only with such arms as were seen in the hands of the natives. It was curious that men capable of constructing so elaborate a fortification should have invented simply such weapons as lances, small and large battle-axes, and clubs; for not a sling nor a bow was seen among them, nor any other weapon but those mentioned. When stones were used they were thrown by the hand.

The *Endeavour*, having taken an ample supply of celery on board, sailed from Mercury Bay. The most successful generals of ancient and modern times were able to take advantage of their greatest victories by having paid careful attention to their commissariat; and Cook, for the same reason, could prolong his researches for a greater length of time than any previous navigator, and keep his crew in tolerable health; more especially to preserve them from that fearful scourge of seamen, the scurvy. Of course he was greatly indebted to the experienced botanists on board, who were able to discover any antiscorbutic plants grown on the shores they visited. Probably the lives of thousands of seamen might have been saved had the commanders been acquainted with the wild plants a loving God has everywhere provided for the use of His creatures, capable of preventing that dire complaint.

About fifty miles to the north of Mercury Bay the natives came off and threw stones at the ship, nor would they listen to the expostulations and advice of Tupia, till a musket ball was sent through the bottom of one of their canoes, when they were convinced of the truth of his account respecting the power of the strangers.

On the 19th a large inlet was entered, in which the ship brought

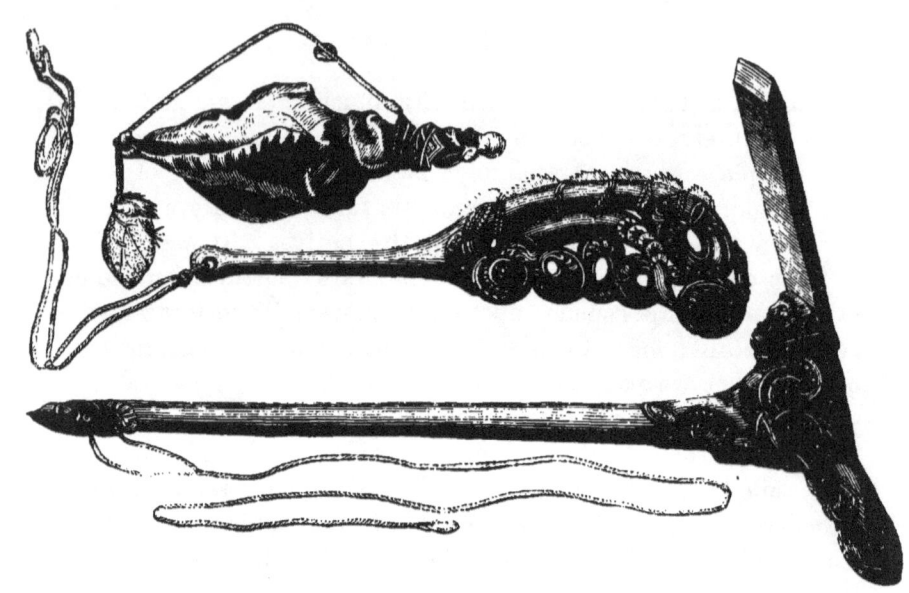

WAR CLUBS AND ADZE MADE BY NEW ZEALANDERS.

A CARVED COFFER IN NEW ZEALAND WORK.

up. Immediately natives came off, who said that they had heard of the strangers from Toiava. One young man introduced himself as his grandson, and received several presents. They also addressed Tupia by name, showing that they had heard of the English from their friends. The commander and his usual companions proceeded in the boats nine miles up the inlet, which they discovered terminated in a river. This they entered with the flood, and found fresh water three miles from the mouth. Here they saw a large village on a sandbank entirely surrounded by mud, probably considered a sufficient protection from their enemies. They were particularly struck by the great size of the pine trees which grew on the banks. One measured nineteen feet eight inches in girth at the height of six feet from the ground. From the root to the first branch it was eighty-nine feet, and as straight as an arrow, tapering very little in proportion to its height. It probably contained, by the captain's computation, three hundred and sixty-six cubic feet of solid timber. Others still larger were seen. A small one was cut down, and found to be similar to the pitch pine, too heavy for masts, but the carpenter was of opinion that, by tapping, the wood would be lightened, and that then the trees would make the finest masts in the world. These trees were the celebrated Kauri pine, from which a valuable gum is extracted. It also makes very fine planking. This tree, the flax plant, and the gigantic fern, are among the characteristic productions of New Zealand.

The name of the Thames was given to the river explored. The natives in the neighbourhood behaved in the most friendly manner; but while the commander and Dr. Solander were on shore, and Mr. Banks with Tupia and some of the natives were below, a lad took possession of a half-minute glass from the binnacle. Mr. Hicks, who was commanding officer, ordered the lad to be triced up and a dozen lashes given to him. His countrymen interfered, and called for their arms from the canoes alongside. In vain Mr. Banks, hearing the noise, and coming on deck, expostulated with the lieutenant. Tupia at length pacified the natives by explaining what was to happen, and they allowed the punishment to proceed. As soon as it was over, an old man, supposed to be the father of the boy, gave him a beating and sent him into the canoe; but the confidence of the natives was gone, and though they promised to come back, no more was seen of them.

The natives on most occasions were ready to steal and cheat whenever they thought that they could do so with impunity. This occurred nearly every day as the *Endeavour* proceeded along the coast. In one day, at different times, nearly five hundred natives were on board or alongside, showing that the country was very populous. One of these was making off with an article of which he had possessed himself without giving anything in return, when the midshipman to whom it belonged hove a lead with a hook secured to it at the end of a line with such aim that the hook caught the thief, but broke off. While at anchor in another part of this bay which is known as the Bay of Islands, the commander gave a piece of cloth to an old chief, one of several hundred natives crowding round the ship. Notwithstanding this, some of them tried to steal the buoy, and not till one of them was hit by a musket-ball would they give it up. After this the commander, with Mr. Banks, Dr. Solander, and two boats' crews, landed in a little cove. They had not been there long, before they saw nearly three hundred people rushing towards them from behind the heads of the cove, and over the tops of the hill. Some of the savages rushed to the boat to seize them, and others, led by a chief, advanced towards the English. The commander, Mr. Banks, and two of the men, fired with small shot. The natives, though at first they fell back, soon again rallied and advanced. On this Dr. Solander fired again and hit the chief, who, with the rest, ran off. The natives still continued in a body, and as seen from the ship, appeared very numerous. A few round shot fired over their heads dispersed them. Happily not a single life was lost, and only two men were slightly wounded. As it happened, the old chief to whom the cloth had been given in the morning had, with some of

BAY OF ISLANDS.

his family, concealed himself in a cave. While the party were collecting celery he was discovered, and was soon put at his ease. He said that one of the men who had been hit with small shot was his brother, and inquired anxiously whether he would die. He was assured that he would not; and a bullet and small shot being shown to him, he was told that those who were hit with the first would die, but that the wounds made by the last were seldom mortal. He and his companions now came and sat down by the English, who gave them a few trifles.

Several days were passed in the Bay of Islands, and a friendly intercourse was maintained during the remainder of the time with the natives. On going out of it, the ship grazed a rock to windward of her with great violence, but received no injury. This part of the country was evidently very densely inhabited; and the people seemed to live on friendly terms with each other, though no head or leading chief was heard of. Fishing seemed to be one of their principal occupations, and nets of great length were seen—one not less than from three to four hundred fathoms. Their towns were all fortified. Farther on, while becalmed, some people who came off, told the voyagers that at the distance of three days' rowing the land would take a sharp turn to the south, and extend no more to the west. It was conjectured, therefore, that this headland was one seen by Tasman and called by him Cape Maria Van Diemen; and an eager look-out was kept for the important headland.

At six in the morning on the 16th of December, land was seen from the mast-head, which proved to be North Cape. It lies in latitude 34° 22′ s., and longitude 186° 55′ w. The isthmus which joins this head to the mainland is low, which gives it the appearance of an island. On the cape a hippah, or village was seen, with several inhabitants. Soon after this, when off Cape Maria Van Diemen, the *Endeavour* met with a gale which, though it was in the middle of the summer of that hemisphere, Captain Cook says, for its strength, and the length of time it lasted, was such as he had scarcely ever been in before. The ship was three weeks getting ten leagues to the westward, and five weeks in getting fifty leagues. During the gale, the ship was a considerable distance from the land, or it is highly probable, he says, they would not have returned to relate their adventures.

It is not necessary to mention the various courses run for several days, as no communication was held with the shore. At length a lofty peak was seen towering above the clouds, and covered with snow, to which the name of Mount Egmont was given. It was surrounded by a flat country of a pleasant appearance, being clothed with verdure and wood. Near it a bay was entered, in a safe and convenient cove of which the ship anchored. Some canoes at once paddled off, and much against the wishes of his people, an old chief from one of them came on board. He was received with all possible friendship, and, after some time, was dismissed with many expressions of kindness, to his companions. This treatment had a beneficial effect, though some of the natives showed an inclination to try how far they might go with the strangers. On one occasion they pursued the long-boat as it was going on shore with casks; but some small shot quickly made them desist.

The bay where they were at anchor was found to be about fifteen miles south of one visited by Tasman, though none of the people among whom Tupia made inquiries had any tradition of his having been on the coast. The commander, with Mr. Banks, Dr. Solander, and others, on their way one day to visit a cove two miles off saw the body of a woman floating, to all appearance dead for some days. Immediately on landing they found a family who seemed greatly alarmed at their approach, and ran away. In a short time, however, they were induced to return, and confidence being established became very communicative. The body of the woman was that of a relation whom they had buried at sea fastened to a stone, from which they supposed it had broken. The family were dressing some provisions, and as the gentlemen cast their eyes into one of the baskets which stood near, two bones were perceived, which, upon nearer examination were found to be those of a human body. The natives, on being questioned by Tupia, acknowledged, without the slightest hesitation, that they were the bones of a man whom they had eaten; that a canoe belonging to their enemies had come into the bay five days before; that seven persons in her had been killed, and that this man was one of them. On Tupia asking why they did not eat the body of the woman, they replied that she was a relation, and that they only ate the bodies of their enemies killed in battle. One of the natives took hold of his own forearm, and intimated that the bone Mr. Banks held in his hand had belonged to that part of the human body; he also bit and gnawed the bone which Mr. Banks had taken, drawing it through his mouth, and showing by signs that it had afforded a delicious repast. A woman of this family of cannibals had her arms, legs, and thighs, frightfully cut, in token of her grief for the loss of her husband, who had lately been killed and eaten by their enemies.

Mr. Banks and Dr. Solander were several times on shore, but their walks were much circumscribed by climbing plants of luxuriant growth, which completely filled up the spaces between the trees, so as to render the woods impassable. Preparations had been made for erecting a durable memorial of the *Endeavour's* visit, and their old friend promised that it should never be removed. Presents of coins and spike-nails, with the king's broad arrow on them, were given to the natives, and two posts, of which the memorial was to be constructed, were taken to the highest part of the island near which the ship lay. The union-jack was then hoisted, and formal possession was taken of the country in the name of His Majesty King George the Third, the name of Queen Charlotte's Sound being given to the inlet. A bottle of wine was then drunk to Her Majesty's health, and the empty bottle given to the old man, who seemed highly delighted with it.

The *Endeavour* left the Sound on the 6th of February, and soon after, during a calm, was very nearly driven on shore by the strong current setting through the straits between the northern and middle island, now known as Cook's Straits. Over the land was seen a mountain of stupendous height, covered with snow. Passing through the straits the *Endeavour* steered north again, and continued on till, the weather clearing, Cape Turnagain was distinctly seen. Captain Cook on this asked his officers whether they were satisfied that Eaheinomauwe was an island. They replying in the affirmative, the *Endeavour* hauled her wind and stood to the eastward. Eaheinomauwe was the name given by the natives to the northern island; Poenammoo to the southern, or rather, as it is now called, the middle island.

The *Endeavour* was now steered down the eastern coast of the last named portion of New Zealand. Some lofty mountains were seen partially covered with snow, and inferior in height to Mount Egmont. During a calm, when close in shore, Mr. Banks went out in a small boat for the purpose of shooting. While he was away four double canoes were seen to put off from the shore, and to pull towards him. Captain Cook trembled for his friend's safety, for Mr. Banks could not see the signals made to hasten his return. At length he noticed the natives, and his boat's head was turned towards the ship. The natives also approached. He, however, got on board before them, thankful for his escape. Probably indeed their attention had been so engrossed with the ship that they had not seen him. When they came about a stone's throw off, they stopped and gazed at the ship with vacant astonishment; but even Tupia's eloquence could not induce them to come on board. After surveying the ship they made towards the shore, but it was dark before they could have reached it. This was the only sight Captain Cook had of the inhabitants of the middle island, or *Tovy Poenammoo*.

An island about twenty-four leagues in circumference, and five leagues from the main, was discovered, to which the name of Banks' Island was given. Some persons on board asserting that they saw land to the south-east, the commander, though believing that they were mistaken, steered in that direction; but no land being discovered the ship wore, and was steered east-south-east. Tovy Poenammoo was found to be very much larger than Captain Cook expected to find it, from the description of the natives in Queen Charlotte's Sound. Heavy gales and rough seas were encountered, and on one occasion, at dawn, rocks were seen close under the ship's bows, she having in the night passed close to another dangerous reef, some leagues from the main. The land discovered appeared green and well wooded, but destitute of inhabitants. Several whales and seals were observed, whereas none had been seen off the north island. At length, on the 5th of March, the south cape was rounded. At the time Captain Cook was doubtful whether it was part of the large island or a separate island; though he marked it in his chart as the former. Nothing of importance occurred during the passage back to the entrance of Cook's Straits, on the northern shore of which, in a bay called Admiralty, the *Endeavour* again anchored that she might fill up with wood and water. This was accomplished by the 31st March, 1770, when a course was shaped by which it was hoped the eastern coast of New Holland would be reached. It was intended, after visiting that coast, to return home by the East Indies and the Cape of Good Hope. Captain Cook himself had wished to return by Cape Horn, with the view of settling the question of a great southern continent; but the ship was deemed unfit to brave the tempests to be expected in a high southern latitude in the most inclement season of the year. The name of Cape Farewell was given to the last point of land seen as the *Endeavour* quitted the coast of New Zealand. The manners and customs of the inhabitants as well as the features of New Zealand are now almost as well known as those of any country in Europe; and we are able to judge of the extraordinary accuracy of all Captain Cook's descriptions whenever he had an opportunity of observing them.

Cape Farewell was left on the 31st of March, and the *Endeavour* sailed westward. Nine days afterwards, a tropical bird was seen; and on the 15th, the voyagers caught sight of an egg-bird and a gannet; and as these birds never fly far from land, the lead was constantly heaved through the night. No bottom, however was found; and it was not till six o'clock on the morning of the 19th of April that land was seen by Mr. Hicks, the first lieutenant. This land proved to be part of the vast country of New Holland, since better known as Australia. The coast first seen was that of New South Wales.

The *Endeavour* now coasted along about three leagues from the shore, and as the weather was clear a pleasant landscape presented itself before the eyes of the explorers. The land was of moderate elevation, diversified by hills and valleys, ridges and plains. Here and there were open spaces clothed with verdure, but in general the country was covered with timber. Smoke was in several places seen, showing that the country was inhabited.

Several days were spent—the *Endeavour* coasting along the shore to the northward; but on account of a northerly wind the voyagers were seldom near enough to remark the features of the country. At last a bay was discovered which seemed to be well-sheltered from all winds, and Captain Cook determined to anchor in it. Just before this several natives had been seen on the shore, four of them carrying a canoe, but they did not come off, and when the yawl, in which the commander attempted to land, approached, they all ran away. So heavy a surf broke on the beach that it was found impossible to go ashore.

The pinnace was now sent ahead with the master to sound, while, the wind being out, the ship beat into the bay. A smoke being seen on shore the glasses were directed towards it, when ten men were observed sitting round a fire, which they presently left, and then ascended a slight eminence, whence they could observe the proceedings of the English visitors. As the pinnace pulled along the shore most of the natives kept abreast of her. Some of them used threatening gestures, brandishing their weapons: there were two especially whose faces seem to have been dusted with a white powder, and their bodies painted with broad streaks, also white, which passing obliquely over their breast and backs looked not unlike the cross-belts worn by soldiers. The same kind of streaks were also drawn round their legs and thighs, like broad garters. They were armed with long spears, and each of these men held in his hand a weapon curved like a scimitar, and which appeared to be about two feet and a half long. The *Endeavour* anchored two miles within the bay, in six fathoms water, abreast of a small village consisting of six or eight huts. On the two points on either side of the entrance a few huts, and men, women, and children, were seen, as were four small canoes, with a man in each engaged in fishing, so intent on their occupation that they took no notice of the ship. An old woman also, followed by three children, came out of a thicket laden with fire-wood, each of the children having its burden. When she reached the huts three more children came out to meet her. She looked often at the ship but manifested no surprise, and went on with her occupation and kindled a fire. Presently the men landed, hauled up their canoes, and began to dress the fish, apparently unconcerned at the stranger ship within half a mile of them. None of the savages had on a particle of clothing. It was a curious scene, like that of a drama in which the actors take no notice of the spectators.

FIRST LANDING-PLACE, BOTANY BAY.

In this instance, however, the actors were not so indifferent as they at first appeared; for when Captain Cook and several companions approached the shore in one of the boats, although the greater number of the people ran away, two men armed with lances came down on the rocks to dispute the landing of the strangers.* It was not an inapt representation on a small scale of the contest which, ere many years had rolled by, was to begin on these shores between savagedom and civilization, when the latter would with giant strides sweep over and subdue the land. The two brave savages kept flourishing their lances and shouting in discordant tones, and Captain Cook, unwilling to injure them, ordered his crew to lie on their oars while he tried to parley with them. To show also his goodwill he threw them nails, beads, and other trifles, which they took up and seemed pleased to obtain. They then waved their hands and seemed to invite their visitors on shore, but as soon as the boat approached they hurried again to oppose a landing. Captain Cook, as a last resource, fired a musket between them. On hearing the report the youngest dropped a bundle of lances, but quickly picked them up, while the eldest, as if in defiance, threw a stone at the intruders. Upon this a musket with small shot was fired at his legs, on which he scampered off to the huts. It was hoped that the contest was now over, and accordingly the English stepped on the shore of that vast territory which was to become the heritage of millions of the Anglo-Saxon race. Still the savage was not subdued, and appeared once more with a shield on his arm, and advancing, made one more significant protest against the intrusion of the white man, by hurling a spear into the very midst of the strangers. Happily no one was hurt, and a third musket loaded with small shot being fired at them, after another spear had been thrown by one of the brave natives, they both took to flight, and the English claimed to be by right of conquest the lords of the soil. They might have

* A tablet has been placed to mark the spot where Captain Cook and his party landed, as may be seen in the engraving.

pursued and overtaken the savages, but Mr. Banks suggested that the spears were possibly poisoned, and that it would be imprudent to venture into the woods.

On entering one of the huts some little children were seen partially concealed, but they were not disturbed, and when the English went away, some beads, ribbons, and pieces of cloth were left in the huts as presents, which it was hoped would gain the good-will of the natives. Fifty spears, from six to fifteen feet long, found lying about were carried off. It was at first supposed that they were poisoned; but on further examination it was found that they were used for spearing fish, and that the green substance found sticking to them was seaweed.

The next morning, a stream was found at which the casks could be filled. While this operation was going on, the natives came down and watched the proceedings with wonder, but did not venture to approach the strangers, though Mr. Hicks advanced towards them with presents in his hands, making every sign of friendship he could think of. That the bay was full of fish, and capable of giving food to a large population, Captain Cook had ample proof; for going with Mr. Banks and Dr. Solander to a cove on the north side of the bay, in three or four hauls with the seine, they took above three hundred weight of fish.

An expedition into the country was planned the same day by the commander, Mr. Banks, Dr. Solander, and seven others, and from it a very fair idea of the general face of the country was obtained. On visiting the huts they found that the natives had not taken away the presents that had been left for them; and others therefore of greater value were added. Presents were left also at all the huts which were passed, in the hopes of thus gaining the good-will of the natives. The trees were tall, straight, and without underwood, and at such a distance from each other that the land might be cultivated without cutting down a tree. The

H

ground was covered with an abundance of grass, growing in tufts close together, about as large as could well be grasped in the hand Although numerous huts were seen the natives kept themselves carefully concealed, though probably watching the strangers at a distance; a glimpse only was caught of one man, who instantly ran away. A transient view was got of an animal as big as a rabbit, and of the tracks of another of the size of a wolf, clawed like a dog; traces of a third which fed on grass, and judged to be not less than a deer in size were also seen. The trees overhead abounded with birds of various kinds, among which were many of exquisite beauty, particularly loriquets and cockatoos, which flew in scores together. The trees however were not of many species; among others was one which yielded a gum not unlike the *sanguis draconis*.

Many other excursions were made on shore, especially by Mr. Banks and Dr. Solander, in search of plants, of which they found vast quantities; and from this circumstance Captain Cook gave the place the name of BOTANY BAY, a name the whole country commonly bore for more than half a century afterwards.

Every effort to establish a friendly intercourse with the natives failed. They had undoubtedly watched, though unperceived, the effect of the white men's weapons; and from awe and terror kept at a distance; still, when they had an opportunity, they showed their hostility to the strangers, and Mr. Monkhouse narrowly escaped a spear thrown at him while he was wandering in the woods.

During the ship's stay in Botany Bay, Captain Cook had the English colours hoisted every day on a flag staff on shore, and caused the ship's name and the date of her visit to be engraved on a tree near the watering place.

At daybreak, on Tuesday the 6th of May, 1770 the *Endeavour* sailed from Botany Bay, and at noon the same day, in latitude 33° 50′ s., she was abreast of a fine looking harbour to which

Captain Cook gave the name of Port Jackson. Northerly winds prevented the ship from making much progress till, in latitude 32° 40′, another harbour was seen, and called Port Stephens. The ship continued her course to the north; smoke was frequently seen, and occasionally the natives were observed. The land increased considerably in height as she advanced, and in many places exhibited a pleasing variety of ridges, hills, valleys, and plains, all clothed with wood. A wide open bay was passed in latitude 27° 6′, and called Moreton Bay.

It had now become necessary to lay the ship ashore, and Captain Cook's object was to find a place where this might be accomplished with safety. Had he entered Port Jackson, he would have found one of the finest harbours in the world for his purpose. He several times anchored while proceeding along the coast, and landed to explore the country—the natives, as before, running off and hiding themselves. Rockingham Bay was passed and named, in latitude 17° 59′. Hitherto the *Endeavour* had met with no misfortune; but as she was now to make acquaintance with it, the point seen farthest to the north was called Cape Tribulation. It lies in latitude 16° 4′ s. and longitude 145° 26′ E.

One beautiful moonlight night, as the ship was speeding on her course with a fair wind, among the shoals of that coral sea, and while most of the officers and crew were tranquilly asleep, she suddenly struck upon a reef, and instantly roused every one on board to the horrors of shipwreck on an inhospitable coast, where they might linger for years without succour. However, the captain and his officers and crew were equal to the emergency, and by throwing everything weighty overboard that could be spared, the ship floated, but was making water rapidly. Had the weather been at all stormy, no human power could have saved their vessel. As it was, the fine weather continued long enough to enable them to draw a sail over the leak. This served the purpose of keeping her in sailing trim, until she was safely moored at the mouth of a creek, which was named Endeavour River. This was on the 17th June, and they remained there repairing the damage to the ship, as well as circumstances permitted, until the 4th of August.

Although the *Endeavour* was now out of danger, her captain had still abundant cause for anxiety on another account:—in spite of all his care, the fearful malady of scurvy had gained, and was

THE ENDEAVOUR LAID UP ON SHORE FOR REPAIRS.

still gaining ground among the ship's company. Poor Tupia, who all his life had been accustomed to fresh fruit and vegetables, was among the chief sufferers, and symptoms were showing themselves which proved that the malignant disease had already made rapid progress. Mr. Green the astronomer, was also, among many others, stricken and disabled. As soon as possible therefore, a tent was put up on shore for the reception of the sick, and recourse was had to nets, for providing fresh fish for the invalids.

The ground in the immediate neighbourhood of the river, was either swampy, sandy, or stony. Mr. Banks, who went on shore with his gun, saw great quantities of pigeons and crows: of the former, which were very beautiful, he shot several. He also saw some deserted human habitations, but no natives.

Four guns having been got up from the hold, were mounted on the quarter deck of the ship, and the heavy stores and powder were landed, that her damages might be examined. It was indeed both wonderful and providential that she had escaped destruction; for not only had the sharp rock torn off the planking and worked its way into the timbers, but one point had cut a hole right through the bottom, and, breaking off, had happily remained fixed. Had it fallen out, no human power could have prevented the ship from foundering. Besides the leak, which was on the starboard side, the ship had sustained very extensive injury on the larboard. The sheathing from the bow on that side was torn off, and a great part of the false keel was gone. The carpenters at once commenced their work; and the forge was set up, that the smiths might make bolts and nails.

While this was going on, some of the people were sent on shore to shoot pigeons for the sick, and on their return they reported that they had found a stream of fresh water, and had seen several native huts, and an animal as large as a greyhound, of slender form, mouse-coloured, and very swift. The next day Captain Cook himself saw the same animal; it had a long tail, and leaped like a hare or deer, and the print of its feet were like those of a goat. For some time afterwards nothing more was seen of the animal, which Mr. Banks, the naturalist, considered must be of some hitherto unknown species; so indeed it was, for it had no congeners in any quarter of the globe previously visited, though now the kangaroo is familiar enough to all readers of natural history, and it forms part of the arms of the colony of New South Wales.

Mr. Banks likewise captured an Australian opossum, a female, with two young ones. This class of animals was formerly supposed to be peculiar to America, from whence its name is derived. Being nocturnal in their habits, nothing is to be seen of them in the day-time, unless you can catch a glimpse of one at noon-tide, sleeping soundly in the hollow of a tree. When night comes, they leap from bough to bough with the greatest animation, especially if it be moonlight. Some species, with thin membranes between the fore and hind paws, can take a flying leap of, sometimes, thirty yards from tree to tree; and hence they are called flying squirrels, though perfectly distinct in their nature, and in some of their habits, from that animal.

THE KANGAROO.

The carpenters continued to work hard on the ship whenever the tide permitted them. The position in which she was now placed, with her bow on the bank, naturally threw all the water aft, and from this circumstance the world was very nearly losing the results of Mr. Banks' labours. For greater security he had placed his collection of plants in the bread room, into which the water ran, and covered them completely. By great care most of them were dried, but many were entirely spoilt.

In consequence of the carpenters being able to work only at low tide, the repairs of the ship proceeded very slowly. In the meantime, however, the people benefited from being on shore, and every effort was made to obtain fresh provisions, calculated to improve their health. The commander himself went to superintend the hauling of the seine; but this was attended with little success, for during one evening only between twenty and thirty fish were caught. A root with leaves like spinach, many cabbage trees, and a wild plantain, were found, with a fruit of a deep purple colour, of the size of a pippin, which improved on keeping; Mr. Banks also discovered a plant, called in the West Indies, Indian kale, which served for greens. These greens, with a large supply of fish afterwards caught, afforded great relief to the voyagers, who had so long been compelled to live on salt meat. Their fresh provisions were further varied by some large cockles, one of which was of such size that it furnished an ample meal for two men. What was of still greater value was the discovery of some fine turtle by the master, three of which he caught when out surveying; though afterwards, when sent out expressly to find more, he seems to have purposely thwarted the wishes of his commander, who, indeed, had too much cause to complain of the narrow-mindedness and ignorance of several of his officers. Many other turtles were, however, afterwards caught, of a species called the green turtle.

Some time elapsed before one of the animals which had been so much the subject of speculation was shot by Mr. Gore. This was a young one—but others were seen equal in size to sheep—the larger sort are indeed much larger than sheep. The fore legs of this specimen were only eight inches long, and the hind legs two and twenty; its mode of progress being by a succession of hops and leaps, helped by its long tail, with which also it balances itself in its progress. It is easy to imagine the interest with which this curious animal, now seen for the first time by civilized men, was examined by Mr. Banks and his brother naturalists. The next day their kangaroo (for so the animal was called by the natives) was dressed for dinner, and proved most excellent. The explorers might now have been said to fare sumptuously every day; for they had an abundance of green turtle, fish, and vegetables of different sorts, with an occasional kangaroo. It was indeed fortunate for the crew of the *Endeavour* that the accident happened to her in this latitude, instead of farther south, where although the soil amply rewards the labours of men, yet its spontaneous productions are very inferior to those of the north. Kangaroos certainly would have been found in abundance, and perhaps fish; but scarcely any vegetables fit for the food of man.

Favourably, however, as the navigators were situated for diet, their position in other respects was unsatisfactory. This was ascertained by the captain who, with Mr. Banks, one day started on a long walk northward, partly to obtain a view of the country, but chiefly to take note of appearances seaward. After traversing the country about eight miles they ascended a high hill, and were soon convinced that the danger of their situation was at least equal to their apprehensions, for in whatever direction they turned their eyes, they saw rocks and shoals without number, and no passage out to sea, but through the winding channels between them, which could not be navigated without the last degree of difficulty and peril. The reports of the master was equally unsatisfactory with regard to the shoals and dangers off the mouth of the harbour, and it seems surprising that the ship should have escaped them on her passage up the coasts. Still, as she had got in, there was no doubt that she might get out, could the right passage be found. They had other causes for hope and thankfulness: the natives were not likely to prove troublesome, the climate was healthy, and food abundant.

Besides kangaroos, wild dogs were seen, which were supposed to be foxes or wolves, as they partly resembled both these animals. With the natives for some time no intercourse was opened. At last, some appeared on the opposite side of the river, very black, totally naked, and with lances in their hands. The commander judiciously ordered his people to take no notice of them, as the best means of drawing them near. This plan succeeded so well that two of them came off in a canoe to within a musket shot, and talked very loudly. They were answered in the same tone, and by degrees they drew nearer, when some cloth, nails, beads, paper, and other trifles, were thrown to them. Of these things, however, they seemed to take no notice; but were highly pleased when a fish was offered them. Some of them afterwards landed, where Tupia and the rest of the crew were sitting, and he prevailed on them to lay down their arms, and to come forward without them. He then made signs that they should sit down by him. With this they complied, and seemed to be under no apprehension or constraint, although on more people going on shore they expressed by their gestures some fear lest the new comers should get between them and their arms. More presents were made to them, to show the good will of the strangers, and their desire to continue on friendly terms. To prove this the Englishmen made signs that they were going to dinner, and invited the blacks to eat with them; the latter, however, declined the honour, and went away in their canoes. These men were of the common stature, but their limbs were remarkably small, their hair was black, but not woolly, some of them wearing it short cropped, others lank and long, and others had it curled. Their colour was dark chocolate, but the tint was owing somewhat to the dirt which covered their skins. They had lively eyes, and their teeth were even and white. The tones of their voices were soft and musical, and there was a flexibility in their organs of speech which enabled them to repeat, with great facility, many English words.

The next day three of the same party of natives paid the strangers a visit, with a fourth whom they introduced as Yaparico. This personage was distinguished by having the bone of a bird, six inches long, thrust through the cartilage of his nose. He seemed to prize this strange ornament as much as a young dandy does his newly raised silken moustache. On examination, all his companions were found to have holes in their ears as he also had, while on the upper part of their arms they wore bracelets of plaited hair; thus evincing a taste for ornament, although they had not a rag of any sort of clothing. The previous day the only gift they seemed to prize was a fish, which was offered them. To day they brought one in return. They were, however, excessively jealous and suspicious, and in consequence of one of the gentlemen examining their canoe they at once jumped into her and paddled away.

The following day, three natives ventured down to Tupia's tent, and were so well pleased with the way he received them, that they went away and brought two others, whom they introduced to him formally by name, a ceremony they never omitted. Some fish were given to them, but after eating a small portion they threw the rest to Mr. Banks' dog. They could not be persuaded to go far from their canoe, which was about ten feet long, fitted with an outrigger, and, though very inferior, like those of the Society Islands. They used paddles, and in shallow water poled it along.

One day, on the commander's return from an excursion on shore, he found several natives on board. Of all the articles exhibited to them, nothing seemed to have attracted their attention so much as the turtles, of which there were no less than twelve on deck. Two days afterwards, they came again, bringing with them a greater number of lances than before. These they placed in a tree, with a man and a boy to watch them. It was evident that their object was to get one of the turtles. They asked for one by signs, and being refused, appealed to everybody who appeared to them to have any authority. Then seizing one, they attempted to drag it overboard. On its being taken from them, they jumped into their canoe in a rage, and went on shore. Here Mr. Banks and others followed them. Before they could be stopped they seized their arms, and, snatching a brand from under

CHLAMYDOSAURUS, OR FRILLED LIZARD OF NEW HOLLAND.

a pitch kettle, they whirled it round with great dexterity and rapidity, and set fire to the grass, which was six feet or more high, and dry as stubble. The fire burnt with fearful rapidity. The woodwork of the smith's forge was destroyed; it caught a sow and some young pigs, one of which was scorched to death, and Mr. Banks had great difficulty in saving his tent, which had been set up for Tupia on shore. Happily, most of the stores, with the powder, had been taken back to the ship, or the consequences might have been more serious.

In another place the seamen were washing, and a quantity of linen and the nets were spread out to dry. Here the natives, disregarding all threats and entreaties, again set fire to the grass. By great exertions the fire was extinguished before it had done much damage, but where it had first been kindled, it burnt with great fury, and spread into the woods to a long distance. A gun loaded with small shot was now fired at the natives, which put them to flight, one of them being wounded; and to give them a lesson, a bullet was fired to pass near them, and this of course hastened their retreat. It was thought that now they would give no more trouble; but in a short time they came back, and Mr. Banks and others went out to meet them.

An old man among the natives then advanced, having a lance in his hand, without a point. He came forward slowly, stopping several times, and the English made signs to him that they wished to be friends. On this, he turned round and addressed his companions, and they, having set up their arms against a tree, also came forward in a friendly manner. The lances which had been taken from them were then returned; this evidently afforded them great satisfaction; and the reconciliation was considered complete.

Several strangers who were among the party were now introduced by name; and on receiving some presents they went away highly contented.

The next day no natives appeared, but the hills all round, for many miles, were on fire, the effects of which by night were very striking. Had the voyagers been compelled by circumstances to remain on that coast, the result of these fires would have been serious, as the conflagration would have driven the kangaroos and the feathered tribes to a distance, and thus deprived the crew of the *Endeavour* of some of their principal means of support. But the ship was now ready for sea, though the master had been unable to find any channel to the northward by which an escape could be made from among the coral reefs which hemmed her in.

It was necessary, however, to make the attempt without delay, as provisions and stores were running short, and the proper time for navigating the Indian seas was passing by. They were doomed to have their patience yet further tried, for when all was ready heavy gales prevented the ship from putting to sea.

On the 29th of July the weather moderated, the wind came off the land, and everything appeared favourable for sailing, when it was found that there was not sufficient water on the bar for the ship to pass over it. For several days more the ship was detained by the unfavourable state of the weather: the detention would have been of still greater consequence had not the boats sent out to catch fish and turtle been tolerably successful. At length, on the 4th of August, Captain Cook had the satisfaction of sailing out of Endeavour Harbour. The ship was surrounded by shoals, and he was yet in doubt whether he should beat back to the southward, or seek a passage to the north or east. He had now a most anxious time, for it was clear that there was no way to sea except through the labyrinth of shoals amid which the ship lay. The navigation of a ship among coral rocks is at all times dangerous, for the lead gives no notice of their vicinity, their sides rising up like walls from almost unfathomable depths.

Night now approaching, the *Endeavour* anchored, when soon afterwards it came on to blow very hard, and at eleven she began to drive. More cable was veered away, and this brought her up; but in the morning it coming on to blow harder she drove again. All the appliances of seamanship were put into operation but still she drove, when topgallant masts were got down, and yards and topmasts struck, and now at length she rode securely.

In this position she continued till the 10th, when Captain Cook, having resolved to search for a passage close in shore to the northward, she got under weigh and stood in that direction with the boats exploring ahead. Nothing but the greatest caution, perseverance, and first-rate seamanship, could have taken the *Endeavour* free of the dangers which surrounded her. Hour after hour the sagacious commander was at the mast-head, or away in a boat searching for a passage, while the rest of the boats were employed in a similar service. At length a passage was discovered and, with the boats piloting ahead, the *Endeavour* stood through it.

A long rolling swell convinced the voyagers that they had no rocks or shoals to fear, but at the same time proved to them that they must not place the same confidence in their ship as before she had struck; for the seas she now encountered so widened the leaks that they admitted no less than nine inches of water an hour, which, considering the state of the pumps, and the navigation before them, was a matter of serious consideration.

The great object Captain Cook had now in view was to ascertain whether the coast of New Holland, along which he was sailing, was or was not united to that of New Guinea. He was afraid that, if he stood on long to the north, he might overshoot the passage, should one exist. At six in the evening, therefore, he brought the ship to with her head to the north-east, no land being in sight. The next morning sail was made, and land seen, and as the day advanced a reef appeared over which the sea broke heavily, extending from north to south as far as the eye could reach, with an occasional break between the ship and the land. The wind was then east-south-east; but scarcely had the sails been trimmed to haul off it than the wind shifted to east by north, which

DRIVING ON TO A CORAL REEF.

made it very doubtful whether the ship could clear the reef. The lead was kept going all night while the ship stood to the northward, but no bottom was found, yet at four o'clock the roaring of the surf was distinctly heard, and at break of day it was seen foaming to a vast height at not more than a mile off. The seas, too, which rolled in on the reef rapidly carried the ship towards it. The wind fell to a dead calm, and the depth made it impossible to anchor. The only prospect of saving the ship was by rowing; but the pinnace was under repair and useless, the long boat and yawl were, however, sent ahead to tow, and sweeps were got out.

Still these efforts could only delay the destruction which seemed inevitable. The ship continued to drive on towards the fatal reef; she was within a hundred yards of it, and the same billow which washed her side broke on the reef to a tremendous height the very next time it rose. The carpenters had been working at the pinnace, and she was now lowered, but even with her assistance the *Endeavour* drove nearer and still nearer to the reef. At the very moment that her doom seemed fixed a light air sprang up, and, with the help of the boats, gave her once more head-way. Scarcely, however, had ten minutes passed before the wind again dropped, and the ship was driven back towards the roaring breakers. Again the gentle breeze returned and lasted another ten minutes. During this time an opening had been discovered, and the ship was towed towards it, but so strong a current set through it that she was driven fully a quarter of a mile away from the reef. Aided by the boats the ebb tide carried her nearly two miles away by noon. When the flood made, however, she was once more carried back towards the reef; but in the meantime the first lieutenant had discovered a passage, and a light breeze springing up it was resolved to attempt it. The boats continued towing ahead, the raging, roaring sea leaped up on either side, the breeze filled the sails, the tide swept rapidly onward, and in

I

a short time the *Endeavour* was within the reef, safe from present danger, and anchored in nineteen fathoms water.

Captain Cook now resolved to keep the land close on board, in spite of all dangers, for fear of missing the channel. Numerous islands and headlands were passed and named, and rocks and reefs were escaped, and at length perseverance and sagacity were rewarded by the discovery of York Cape, the northern promontory of the country, and the southern side of Torres Straits, through which the *Endeavour* triumphantly passed.

As Captain Cook was now about to leave the eastern coast of New Holland, which he had followed up from latitude 38°, and which he was confident no European had ever before seen, he landed on an island, which he named Possession Island, and once more took formal possession of the whole eastern coast of the mainland, in right of His Majesty King George the Third. He gave to the country, with all its bays, rivers, and islands, the name of New South Wales. Three volleys of small arms were then fired, and these were answered by the same number from the ship. Ten natives were seen on the island when this ceremony was performed, and seemed astounded, as they very well might be.

They were seen to be armed with spears; one of them had also a bow and a bundle of arrows, which weapons had not before been seen. Two of them had large ornaments of mother of pearl hanging round their necks. It was expected that when the boats approached they would have made a show of opposing a landing, but, instead of that they walked leisurely away. They and their descendants have never been disturbed in their possession of the island, and at the present day it is exactly in the state it was when Cook visited it.

Some time was occupied in the intricate navigation of the straits, and the *Endeavour* then steered north, along the south-western coast of New Guinea, but, the water being shallow, at such a distance from the shore it could scarcely be seen from the ship. Still, as the commander wished to ascertain the character of the country, and the appearance of the inhabitants, he steered in for the land till about three or four miles from it, and in three fathom water, when the ship came to an anchor on the 3rd of September.

The pinnace being hoisted out Captain Cook, with Mr. Banks and his servants, Dr. Solander, and the boat's crew, in all twelve persons, well armed, embarked in her and pulled directly for the shore. But the water was so shallow that they could not reach it by about two hundred yards, they therefore waded the rest of the way, and left two seamen to take care of the boat. As yet no inhabitants had been seen, but when the party landed they discovered the print of feet on the sand below high water mark, showing that people had lately been there. A thick wood came down to within a hundred yards of the water. To avoid the risk of being cut off by an ambush the explorers proceeded cautiously, skirting the wood till they came to a grove of cocoa-nut trees of small growth which stood on the bank of a little stream. The trees were well hung with fruit, and near them was a small hut round which lay a number of the freshly picked shells. Tempting as was the fruit it was not considered safe to climb the trees to obtain it; they were obliged, therefore, to leave the grove without tasting a nut. Farther on they met with a bread-fruit tree and some plantains, and had got about a quarter of a mile from the boat when three blacks rushed out of the wood with a hideous shout and ran towards them. The foremost threw something from his hand which burnt like gunpowder, and the other two darted their lances at the strangers. As it was necessary to keep these savages at a distance they were fired at with small shot, but as this did not make them retreat, and they threw another dart, some bullets were discharged at them. The effect was to make them run; but it was hoped that none of them were wounded. As Captain Cook says, he had no desire to invade the country either to gratify appetite or curiosity, he judged it right and merciful to retreat at once so as not to have to destroy more of the ignorant savages. There was no time to lose, as the men in the boat made signs that more natives were collecting. They had succeeded in getting safely on board, when they saw nearly a hundred savages who shouted and threw fire-darts, several at a time, towards them. On board ship it was supposed, from the effect produced, that the natives had fire-arms, and even from the boat, had they not been so near, the English would have fancied from the flash and smoke that the blacks were firing musketry; the sound only was wanting. Some muskets being fired over their heads they walked leisurely away. In appearance these natives were very similar to those of New Holland, though their skin was not quite so dark. They were all stark naked. The land was low and covered with a luxuriance of wood and herbage that can scarcely be conceived. Some of the officers wished to send on shore to cut down the cocoa-nut trees for the sake of the fruit, but the commander refused to comply with their proposal, feeling that it would be cruel and criminal to

ORNITHORYNCUS PARADOXUS OF AUSTRALIA.*

* This remarkable animal is peculiar to Australia. It is commonly called the "duck-billed water-mole," and in appearance and structure seems to be allied to both reptile, quadruped, and bird. It was first discovered in 1797

risk the lives of the natives, who would certainly try to defend their property, merely for the sake of a transient gratification. The boat was therefore hoisted in and sail made to the westward.

The more interesting portion of Captain Cook's first voyage round the world was now accomplished. He had successfully made the important observation for which he was sent out; he had become intimately acquainted with the inhabitants of Otaheite and several of the adjacent islands, though, from the cunning of the people, he had failed to discover that it was among the darkest of "the dark places of the earth." He had shown that if there was a great southern continent, it must be in a very high latitude; he had proved that New Zealand consisted of two great islands, and had cause to suspect the existence of a third smaller one; he had sailed along the coast of New Holland, and had made the acquaintance of its inhabitants, and many of its animal and vegetable productions. Though he had seen the coast of Tasmania, and admired its beauty, he had not discovered that it was separated from New Holland; but he had settled the point before in dispute, whether that little known land was or was not joined to New Guinea, by sailing between them; and he had shown that the eastern coast of the island-continent of Australia—was fit to become the habitation of civilized men. This great fact was, after all, the most important result of the voyage.

The condition of the *Endeavour* had, by this time, become very critical. So battered were her lower timbers and planks, and so out of order were her pumps, that a heavy sea might at any moment have sent her to the bottom. It was absolutely necessary to find a harbour where she might be hove down to undergo a complete refit. Under these circumstances the commander of the expedition determined to go to Batavia, the capital of the Dutch settlements in the island of Java, and at that time the centre of commerce in those seas. He had indeed no option, for there was not another port which he could hope to reach, where the ship would receive the necessary repairs. He was not, indeed, ignorant of the unhealthiness of the climate; but he hoped not to be detained there long, and that his hardy crew would be able for a short time to withstand its ill effects.

The first island of any size which the *Endeavour* sighted after leaving New Guinea was Timor, along the shore of which she coasted. Notwithstanding the wishes of some of his officers, Captain Cook declined to put in there, as he was anxious to reach Batavia without delay. Between that island and Java, however, he fell in with a small island, which at first he thought was a new discovery; but on steering for it and getting close in with the north side, houses, plantations, and numerous flocks of sheep were seen. The temptation of obtaining fresh meat and vegetables was not to be resisted, as there were many sick on board; and accordingly Mr. Gore was sent on shore to open a communication with the natives. Two persons were seen riding on the hills as if for their amusement, and often stopping to look at the ship. This made the voyagers suspect that there must be a settlement of Europeans on the island. Such was in fact the case. The Dutch East India Company had a short time before taken possession of it, and sent a resident to superintend their affairs, though the native rajah or chief was still retained as the nominal ruler of the island. This island proved to be Savu, at that time so little known, that it was not to be found on any of the charts on board. It is about thirty miles long, and was then very thickly populated.

In the evening, the ship entered a bay before a large native town, over which the Dutch colours were flying, and three guns were fired. The native chief treated the strangers very courteously, and was evidently ready to supply them with all they desired. They were informed that the island abounded in buffaloes, sheep, horses, asses, goats, hogs, dogs, cats, fowls and pigeons, with most of the fruits of the tropics. The resident, Mr. Lange, however, though polite in his manners, very soon showed that he was determined to make a gain of the visitors, and asked the most exorbitant prices for all the provisions they required, besides insisting that they should be paid for in gold. Fortunately, by a well-timed present to an old man, the rajah's prime minister, his services were engaged, and ultimately through his means, all the provisions which were required were procured at fair prices. The island was divided into five provinces, with a rajah over each, who could altogether muster upwards of seven thousand fighting men. All the rajahs were said to live on friendly terms with each other, and the inhabitants were described by Mr. Lange as being particularly well conducted and moral. Their religion was a kind of paganism, but of a most liberal description, according to the account given by Mr. Lange; each man having the liberty to set up a god in his own house, and to worship it after his own fashion. Although in many instances the Dutch have been sadly unmindful of the spiritual as well as temporal interests of the inhabitants of their colonial possessions, they had sent to this island a Dutch officer and a native woman, who had been brought up a Christian, charged with the education of the people, and their instruction in the principles of Christianity. The Dutch had also printed versions of the New Testament, a catechism, and several tracts in the language of this and the neighbouring islands. The number of Christians in the township of Seba alone, was estimated at six hundred. If the character given by Mr. Lange of these islanders was correct, a true Christian missionary would have found a prolific field open to him among them.

The *Endeavour* left the interesting island of Savu on the 21st of September, 1770, and made Java Head at the west end of Java, on the 1st of October. Poor Tupia was very ill, and on the morning of the next day a boat was sent on shore to procure some fresh fruit for him, and some grass for the buffaloes, which, with sheep, pigs, and fowls, had recently been got on board. On passing through the Straits of Sunda, the *Endeavour* was boarded by the Dutch authorities, and various official enquiries were made as to whence she had come, and the object of her voyage. These being answered, she proceeded to Batavia.

Captain Cook and his companions were received into port by the Dutch governor with all the courtesy and kindness which could be expected. Permission was given them to take up their abode in private residences, although strangers were, as a rule, compelled to live at a hotel, under the direct supervision of the authorities. Leave was also obtained to heave down the ship in order to repair her damages, which were found on inspection to be of a very serious nature. Indeed, in one place the planking was so worn by the grinding on the rocks, that it did not exceed the thickness of the sole of a man's shoe. Her frame in many places was much shattered, and her pumps had become rotten and utterly useless.

Batavia had long had the reputation of being very unhealthy. The crew, however, thought themselves thoroughly seasoned to all climates, and their rosy countenances contrasted favourably with the pale faces of those who had been even a few weeks at the place. All indeed, with the exception of Tupia, were in good health when they entered the port. Even he revived at the strange sights which met his gaze as he entered for the first time a civilized town. The houses, carriages, streets, people, and a number of other novel objects, had the effect on him of fascination. Tayeto expressed his wonder and delight with still less restraint, and danced along the street in a kind of ecstasy, examining every object with a restless and eager curiosity. Tupia, remarking the various dresses of the people of different countries, desired likewise

BATAVIA, FROM THE SEA.

to put on his native costume. South Sea cloth was therefore sent for from the ship, in which he immediately equipped himself.

In the course of a few days, however, the effects of the climate began to be felt. Poor Tupia, after the excitement caused by the novelties he witnessed had subsided, experienced a reaction, and every day grew worse and worse. Young Tayeto also was seized with an inflammation of the lungs, and both Dr. Solander and Mr. Banks and his two servants were taken seriously ill; indeed, almost all the people belonging to the ship, on board or ashore, were sick; affected by the low swampy situation of the place, and the numberless dirty canals which intersected the town in all directions.

Tents were then set up on shore, on Cooper's Island, for the ship's company, and one was also pitched by Mr. Banks' desire for Tupia, who was anxious to escape from the close air of the town. Mr. Banks accompanied him, and remained with him for two days, till compelled by his own illness (a regular tertian ague) to return to his lodgings. Mr. Monkhouse, the surgeon of the ship, was the first victim, and Dr. Solander could with difficulty crawl out of bed to attend his funeral, which Mr. Banks from illness was unable to do. On the 9th the poor young boy Tayeto died, and Tupia, who loved him as a son, was so much affected that he rapidly sank, and in two days followed him to the grave. The lives of Mr. Banks and Dr. Solander were saved by their removal to a healthy spot, some miles from the city. Altogether, seven persons who had come in the ship were buried at Batavia; but many others imbibed the seeds of disease, which, in a short time, proved fatal.

Every possible assistance which Captain Cook required was given by the Dutch governor, and on the 26th of December, 1770, having taken leave of him and the principal people in the place, the voyagers set sail from Batavia with a light breeze from south-west. At that time the number of sick on board amounted to forty, and the rest of the ship's company were in a very feeble condition. Every man had been ill except one, the sail-maker, who was upwards of seventy years of age; he, however, was among those who died on the passage to the Cape of Good Hope.

After leaving Java, the *Endeavour* touched at Prince's Island, where she took in water and fresh provisions. Shortly afterwards, dysenteries and slow fevers appeared, and so violent were the symptoms that the ship was a complete hospital, those who were able to move about being insufficient to attend to the sick in their hammocks. Mr. Banks was so ill that his life was despaired of. Mr. Green, Mr. Sporing, Mr. Parkinson, the natural history painter, with Mr. Monkhouse, and many others, three-and-twenty persons in all, in addition to the seven buried at Batavia, died before the ship reached the Cape of Good Hope. On the 15th of March, the *Endeavour* anchored in Table Bay, near the Cape of Good Hope, where Captain Cook's first care was to provide a place for the sick on shore. Here the greater number recovered, though some were still ill when again taken on board. The country appeared to the voyagers to be of a most sterile and forlorn character, and from the accounts they received of the great distances from each other at which the settlers were situated, they conjectured that such must be the general nature of the country in the interior. Possibly the Dutch settlers may not have been anxious to praise it to the English, as it must have been obvious that it would prove a very important possession, on account of our extensive commerce with the East Indies.

Cape Town, at that time, consisted of about a thousand houses, neatly built of brick, and whitewashed on the outside, with thatched roofs. The streets were broad and commodious, and through the principal street ran a canal with rows of oaks planted on either side; but, on account of the slope of the ground, having numerous locks. The healthiness of the climate of Cape Town contrasted

ST. HELENA, SHOWING THE LADDER UP TO THE FORT.

favourably with that of Batavia, and most of the sick rapidly recovered. The Dutch, at this time, appear to have been living on friendly terms with all the neighbouring tribes of natives, nor did Captain Cook seem to be aware that any of the Hottentots were reduced to a state of slavery. He speaks only of their being servants to the Dutch farmers, and taking care of their cattle. Their only enemies were the bushmen, who never engaged in open warfare, but stole the cattle of their neighbours at night, being armed with lances and poisoned arrows.

The *Endeavour* left Table Bay on the 14th of April, and, after calling at Robin Island, a Dutch convict station, she proceeded with her voyage on the 25th. On that day she lost her master, whose health had been destroyed by intemperate habits, and just before she reached England her first lieutenant, Mr. Hicks, died of consumption, from which he had been suffering the greater part of the voyage; thus making up a long catalogue of deaths since the ship left England. Mr. Hicks was succeeded by Mr. Charles Clerke, who accompanied Captain Cook in his subsequent voyages, and was highly esteemed by his commander, as well as by all who sailed under him.

On the 1st of May, the *Endeavour* called off St. Helena, then known only as the summit of a submarine mountain, the water round it being of unfathomable depth; although the island was of especial importance to Indiamen, as it was the only British possession at which they could call on their voyage. Here the *Endeavour* found the *Portland* man-of-war, commanded by Captain Elliot, and twelve sail of Indiamen. In company with this fleet, she stood out of the roads on the 4th of May. But finding that his ship sailed more heavily than the rest of the fleet, Captain Cook deposited his logs, or ship's papers, and some of the journals of his officers, with Captain Elliot; and, on the 23rd not one of the ships was in sight.

By this time the rigging and sails of the *Endeavour* had become so bad, that every day something was giving way. But, notwithstanding this, she continued her course in safety; and, on the 10th of June, land which proved to be Lizard Point, was seen by Nicholas Young, the same boy who first sighted New Zealand. On the 12th, the ship came to anchor in the Downs, and Captain Cook went on shore at Deal.

The importance of the voyage just described can be better appreciated by the present generation than it could have been by those who were alive at the time of its conclusion. Captain Cook's own modest summary of it is interesting. He says,—

"I sailed from Deptford the 30th of July, 1768; from Plymouth the 26th of August; touched at Madeira, Rio de Janeiro and Straits of Le Maire; and entered the South Pacific Ocean, by Cape Horn, in January, the following year.

"I endeavoured to make a direct course to Otaheite, and, in part succeeded; but I made no discovery till I got within the tropic, when I fell in with Lagoon Island, Two Groups, Bird Island, Chain Island, and, on the 13th of April, arrived at Otaheite, where I remained three months, during which time the observations on the transit of Venus were made.

"I then left it; discovered and visited the Society Isles, and Oheteroa; thence proceeded to the south till I arrived in the latitude of 40° 22′, longitude 147° 29′ W.; and on the 6th of October fell in with the east side of New Zealand. I continued exploring the coast of this country till the 1st of March, 1770, when I quitted it and proceeded to New Holland, and having surveyed the eastern coast of that vast country, which part had not before been visited, I passed between its northern extremity and New Guinea; landed on the latter, touched at the island of Savu, thence to Batavia, the Cape of Good Hope, St. Helena, and arrived in England on the 12th of July, 1771."

On their arrival in London, Cook and his companions were received by the scientific as well as by the great and fashionable world, with the attention and respect they so well deserved; for no previous expedition undertaken by England had been more generally successful. Cook was promoted to the rank of commander, his commission being dated the 29th of August, 1771. He was also introduced to the King at St. James's palace, and had the honour of presenting the journal of his voyage illustrated by maps and charts; while their Majesties the King and Queen, and numerous people of high rank and attainments took delight in listening to the accounts given by the explorers of their adventures, and in examining the specimens of manufactures and of natural history which they had brought home.

It was not, however, present *eclât*, nor the apparent magnitude of the discoveries made, but their consequences, which rendered this voyage of real importance. The ultimate result was the founding of two nations of the Anglo-Saxon race; and whatever cause there may be to question, if not to condemn, the manner in which possession has been obtained of distant countries, and, in which, also, their colonization has been effected, in almost every instance, and by almost all nations having the power which civilization gives, it must still be borne in mind that God has overruled, and is overruling these transactions, for His own glory and for the spiritual benefit of the world. He makes not only " the wrath " but the ambition and pride and cupidity of man " to praise Him ;" and then, the remainder " He restrains." And all circumstances are made, in His infinite wisdom and power, to advance the spread of " the glorious gospel of the blessed God," and to usher in the kingdom of Him whose right it is to reign, even of Christ Jesus; the Prince of peace, the Lord of lords, and the King of kings.

With regard to the discoveries made in the voyage just recorded, it is almost superfluous to say that the countries then visited for

K

the first time by our countrymen, have, after the lapse of a century, become familiar as household words to the whole world. Australia, Tasmania and New Zealand have become component parts of the British empire, and have already been made the home of hundreds of thousands of the crowded population of the British Isles, as well as of emigrants from other European countries; and these lands will probably, before another century has passed away, become centres, not only of civilization, but of evangelical truth and saving faith. And herein the Christian reader will and must rejoice.

HARBOUR OF PANGO PANGO, TUTUILA.

CHAPTER III.

SECOND VOYAGE OF DISCOVERY.

June 1772 to July 1775.

IT had long been the opinion of geographers, that a great southern continent existed; and in 1738, a French expedition, under M. Lozier Bouvet, had been sent out in search of it. On the 1st of January, 1739, he got sight of land, in latitude 45° 20′, and longitude 25° 47′ E. from Teneriffe. It was, according to his description, a lofty and steep cape, backed by mountains mostly covered with snow, while the coast had so broad a fringe of ice that it was impossible to approach it near enough to make any thorough examination. In remembrance of the day of discovery, the cape, which was supposed to be part of the southern continent, was called, "Cape de la Circoncision."

It had been supposed, before the return of Cook from his first voyage, that New Zealand, New Holland, and New Guinea, formed part of the great southern land, which was generally denominated TERRA AUSTRALIS INCOGNITA. Cook, indeed, dispelled this idea, by proving that these three territories were islands; but the question as to the existence of the great southern land, still remained to be proved.

The subject was under discussion by men of science when the *Endeavour* returned from her first voyage; and the Royal Society soon afterwards resolved to recommend the despatch of another expedition, for the purpose of attempting to settle the question. An offer of the command of this exploratory voyage was at once made to Captain Cook, who gladly accepted it,—the selection of ships suitable for the purpose being wisely left to his judgment. The qualities he considered essential were, great capacity, or stowage room; a rig easily worked, a size not too large to enter small harbours; and a build which would enable the vessel to take the ground and be easily got off again.

The *Endeavour* having been sent out to the Falkland islands as a store ship, was not available; two more vessels, therefore, made by the same ship-builder as the *Endeavour*, were purchased at Hull. The largest, named the *Resolution*, was of 462 tons burden; and the other, called the *Adventure*, was 336 tons. Captain Cook took possession of the former, as commander of the expedition; and Tobias Furneaux, who had been second lieutenant with Captain Wallis, was promoted and appointed to serve under Cook in command of the *Adventure*.

Captain Cook's first lieutenant was Robert Cooper; his second, Charles Clerke, who had accompanied him on his previous voyage, as had also his third lieutenant, Richard Pickersgill, and the lieutenant of marines, John Edgcumbe, with two of the warrant, and several of the petty officers.

Mr. Banks and Dr. Solander had intended going, but not finding the accommodation on board which they considered necessary for the comfort and convenience of themselves and their attendants, they gave up the project. So great, however, was the public enthusiasm on the subject of the expedition, that, according to Boswell, even Dr. Johnson thought of applying for leave to accompany it, though, if he ever seriously entertained the wish, it was speedily abandoned.

Two astronomers, Mr. William Wales and Mr. William Bayley, were engaged by the Board of Longitude,—the former sailing in the *Resolution*, the latter in the *Adventure*. The Admiralty appointed, as landscape painter, Mr. William Hodges; and Mr. John Reinhold Forster, and his son, were engaged to attend to the department of natural history. The Board of Longitude also amply furnished the expedition with the best astronomical and other instruments which might be required, and with four watch-machines, as chronometers were then called. Lord Sandwich, who was at the head of the Admiralty Board, anxiously watched the equipment of the ships, visiting them from time to time to satisfy himself that everything was done in the best way to secure the success of the undertaking, and the comfort and health of those on board.

Captain Cook had, in his former voyage, paid great attention to the means best adapted for preserving the health of his crew; and he had seen the importance of having an ample supply of provisions of an antiscorbutic character. He also endeavoured to have the ship well dried and ventilated, and determined, as far as possible, that the men's clothes should be kept dry, and their persons clean. Each ship had two years and a half provisions on board, and among other articles were wheat and sugar (in lieu of oatmeal), oil, malt, salted cabbage, portable broth, mustard, marmalade of carrots, and inspissated juice of wort, from which beer could be at once made. The frame of a vessel of twenty tons was put on board each ship, to be set up, if found necessary, to serve as tenders, or to enable the crew to escape should the ships be wrecked. The *Resolution* had a complement of 112 officers and men, and the *Adventure* of 81. Fishing nets and hooks of all sorts, articles to barter with the natives, or to bestow as presents, and additional clothing for the crews, were put on board. Medals also were struck, with the likeness of His Majesty on one side, and of the two ships on the other, to be given to the inhabitants of newly discovered countries, as memorials of the explorers' visit. Indeed, no expedition with a similar object in view had ever left the shores of England so well equipped in every respect as was the one now about to sail.

The *Resolution* being ready for sea, sailed from Deptford on the 9th of April, 1772; but after being joined by the *Adventure* she was detained by contrary winds till the 10th of May, when, both again sailing, the *Resolution* was found to be so crank* that it was necessary to lower her upper works, and for this purpose she put into Sheerness. Lord Sandwich and Sir Hugh Palliser went down to see the alterations made in an effectual manner. On the 22nd of June, the ship being again ready for sea, sailed from Sheerness and joined the *Adventure* in Plymouth Sound on the 3rd of July. Thus it will be seen that there was a delay of nearly three months after the expedition was supposed to be ready, before it was fully prepared for sea. Lord Sandwich and Sir Hugh Palliser again visited the ships in Plymouth Sound, and the chronometers being set going in the presence of the astronomers and the chief officers, the ships at length, on the 13th of July, set sail, and shaped a course for Madeira.

Anchoring in Funchal Roads on the 29th, and having taken on board fresh beef and vegetables, including onions, for sea stores, the ships sailed again on the 1st of August. Finding their water run short, they put into Porto Praya in the island of St. Jago, one of the Cape de Verde Islands, for a supply. On the 29th of October, the land of the Cape of Good Hope was made, but as the ships

* Among sailors, a ship is said to be *crank* when the rigging is too weighty for the hull, so as to risk being upset.

were unable to get in before dark, they stood off and on during the night. In the evening the phosphorescence of the sea became unusually brilliant; and to convince Mr. Forster, who differed from Mr. Banks and Dr. Solander, that it was caused by insects, some buckets of water were drawn up from alongside. On examition he found that the water was full of globular insects of the size of a pin's head, and quite transparent.

The next day the ships anchored off Cape Town, where Captain Cook and his officers were received by the governor and other authorities with attention and respect. The governor informed Captain Cook that a French ship had discovered land in the meridian of the Mauritius, in latitude 48° s.; and also that in the previous March two French ships, under M. Marion, had touched at the Cape on their way to explore the South Pacific.

The expedition quitted the Cape of Good Hope on the 22nd of November, and steered a course towards Cape Circumcision which was the first object for which they were directed to search. They soon found the weather very cold, when warm clothing was issued; and having encountered a heavy gale, with hail and rain, which drove them far to the eastward of their course, all hope of reaching the looked-for cape was given up. Owing, also to the severity of the weather, and the sudden transition from dry heat to extreme cold and wet, the ships' companies suffered a severe misfortune in the loss of nearly all the live stock (consisting of sheep, hogs, and geese) which they had brought with them from Cape Town. This weather continued for the greater part of the time the ships remained in that high latitude. On the 10th of December an island of ice was seen in latitude 50° 40′ s. and 2° 0′ E. of the Cape of Good Hope. After this, thick hazy weather again came on with sleet and snow. The ships continued their course, the *Resolution* leading, when an iceberg, directly for which they were steering, was discovered, through the mist, not a mile off,

It was about fifty feet high, flat at top, about half a mile in circumference, and its sides, against which the sea broke furiously, rose perpendicularly from the ocean. Captain Furneaux, who was astern, took this ice for land, and hauled off from it; and there is no doubt that many navigators who have reported land in these latitudes have been deceived in the same way.

Nothing could be more trying to the explorers than the navigation in which they were now engaged; day after day tacking off and on among large fields of ice, through which they in vain endeavoured to find a passage to the southward, with the constant risk, in thick weather, of running foul of icebergs, or of getting fast in the packed ice which might any moment enclose them, while all the time they were exposed to storms of snow and sleet, with a constant frost, although it was the middle of summer. Dangerous as it was sailing among icebergs, or, as Captain Cook calls them, ice rocks, especially in thick weather, the ships were in still greater peril when surrounded by packed ice, which consisted of huge slabs of great thickness, varying from thirty or forty feet down to three or four feet square, packed close together and often piled one on another. Stout as were the ships, it was not expected that they could resist the enormous pressure to which they would be subjected should they get caught in such frozen bonds. It was the opinion of those on board that this sort of ice was formed only in bays and rivers, and that therefore they must be near land, which was eagerly though vainly looked for. So severe was the cold that an iceberg examined by the master had no water running down it, as is generally the case in summer.

Captain Cook now steered to the west, in the hopes of getting round the ice; but though he held on this course for some time both to the south and west of the supposed position of Cape Circumcision, he neither fell in with it, nor did he observe any of the usual indications of land. Various birds, however, were seen, and several of them were shot; but as they would find roosting places on the ice islands, they might have come a very great distance from the land. Thus the penguins, which were seen in great numbers on some icebergs, and are supposed never to go far from land, might have come a very great distance over the ice from their native haunts. Be that as it may, no land was seen by either vessel, notwithstanding the diligent search made for it.

On the 31st of December, while the ships were still surrounded by ice, a strong gale sprung up with a heavy sea, which made it very dangerous for them to remain in the position in which they then were. The peril was yet further increased by an immense field of ice which appeared to the north, extending from north-east by east, to south-west by west, and between two and three miles off. The

GREAT PATAGONIAN PENGUIN.

ships received several severe blows from masses of ice of the largest size. Providentially they got clear by the afternoon, for at that time the wind increased so much that it was necessary to haul the topsails and to strike top-gallant masts. The next day the wind abated, but the weather continued thick and hazy, with sleet and snow which froze on the rigging as it fell, and ornamented the whole of it with icicles. At length the longitude in which the looked-for cape was supposed to lie was reached, and as the ships were far to the southward of the latitude in which Captain Bouvet stated he had seen it, no doubt remained that he had mistaken lofty icebergs surrounded by loose or field ice for land, as Captain Cook and his officers had already been deceived on the first day they fell in with field ice.

ICE-BOUND.

When the weather became finer the ships were able to fill up their water casks with pure fresh water, by collecting masses of ice and then hanging them up to allow any salt which might have adhered to them to run off. Whenever the weather permitted, the astronomers were employed in making observations, and the naturalists in collecting birds, the only objects they had the means of obtaining.

The antarctic circle was crossed on the 17th of January, in longitude 39° 35′ E.; and on the evening of that day the whole sea to the south and west appeared covered with ice, though shortly before none was in sight. In this space thirty-eight ice islands, great and small, were counted, besides loose ice in abundance, so that the ships were obliged to luff to avoid one piece, and to bear up to escape another, as they proceeded to the south. At length a compact mass, from sixteen to eighteen feet high, appearing to the south, without any opening, Captain Cook altered his course to the north. A number of whales were now seen sporting about the ice, and several flocks of antarctic petrels. The ships did not alter their course an hour too soon, for that night a heavy gale sprang up which would have rendered their position very dangerous. After this, search was in vain made for the land said to have been seen by the French captain in the longitude of the Mauritius.

On the 8th of February, during thick weather, the *Adventure* was separated from the *Resolution* and though, according to arrangement, Captain Cook cruised for three days about the spot where his consort had last been seen, and continued burning blue lights and firing guns, he was compelled at last to give up the search. On the night of the 17th the aurora presented a very beautiful appearance. It was first seen in the east, and gradually rising formed a brilliant arch across the heavens, with a light sufficiently strong to cast shadows on the deck, and at one time to allow a book to be read. A description of the incidents met with during this part of the voyage would not prove generally interesting. One, however, must not be omitted.

The *Resolution* being off a large ice island round which there was a quantity of loose ice, Captain Cook sent two boats to take some

AURORAL LIGHTS.

on board. The island was not less than half a mile in circumference, and its summit three or four hundred feet above the surface of the sea. While the boats were thus engaged in its neighbourhood, it was seen to bend over till it turned nearly bottom up, though it seemed by the change not to have lost either in height or size. The boats escaped without damage from their dangerous position.

During all the time, up to the separation of the two ships, the crews had enjoyed generally excellent health. A few slight symptoms of scurvy had appeared, but they were quickly subdued by a liberal use of the remedies which had been supplied, the fresh wort made from malt seems to have been very efficacious in arresting the malady. Occasionally too, when the weather allowed, the men's bedding and clothes were spread on deck to air, and the ship was smoked and cleaned between decks. This prevented the crews from contracting those diseases which have proved so fatal on board ships where they have been neglected.

At length, by the middle of March, the antarctic summer being nearly over, and his crew requiring rest and his ship refitting, Captain Cook shaped a course which would soon bring her into a more genial clime. He had purposed visiting Van Diemen's Land, but as the wind would not allow him to shape a course for that country he steered for New Zealand, which was sighted on the 25th of March. A heavy gale compelled him to keep at sea, but the following day he entered Dusky Bay at the south-west end of Tavai Poenammoo, or the Middle Island, as it is now called. This was on Friday the 26th of March, after having been 117 days at sea, and sailed over 3,660 leagues, or nearly 10,000 miles, without having once sighted land. Only one man, and he of a naturally bad habit of body, had been seriously ill; and Cook attributed the excellent health of his crew, partly to the frequent airing and sweetening of the ship by fires, etc., and partly to the portable broth, sweet wort, pickled cabbage, and sour kraut.

Although no discovery, except of a negative character, was made during this part of the voyage, we cannot but admire the hardihood and perseverance, the skill and courage exhibited by the great navigator during the whole of that trying time.

A secure harbour having been found by Lieutenant Pickersgill in Dusky Bay where the ship could lie close to the shore, she was warped into it and moored, her yards being locked in the branches of the trees; there being also, a hundred yards from her stern, a fine stream of fresh water. No place could have been better suited for refitting the ship and refreshing the crew; and both officers and men enjoyed their stay at this healthy and beautiful spot. Places were forthwith cleared of trees to set up the observatory, the forge, and the tents for the sailmakers and coopers. At the captain's suggestion wholesome beer was brewed from the leaves of a tree resembling the American black spruce, mixed with the inspissated juice of wort and molasses. The constant attention of the great navigator to the most minute points calculated to maintain or improve the health of those placed under his charge cannot be too strongly commended. Throughout his journals notices constantly occur which shew that whenever antiscorbutic vegetables or herbs of any sort were required he did not entrust the search to others, but went himself to look for them. It is sad to reflect how indifferent to his example many other navigators have been, especially the masters of merchantmen; and that even at the present day, notwithstanding all the assistance which science is able to render, their crews often suffer fearfully from scurvy.

Shooting and fishing parties now went out constantly, and an ample supply of wild fowl was obtained. The bay was also surveyed, and found to contain several good harbours. Some exploring expeditions for short distances into the interior were also started—but very few natives were met with. There appeared, indeed, to be only three or four families settled in the neighbourhood, and it was not understood why they had separated themselves from their countrymen; but it was conjectured that they were the remnant of a tribe which, in one of the frequent native wars, had escaped massacre. Only one of these families became intimate with the strangers, in whom they showed unusual confidence by taking up their quarters very near to the watering place.

These people evinced little astonishment at sight of a few sheep and goats which, having escaped the effects of the cold, were taken on shore: but stared at them with what appeared to be stupid insensibility, and when various articles of European manufacture were offered to them, they received these gifts with indifference, except indeed, hatchets and spike-nails, the value of which they could comprehend.

After some further acquaintance, the head of this family, and his daughter, were persuaded to visit the ship. Before venturing on board, he presented to the captain a piece of cloth, and a green talc hatchet; he gave another to Mr. Forster, and the girl gave one to Mr. Hodges. This custom of making presents had been found common with the natives of the South Sea Islands, but had not before been observed among the New Zealanders. After these propitiatory gifts were received, and before stepping on to the stage which led to the deck, the native took a small green branch in his hand, with which he several times struck the ship's side, while he also repeated a speech or prayer. When this ceremony was concluded he stepped on deck.

On taking leave of this New Zealander, Captain Cook was presented by him with another piece of native cloth, with the expression of a wish for a cloak in return. One of red baize was accordingly given to him, and seemed to afford great satisfaction. Thus far, therefore, on this visit intercourse with these aborigines of the new country was pleasant and successful.

Other natives were afterwards seen by some of the explorers, who were on a shooting expedition. These set up a hideous noise, and were with difficulty persuaded to approach and lay down their spears. At last one of them came forward, with a plant in his hand, one end of which he presented to Captain Cook, while he himself held the other. He then began a long speech with frequent pauses, and as soon as the captain replied, of course not understanding a word that was said, the savage proceeded in his harangue. This done, he took off his cloak which he put on the captain's shoulders, and seemed to consider that their peace was established. The natives followed the English to the boat, and seeing some muskets lying across the stern, desired them to be taken away, having probably observed their effects on the wild ducks. They then assisted to launch the boat, but it was necessary to keep a watchful eye on them, for they wanted to take away everything in the boat on which they could lay hands. No canoes were observed belonging to these people, two or three logs of wood tied together serving them for crossing rivers; indeed fish and fowl were so plentiful that they had not far to go in order to procure food.

In accordance with Cook's desire to benefit the countries he visited, he took five geese which he had brought from the Cape of Good Hope, and left them in a retired cove (which was on that account called Goose Cove), in hope that they might there multiply and be useful to future inhabitants. A garden was also dug, and, with the same object in view, various sorts of garden seeds were sown in it.

On the 28th of April the tents and other articles being taken on board, the *Resolution* once more got under weigh, though, owing to light and contrary winds, it was not till the 11th of May that she was fairly at sea. She then proceeded along the west coast, towards Queen Charlotte's Sound, in Cook's Straits, between the two islands. Nothing of importance occurred till the ship was about three leagues to the westward of Cape Stephens when just as it fell calm, six waterspouts appeared round her, four between her and the land, and one outside; the sixth in the south-west, two or three miles off.

Progressing in a crooked line to the north-east, it passed within fifty yards of her stern. A gun had been got ready to fire into it when it should come nearer. The diameter of the base was about sixty feet,—the sea within which was much agitated, and foamed up to a great height. From this the water appeared to be carried in a spiral stream up to the clouds. Some of the seamen said that they saw a bird in it, which was whirled round like the fly of a jack. During the time the waterspouts were in sight, there were light puffs of wind from all points of the compass, while occasionally large drops of rain fell.

WATERSPOUT

On the 18th, the *Resolution* appeared off Queen Charlotte's Sound, where, greatly to the satisfaction of all on board, her consort the *Adventure*, was found to be awaiting her. Her boats soon came out, and the *Resolution* was brought to an anchor in Ship Cove close to her. Captain Furneaux at once came on board, and gave Captain Cook a narrative of his proceedings after being separated from him. Having in vain looked for the *Resolution*, he bore away to the north, till Van Diemen's Land was sighted. He sailed along the east coast for some distance, some parts of which appeared fertile and thickly populated. The *Adventure* lay within Maria Island for five days to take in wood and water, and then proceeded to the north along shore. For some distance no land was seen, but as the soundings were very regular, Captain Furneaux was of opinion that no straits existed between New Holland and Van Diemen's Land, but only a very deep bay. Having come to this erroneous opinion, he bore away for New Zealand, and had been five weeks in Ship Cove when the *Resolution* appeared. He had kept up a friendly intercourse with the natives, who frequently asked for Tupia, and seemed much concerned when told that he was dead.

While at Queen Charlotte's Sound, Captain Cook had a garden planted, as before, and gave the natives some potatoes, explaining their use and the mode of cultivating them. A pair of goats and a boar and two sows were put on shore, in the hopes of their multiplying. A ewe and ram which had been brought with great trouble and care to the place, were also landed, but the following day were found dead, from having eaten some poisonous plant.

An idea had prevailed on board the *Adventure* that the natives were ready to sell their children. This Captain Cook soon proved to be incorrect. Their object in bringing them on board was to obtain presents for them. A man brought his son, a boy of about ten years of age, and at first Captain Cook fancied from what he had heard that the object of the father was to sell him, but he soon found that it was merely to obtain a white shirt, which was given. The boy was so proud of it that he went about, showing it to everybody he met, till he encountered old Will the goat, who making a butt at him knocked him over into some dirt, sadly soiling his shirt. The boy considered the mischief irreparable, and was afraid of appearing before his father. At last he was brought in by Mr. Forster, when he told a lamentable story against the great "dog"— nor was he comforted till his shirt was washed and dried. Captain Cook justly remarks in his journal that this incident shows how easily people can be deceived, when ignorant of the language, as to the customs and habits of the natives of foreign countries.

While these friendly natives were on board, a strange canoe full of people entered the harbour. The natives on seeing them said they were enemies, and two of them mounted the arm chests on the poop, one armed with a native hatchet, and the other with a spear; and, in bravado, bade their enemies defiance. The rest who were on board, jumping into their canoe went on shore, probably to secure their women and children. The two who remained begged Captain Cook to fire at the strangers. The latter, however, came on board, apparently without having had any evil intentions; and peace was soon established among all parties. The strangers at once asked for Tupia, and hearing that he was dead, one or two expressed their sorrow in a way which appeared more formal than real.

A brisk trade was soon established with the new comers; but the thoughtless seamen were so ready to give even the clothes off their backs for the merest trifles, neither useful nor ornamental, that the captain was compelled to dismiss the strangers. He afterwards crossed the harbour with Mr. Forster and one of the officers, to a spot where a hundred natives, men, women, and children, were collected, with six canoes, and apparently all their utensils. These they seem always to carry with them when they go even a short distance from home lest they should be stolen by their enemies in their absence.

The state of constant warfare and consequent distrust in which they lived, especially in the middle island, was very evident, for they were generally found on their guard, travelling or working with their weapons in their hands; even the women were seen occasionally armed with spears. Captain Cook had reason to believe that the entire population of the Sound had changed since he was there in 1770, as he could not recognise the face of a single person he then knew. Those who asked for Tupia had possibly not seen him, but had only heard of him from their countrymen, among whom he was very popular. The immorality of the natives met with during their visit to New Zealand, appears to have been very flagrant; and it is sad to reflect that advantage was taken of it by the seamen, without the slightest rebuke or censure from their superiors; indeed, it cannot be discovered from the journals of the officers that they were at all aware of their duties as a Christian people with regard to heathen savages whose shores they visited.

The king's birthday was spent with the usual festivities, the officers of the two ships dining together.

On the 7th of June 1773, the two ships put to sea, with the intention of exploring all the unknown parts of the ocean between the meridian of New Zealand and Cape Horn. In case of separation they were to rendezvous at Otaheite, where Captain Furneaux was to wait till the 20th of August, and then to proceed to Queen Charlotte's Sound. If not joined at that place before the 20th of November by Captain Cook, he was to put to sea and carry out the instructions he had received from the Admiralty. Cook's object in attempting to explore in so high a latitude during the winter season, was to get some of the work done which would otherwise have occupied the precious months of summer; and besides, he wished to show future navigators that it would be practicable to make discoveries even in the depths of winter.

After leaving New Zealand, the course steered was generally about north-east, so that the ships soon got into a warm latitude, and the men once more put on their cool clothing. Sad news was brought on board the *Resolution* at this time, the 29th of June. It was that scurvy had broken out on board the *Adventure*; that her cook had died, and that twenty men were ill with that complaint and the flux. The *Resolution* had only three men on the sick list, and but one of those had the scurvy. A few others, showing symptoms of it, were supplied with wort, marmalade of carrots, and thickened juice of lemons. It appeared that the crew of the *Adventure* during the six weeks they were in Queen Charlotte's Sound had eaten no vegetables, partly from not knowing what herbs to gather, and also from the inveterate dislike of the seamen to a new diet. Captain Cook had, from the first, when he thought it necessary, insisted on having wild celery, scurvy grass, and other herbs, boiled with the peas and wheat, both for officers and men; and though some refused to eat it, he was firm, and would allow no other food to be served out, so that at last the prejudice wore off. Captain Furneaux instantly made use of all the remedies in his power, and his people improved in health. Still it was necessary for their sakes to put into a harbour where vegetables could be procured, and a course was accordingly steered for Otaheite.

Several small low islands clothed with cocoa-nut trees were seen, but the necessity of reaching a harbour without delay prevented their examination.

On the 15th of August, Osnaburg Island, or Maitea, was seen, and the ships then steered for Oaiti-piha Bay, near the south-east end of Otaheite, in order to procure there such refreshments as the place could afford.

At daybreak they found themselves not half a league from a reef, towards which the scud of the sea rapidly sent them, the wind having completely fallen. The depth was too great to anchor, and the boats failed to tow the ships off. A number of natives came off with provisions, but seemed totally unconscious of the dangerous position of the ships. It was curious that though they recognised Captain Cook and those who had been there before, no one asked for Tupia.

The position of the ships became more and more critical: the captain had hoped to get round the end of the reef, but as they drew nearer and nearer this hope vanished, and shipwreck seemed certain. Just then a passage was discovered through the reef, but a boat being sent ahead to sound, it was found that there was not water sufficient for the ships to pass over; indeed, so strongly did the flood-tide set towards it, that the *Resolution* seemed nearer than ever to destruction. The horrors of shipwreck stared the explorers in the face; there was no wind to fill their sails; the boats were powerless; the only means for saving the ships was to anchor; but would the anchors hold? They were let go, and the *Resolution* was brought up in less than three fathom water, striking at every fall of the sea, while the *Adventure* brought up close on her bow without striking. Kedge anchors and hawsers were now carried out, and found ground; by hawling on these the ship was got afloat, but there was a fear that these would come home or be cut by the rocks, and nothing could then have saved the *Resolution*. Happily they held on till the tide turned, when a light breeze coming off the land, both vessels made sail, and got out of danger, though with the loss of several anchors and cables.

The next day the ships anchored in Oaiti-piha Bay about two cables' length from the shore. Both ships were crowded with natives, who brought off cocoa-nuts, plantains, bananas, apples, yams, and other fruits and vegetables, which they exchanged for nails and beads. Presents of shirts and axes were made to several who called themselves chiefs, or *earees*, and promised to bring off hogs and fowls, which however they did not do. These earees did not scruple to pilfer whatever came in their way, and one of them, who pretended to be very friendly, was found handing articles which did not belong to him out of the quarter galley. As his companions on deck were behaving in the same way, they were all turned out of the ship, and two muskets were fired over the head of the chief offender to frighten him. On this, he jumped out of his canoe, which, with two others, was brought on board, and a gun was fired along shore, but so as not to hurt any one. This soon cleared the coast. In one of the canoes was a little boy, who was, at first, very much frightened, but beads were given to him, and he was sent in safety on shore. This quickly restored the confidence of the natives, and all by the evening were again good friends.

The intercourse with the natives now went on with tolerable smoothness, though their thieving propensities frequently nearly brought about a rupture. On one occasion, in Captain Cook's presence, a native seized the musket of one of the guards on shore, and made off with it. Some of the seamen were sent after him, but he would have escaped had not the natives also given chase, knocked down the thief, and brought back the musket. Although fear may possibly have operated on this occasion with the natives more than a sense of justice, Captain Cook was thankful to them, because he would certainly have lost ten times the value of the weapon in endeavouring to recover it by force.

The following day a chief brought on board a quantity of fruit as a present, among which were a number of cocoa-nuts, which, after the juice had been extracted, had been thrown away by the seamen. These had been so artfully tied up in bundles that at first the cheat was not perceived. The chief did not seem at all ashamed when the trick was discovered, but, having opened a few himself, acknowledged that they were empty. On going on shore, however, he sent off a quantity of plantains and bananas.

A supply of water, fruit, and roots having been got on board, Captain Cook was preparing to sail for Matavai, when it was announced that Waheatoua was coming to meet him. He found the young chief seated in the open air on a stool, surrounded by a large number of attendants, and at once recollected him, having known him when a boy, under the name of Tearee. He had, on the death of his father, Waheatoua, taken his name. The chief begged Captain Cook to remain some months, promising hogs and provisions of all sorts. He insisted on keeping the captain by his side, and whenever they moved about the stool was carried after them, that they might again be seated in the same position.

Before the ships had come to an anchor in Matavai Bay, the decks were covered with natives, many of whom Captain Cook recognised. The king Otoo was among those on board, but he took fright without any apparent reason, and landed again. The next day an encampment was made on shore for the sail-makers, coopers, and the sick. This done, Captain Cook, accompanied by Captain Furneaux, Mr. Forster, and others, set off to visit Otoo. He was found seated on the ground, under the shade of a tree, with a large crowd round him, all standing uncovered, as a mark of respect; that is, not only were their heads bare, but their shoulders, and some wore no clothing above the breast, his father not excepted. Presents were made by Captain Cook, and the king was told that they were given in friendship, and that none would be received in return. The king inquired for Tupia, and for all the officers who were on board the *Endeavour* on the former voyage. Otoo, though a fine tall young man, was very nervous, and acknowledged that he had left the ship because he was afraid of the guns. On the 27th, however, he came to the camp with a large retinue, having first sent on board a quantity of cloth, fruits, a hog, and two large fish. He, a sister, and younger brother, with several attendants, were persuaded to visit the ship, and all received presents, Captain Cook afterwards taking them to their home at Oparree in his boat.

On landing the captain met a venerable old lady, the mother of Toutaha. She seized him by the hands, and, bursting into tears, exclaimed, "Toutaha, the friend of Cook, is dead." Captain Cook says that he was so much affected that he should have wept also, had not Otoo drawn him away. Captain Furneaux made the king a present of a male and female goat, in the hope that they might stock the island.

On another occasion, when Otoo came on board, as he entered the cabin, several chiefs who were there immediately uncovered their shoulders, although they did not rise or show him any other mark of respect. He was entertained with the bag-pipes, which seemed to have especial charms for the natives. The seamen also danced hornpipes and country dances. In return the king entertained the voyagers with a dramatic performance, in which his sister took a part. The drama seemed to have reference to the circumstances of the time, as Captain Cook's name was frequently mentioned. The lady's dress was very elegant, being decorated with long tassels made of feathers, hanging from the waist downwards. The performance lasted about two hours. So far as the disposition of the natives was concerned, the visit seems to have been satisfactory, though fewer hogs were obtained than were required. Mr. Pickersgill was sent about in all directions to obtain them, and in one of his expeditions he saw Oberea, once the person of most importance in the island. She had now become old, poor, and of little consequence.

Otoo was very unwilling that the ships should go, and shed tears when he parted from Captain Cook. A young lad, called

Boreo, was taken on board the *Resolution*. Though he seemed tolerably satisfied, he could not help weeping as he saw his native island left astern. Two days afterwards, the ships anchored in the harbour of Owharre, in the island of Huaheine. The two captains, on landing, were received with the greatest cordiality by the natives, who after a few presents had been distributed amongst them, brought hogs, fowls, dogs, and fruit, which they exchanged for hatchets, nails, and beads; indeed there seemed every prospect of an abundance of provisions being obtained. The chief, Oree, who had, on Cook's former visit, exchanged names with him, was still living, and sent word that he was hastening to see him. Before however the captain was allowed to leave his boat, five young plantain trees—the emblem of peace employed by the natives—were brought on board separately, and with some ceremony. Three young pigs, their ears ornamented with cocoa-nut fibre, accompanied the first three, and a dog the fourth. Lastly, the chief sent the inscription engraved on a piece of pewter which had been left with him in July, 1769.

This ceremony ended, the guide who had come to conduct the English to the shore, requested them to decorate three young plantain trees with looking glasses, nails, medals, and beads. This being done, they landed with the trees in their hands, and were conducted to the chief through a multitude of people, who made a lane for them to pass. They were then made to sit down a few paces from the chief, and the plantains were taken from them. One was for their god, one for the king, and the third for friendship. Captain Cook then wished to advance to the king, but he was told that the king would come to him, which he did, falling on his neck and embracing him, the tears flowing down his venerable cheeks, showing the affectionate feelings of his heart. His friends were then introduced, and presents were made to them. Cook speaks in the most affectionate terms of Oree; indeed all his actions showed him to have been an upright kind-hearted man.

The trading expeditions sent out were so successful that three hundred hogs, besides fowls and vegetables of all sorts, were obtained. It was from this island that Captain Furneaux received on board a young man, named Omai, a native of Ulietea, where he had some property, of which he had been dispossessed by the people of Bolabola. Omai was not a chief, and he was so inferior in figure, complexion, and manners, to the chiefs, that Captain Cook was surprised that Captain Furneaux should have selected him. He was not, indeed, a favourable sample of the natives of the Pacific isles as far as appearance went. Ultimately however, Omai, by his intelligence and good conduct, won the regard of Captain Cook, who afterwards, in his journal, speaks of him in warm terms of commendation.

Here, as elsewhere, there were thieves and rogues. Mr. Sparrman was attacked while wandering in the woods, beaten, and robbed of his clothes and hanger. Oree, on hearing of it, shed tears, and set off in person to recover the clothes, most of which he got back. Altogether, however, the chief and his subjects were among the best disposed of all the people visited during the voyage. He came on board the *Resolution* as she was leaving the harbour, and did not quit her till he had taken an affectionate farewell of Captain Cook, when nearly half a league out at sea. He then went away in a small canoe, paddled by himself and another man, all the other natives having long before left the ship.

The following morning, the ships entered the harbour of Ohamaneno, in the island of Ulietea, where they lay safely moored. The ships were at once surrounded with canoes; and hogs and vegetables were offered in abundance. At first, none of the former would be taken, as the ships were already crowded;

but as killing and salting went on, room was made for them, and in all, four hundred and fifty hogs were collected at this island. Most of them were brought in canoes from different directions to the ship, so that there was very little trading on shore. It was in consequence of the exertions made by Captain Cook in collecting provisions, and the judicious means he employed that he was able to remain away from home so many years, and to make so many important discoveries.

The chief of that part of the island was Oreo. Captain Cook paid him a visit at his own house, and was cordially received. He, as others had done, enquired after Tupia and the captain's

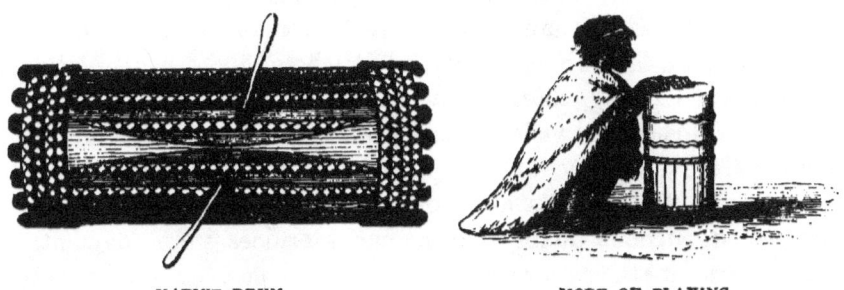

NATIVE DRUM.   MODE OF PLAYING.

companions on his former voyage by name. A play was soon got up—the chief's daughter and seven men being the actors. The plot was as follows: a theft was committed in a masterly manner, but discovered before the thief had time to carry off his plunder. He and his accomplice were attacked by those who had charge of it; but the latter were beaten off, and the rogues escaped in triumph. This incident gives a notion of the moral character of the people in that respect. On another occasion Oreo entertained the strangers with a feast in the native fashion. The floor was strewed thick with leaves, on which hot bread, fruit, and plantains were placed, with two pigs roasted whole—one of about sixty, the other thirty pounds. They were admirably dressed, having been baked in the native underground ovens, all parts being equally cooked. Cocoa nuts supplied the beverage, but the visitors had brought some bottles of wine, which the chief seemed to like, as he both then and always filled his glass whenever the bottle came to him, but seemed not to be affected by it. Plays were got up every day for the amusement of the strangers; indeed the natives seemed anxious in every way to please them. The people of this island appeared to be of a mild, amiable, and timid disposition.

A native lad about eighteen years of age, called Oedidee, joined the *Resolution* at this island, in the place of Boreo, who falling in love with a damsel he met with, remained that he might marry her. Oedidee was a native of Bolabola, and a near relation of the great Opoony, chief of that island.

On this, his second visit to these islands, Captain Cook knowing more of the language of the people, was able to gain a better insight into their habits and customs. Among other points, he discovered, without doubt, that human sacrifices were frequently offered up at their morais. At first the natives would only acknowledge that criminals were killed, but afterwards they confessed that any whom the priest chose to denounce were offered up. Thus a priest who had a dislike to a man might at any moment doom him to death, by pronouncing him a bad man. He then sent out his executioners, who with a couple of blows from their heavy clubs, struck the unsuspecting victim dead at their feet. The corpse was forthwith carried to the morais, when the chief, who was compelled to attend such sacrifices, had the eye offered to him to eat. At some of the islands, the inhabitants of which Captain Cook describes as the most happy on earth, the priests held this terrific power to a fearful extent. At the time of his thus writing he was not aware of the fact which is so strikingly illustrative of the declaration of holy writ, that "the dark places of the earth are full of the habitations of cruelty."

On the 17th of September, 1773, the ships were again at sea. It was the intention of Captain Cook to get into the latitude of Middleburg and Amsterdam, in order to touch there before hauling up for New Zealand. At night they generally lay to, lest any land might be passed in the dark. Some small islets clothed with cocoa-nut trees, were passed on the 23rd, and named Hervey's Island, but no inhabitants were seen on shore.

Middleburg was reached on the 1st of October, and the following day, as the ships were beating up to an anchorage, two canoes came boldly off to them. Directly the anchors were dropped, the ships were surrounded by canoes, bringing cloth and other curiosities. Among the people who came on board was a chief whose good services were secured by the present of a hatchet, spike-nails, and other articles. His name was Tioony. He piloted the boats to a place where the landing was very easy, and where a large concourse of people were assembled to receive them with commodities which they pressed on their visitors, scarcely expecting to receive anything in return. At last, the chief, making the people open right and left, conducted his visitors to his house, which was delightfully situated about three hundred yards from the sea, at the head of a fine lawn under the shade of some shaddock trees. The floor was covered with mats, on which the guests were invited to be seated, the people ranging themselves on the ground in a circle outside. The piper having landed, Captain Cook ordered the bag-pipes to be played, and in return, three young women sang with a very good grace. A present being made to each of these, all the other women commenced singing. Their songs were musical and harmonious, and in no way harsh or disagreeable. The chief had another house in an adjoining plantation, to which his guests were conducted, and where they were entertained with bananas and cocoa-nuts, with bowls of cava; though, on witnessing the mode of preparing that beverage, the thirst of the visitors was sufficiently quenched. They were seated in an open space in front of the house which was surrounded with fruit and other trees, whose fragrance filled the air.

The chief, Tioony, went on board and dined, and then, at their request, conducted the strangers through part of the island. There were numerous plantations of fruit trees and edible roots, laid out with great judgment, and inclosed with neat fences made of reeds. The ships were crowded the whole day with people trafficking, and perfect good order prevailed. In the evening, on the return of the officers on board, they expressed themselves highly delighted with the country, and the very obliging behaviour of the inhabitants, who seemed to vie with each other in doing what they thought would please their visitors.

The group of islands, at one of which the ships now were, were called the Tonga Islands; but Cook from the treatment he received named them the Friendly Islands, by which name they are now generally known. Tasman, who discovered them in 1642-3, named the two principal islands Amsterdam and Middleburg. The former is called by the natives Tongatabu, or the Great Tonga; the latter Ea-oo-we. There are other volcanic islands to the north, belonging to the group not then known.

Leaving Ea-oo-we, or Middleburg, the ships ran down to Tongatabu, keeping about half a mile from the shore, on which the sea broke with a heavy surf. With the aid of glasses it was seen that every part of the shore was laid out in plantations, while the natives were observed running along the shore waving small white flags, which were of course looked on as an emblem of peace. They were answered by hoisting a St. George's ensign. Several canoes paddled boldly alongside, and the people in them after presenting the cava root, came boldly on board. The ships anchored in Van Diemen's Road, just outside the breakers, with a casting-anchor and cable to seaward in forty-seven fathoms water, to prevent them from tailing on the rocks. Their decks were quickly crowded with natives, who brought off only native cloths, for which the seamen too readily gave them clothes. To put a stop to this proceeding, Captain Cook ordered that no sort of curiosities should be purchased by any person whatever. The good effect of this order was visible next morning, when instead of comparatively useless articles, the natives brought off bananas and cocoa-nuts in abundance, and some pigs and fowls.

Proper arrangements having been made for conducting the trade, the captains landed under the guidance of a chief, Attago. who had at once singled out Captain Cook as the principal person, and offered him the usual presents. Cook and Attago also exchanged names, the custom of so doing being practised at the Friendly as well as at the Society Islands. The friendly chief pointed out a creek into which the boats could run, and on landing, the visitors were seated under the shade of a tree, the people forming a circle round them, but no one attempted to push forward, as was the habit of the Otaheiteans. The officers then begged Attago to show them the country. This without hesitation, he at once signified his readiness to do.

The first visit was paid to a sort of temple in an open green, raised on the top of an artificial mound, about seventeen feet above the level ground. The mound was of an oblong form, enclosed by a wall, and the building, which differed little from the ordinary dwelling houses of the people, was of the same shape. On approaching this temple the people seated themselves on the grass, about fifty yards off, when three venerable looking priests appeared, and addressed the strangers, with whom, as soon as their speech was finished, they came and sat down, when some presents were made to them. After this, Attago signified that the strangers were welcome to examine the temple. In the interior were some images, but when Cook enquired if they were Etuas, or gods, Attago kicked them over without any ceremony, to shew that he did not look upon them with reverence. Neither Omai nor Oedidee understood the language spoken by the natives of Tonga, consequently it was difficult to ascertain the exact object of the building.

It appears extraordinary to us at the present day, and it is painful to narrate, that Captain Cook should have conceived it right, as he says he did, to make an offering at the altar. He and his companions therefore laid down some blue pebbles, coins, nails, and other articles, as presents to the gods of these poor heathens. Unhappily, this proceeding was in accordance with the customs of our countrymen, and even of the English government in India, who, to a much later period furnished a money grant to the temple of Juggernaut (one of the principal gods of the Hindoos), and it was only in comparatively modern times that this disgraceful grant was discontinued. In the present instance, however, it did not appear that these offerings were looked upon as particularly sacred, as the chief, Attago, took them up, and, placing them in the folds of his dress, appropriated them to himself.

The green in which this temple stood was at the junction of several roads, two or three of which were very much frequented. The high road along which the chief led the strangers was perfectly level, and sixteen feet broad; many others led into it, and all were enclosed on each side with neat fences made of reeds, and shaded from the scorching sun by fruit trees. Not an inch of ground was waste; the roads occupied no more space than was necessary, while the fences did not take up above four inches on each side, and even this was not wholly lost, for many of them were composed of useful trees or shrubs. Numbers of people were met, some travelling down to the ships with their burdens of fruits and other articles for barter. All courteously got out of the road, sitting down or standing with their backs to the fences as their visitors passed.

At most of the cross roads the temples just described were seen standing on mounds, but were surrounded by palisades instead of stone walls. After walking several miles, a larger temple than usual was reached, and near it was a house, at which the party stopped, and were treated with fruit and other provisions, while an old priest made a long speech. These temples at the cross roads remind us of the shrines set up to legendary saints in Roman Catholic countries.

The party returned on board with Attago, and while at dinner they received a visit from an old chief of superior rank, in whose presence the former would not sit down nor eat. As soon, however, as the old man was gone, Attago took his place, finished his dinner, and drank two glasses of wine.

Here, as at most places, the natives of inferior rank showed a disposition to thieve. Poor Mr. Wales was found seated on the shore, unable to move, for having when landing, in order to wade to the shore, taken off his shoes and stockings, a native had run off with them, and it was impossible for him to follow over the sharp coral rocks. Attago, however, soon discovered the thief, and had the stolen garments returned. On two or three other occasions the boats were pillaged, and a man, having run off with a seaman's jacket, though hotly pursued and fired at, would not abandon his prize till intercepted by some of the English on shore. A native also got into the master's cabin, and had stolen some articles, when, as he was leaping through the port into his canoe to escape, he was discovered. He was pursued by one of the boats, when, taking to the water, he dived under her several times, just as the men thought that they were about to catch hold of him. Finally, he contrived to unship the rudder, and thus rendering the boat unmanageable, made his escape.

Just as the explorers were about to sail, it was discovered that there was a much greater person in the island than any one they had yet seen. Mr. Pickersgill, who had met him, said that the people paid him extraordinary respect, and that some, when they approached him, fell on their faces, and put their heads between their feet, and that no one presumed to pass him without permission. When, however, Captain Cook saw the monarch, he took him for an idiot, from his stolid or sullen manner. On being spoken to, he neither answered nor altered a feature of his countenance, and even when a shirt was put on him, and other articles were placed by his side, he neither lifted an arm of his own accord, nor put out his hand to receive them. Probably, however, this manner was assumed, as adding, in his opinion, to his dignity, as he was afterwards caught laughing at something Attago said to him.

During the whole time of their stay at this island, Attago had proved himself of great use to Captain Cook and his companions. He had presented himself on board the captain's ship every morning, and did not quit his side till dark. On the departure of the ships, he earnestly pressed the captain to return, and to bring cloth and axes, promising hogs, fowls, fruit, and roots in abundance. He asked also, for himself, a uniform similar to that worn by the captain. Among other presents made by Cook to this friendly chief were two dogs, as there were none at that time in the island; indeed, pigs appear to have been the only four-footed animals in the possession of the inhabitants, although they knew of the existence of dogs. Besides fowls, there were pigeons, doves, parrots, and other birds. The whole island was thoroughly cultivated, and produced bread-fruit, cocoa-nut trees, plantains, bananas, shaddocks, yams, and other roots, the sugar-cane, and a fruit like a nectarine. The roads also were so well laid out, that there was an easy communication from one part of the island to the other in every direction. There were no towns or villages, but most of the houses stood in the midst of plantations. They were neatly constructed, but not much superior to those of the Society Islands. The floor, however, was slightly raised, and covered with thick mats; the same sort of matting serving to enclose them on the weather side, while on the opposite they were left open.

The ingenuity of this people was more especially exhibited in the construction of their canoes, which were superior to any that had been seen in the Pacific, though their tools were made of stone, bone, or shells, like those of the other islanders. The canoes are built of several pieces, sewed together in so neat a manner that, on the outside, no join could be seen. They were of two kinds, double and single. The single were from twenty to thirty feet long, and twenty-two inches broad in the middle, with wedge-shaped heads and sterns, and decked over at both ends, leaving only a third part open. They had outriggers, and some few carried sails, but were generally impelled by short paddles, the blades of which were broadest in the middle. The double canoes were composed of two vessels, each from sixty to seventy feet long, and four or five broad in the middle, and sharp at each end. They were fastened together by strong beams placed across their gunwales, which were raised for that purpose, and they were kept about seven feet apart. A platform of boards was placed on these beams, and served as a deck. They were very strongly built, and as the canoes themselves were also decked over, they might be immersed to the very platform without sinking. On the platform was a hut, serving as a cabin for the crew, and there was a hatchway through the platform into the hulls, by which the water was baled out. The canoes also carried as a moveable fire-hearth, a square, shallow trough of wood, filled with stones. They were rigged with one mast, which could be easily lowered, and had a lateen sail or matting, stretched on a long, slightly-bent yard, which could be

DOUBLE CANOE.

quickly shifted round when beating to windward. These vessels were capable of making long voyages, and the Tonga islanders were in the habit of going to Fejee, where they built canoes for the natives, and had probably extended their voyages to the

Navigator's Group, and possibly to New Zealand itself. Indeed, when these vessels are seen, there is no difficulty in understanding the means by which so large a number of the islands of the Pacific have been peopled by the same race, some retaining a portion of the civilization their ancestors possessed, others losing it altogether.

The natives of Tonga were slightly tattooed, and their natural complexion was of a light copper colour. The size of both men and women was that of ordinary Europeans. The dress of both sexes consisted of a piece of cloth or matting, wrapped round the waist, and hanging below the knees, while their shoulders and arms were uncovered, and usually anointed. They wore their hair short, and had ornaments in the form of necklaces, bracelets, and finger rings, made of bone, shells, or mother-of-pearl. Their cloth was of the same material as that of Otaheite, but coarser, and more durable, because glazed so as to resist the rain. They used vegetable dyes of various colours—brown, purple, yellow, red, and black. Their baskets, made of the same material as their mats, were very beautiful. They had different kinds of musical instruments; one of these was a sort of flute, which was made resonant by the breath of the nostril; another was similar to Pandean pipes, and composed of reeds; and a third was a drum made out of a hollow log. Their mode of saluting was like that of the New Zealanders, by rubbing noses together; and when anything was presented to them, they put it on their heads as a sign of its being accepted.

The government of the country was vested in a great chief or king, called the Areoke; and there were other chiefs under him, as governors of districts. It seemed pretty evident to the voyagers that the land of the island was apportioned among certain dignitaries, for whom the rest of the community worked, either as free labourers or slaves. When purchases were made by

CANOE BUILDING.

the English, although the collected goods were brought to market by a number of natives, one person uniformly received payment, and no bargain was struck without his consent.

Captain Cook was unable to obtain information respecting the religion of the people, excepting that he saw their temples and tombs, in his excursions through the island. It was observed, however, that nearly all the adults had lost the little finger of one hand, some, of both hands; and it was conjectured that the amputation was made at the death of parents or other relations. The people also burnt incisions in their cheeks, near the cheek-bone, probably also as a sign of mourning for the dead.

The expedition sailed from Tongatabu on the 7th of October; Captain Cook's last act being to send off by a canoe to his friend Attago, some wheat, peas, and beans, which he had neglected to give him with other seeds. A course was then shaped for Queen Charlotte's Sound, in New Zealand, there to take in wood and water, the commander intending afterwards to continue his discoveries to the south and east. The next day the lofty island of Pilstart was seen. It lies thirty-two leagues south by west from the south end of Eua. On the 21st the north end of New Zealand was made, and the ships ran down the east coast for the purpose of communicating with the natives, Captain Cook being very anxious to give them seeds and animals with which to stock the country. He had, however, no opportunity of doing this till he reached Cape Kidnappers, when a canoe came off with two men, who, by their dress and behaviour, appeared to be chiefs. To the principal of these, pigs, fowls, seeds, and roots were given, and a promise exacted that he would not kill the animals. He seemed more delighted with a long spike nail which was offered him, than with the animals. It was evident that the people on the coast had not forgotten what occurred on the previous voyage, as the first words they uttered on coming on board were "We are afraid of the guns," yet they seemed to understand that if they behaved properly they would be well treated.

Soon after this a heavy gale sprang up which lasted several days. During its continuance the *Adventure* was separated from the *Resolution*, and no more was seen or heard of her during the remainder of the voyage. The stormy weather continued for some time, and the *Resolution* had all her sails split before she at length came to an anchor in an inlet discovered on the east side of Cape Teerawhitte. While she lay at anchor, some natives came off who were tempted on board with the offer of nails, which they highly valued. To one of the men two cocks and two hens were given, but it was feared from his manner on receiving the present he would not take proper care of them.

The next day, the gale having abated, the *Resolution* proceeded to Ship Cove in Queen Charlotte's Sound. Here the sails were unbent to be repaired, and tents were set up on shore. It was now discovered that the bread, which was in casks, was greatly damaged. It was, therefore, examined, the copper oven was set up, and the better portions rebaked. The natives at once visited the ship, several of whom Captain Cook remembered, especially an old man, Goubiah by name. Some of them appropriated whatever they could find on shore unguarded, and, among other things, a seaman's bag of clothes. These were, however, recovered by the captain, who made, he says, a "friendly application for them," a mode of proceeding, which, with a due exhibition of power, might possibly have succeeded on other occasions under similar circumstances. The youngest of the two sows, which Captain Furneaux had put on shore in Cannibal Cove, was seen with these people, but lame of a leg and very tame. It was said that the other had been killed, but this was afterwards found not to be the case. The people proved to be adepts in thieving, and one chief, pretending to keep his countrymen at a proper distance, with furious actions, was discovered putting a handkerchief into his bosom which he had just picked out of Captain Cook's pocket. A fresh party, after bartering fish for cloth very fairly, stole six small water casks, and then made off in a fright, leaving a boar, which had been given them, and some of their own dogs. It is pleasant to have to describe the persevering endeavours of Captain Cook to stock the country with animals likely to prove useful to the inhabitants, little thinking how largely his own countrymen would benefit by his labours, and that, before a century would have passed by, vast flocks of sheep and horned cattle and horses would be feeding on the widely extended pastures of those fertile islands.

Before sailing, when at length one day his visitors had left him, he took on shore three sows and a boar, two cocks and two hens, carrying them some little way into the woods, where they were left with a supply of food to last them for ten or twelve days. The food was left that the animals might remain in the woods, and not roam down to the shore, where they might be discovered by the natives. Some cocks and hens were also left in Ship Cove, but as the natives occasionally went there, there was a risk of the birds falling into their hands. Two more goats were landed, but the he goat was seized with a sort of fit, and was supposed to have rushed into the sea and been drowned, as his mate who followed him when he started off on his mad career, came back without him. The vegetables which had been planted on the former visit had thriven, and most of the potatoes had been dug up.

All the time of the ship's stay a friendly intercourse was kept up with the natives. The best way of securing peace with savages, Captain Cook observes, is by first convincing them of your superiority, and then by being always on your guard. A regard for their own safety will then prevent them from being unanimous in forming any plan to attack you, while strict honesty and kindly treatment will gain their friendship. These principles mainly guided the great navigator in his intercourse with the savages he visited, and it was owing to this that he was so long able to pursue his useful discoveries.

He had ample evidence on this occasion of the savage character of the people by whom he was surrounded. A party of them had gone away on a war expedition, and returned with the body of a youth whom they had killed. Most of the body had been eaten, when one of the officers brought the head and a portion of the flesh on board. This latter was boiled and eaten by one of the natives with avidity, in the presence of Captain Cook and most of the officers and ship's company. This horrid proceeding had such an effect on some of the men, as well as on the captain, as to make them sick.* It had a still greater effect on the native of Otaheite, Oedidee. He at first became perfectly motionless, and looked the personification of horror. When aroused from this state he burst into tears and continued to weep and scold by turns, telling the New Zealanders that they were vile men, and that he would no longer be their friend. He would not suffer them to touch him. He used the same language to one of the crew who tasted the flesh, and refused to accept or to touch the knife with which it had been cut. It would be difficult, to paint more perfectly than Captain Cook has done in the above description, the natural horror felt by human beings when first becoming aware of the existence of cannibalism. It must be remembered that the people of Otaheite and those of New Zealand evidently sprang from the same race; and it is remarkable that the latter should have become addicted to such an abominable practice, while the former viewed it with unmitigated horror. Captain Cook says that he did not suppose the New Zealanders to have commenced the practice for

* It seems strange that this "horrid proceeding" should have been permitted on board the English ship; and that Captain Cook, with his well-established character, should have stood by and witnessed it, is unaccountable.

From the "Picture Gallery of the Nations."
NEW ZEALANDERS.

want of food, as their coasts supplied a vast quantity of fish and wild fowl, and they had also numerous dogs which they ate. They had also some vegetables and many land birds. He was not aware that at the distance of a few days sail there was a race of men equal, if not superior in intelligence, to the New Zealanders, still more addicted to the horrible practice, the accounts of which, thoroughly authenticated as they are, make the heart sicken at the thought of the depths of depravity to which human nature can sink.

In vain the *Adventure* was looked for. The unanimous opinion was that she was not stranded, nor likely to be in any neighbouring harbour; and as no actual rendezvous had been appointed, all hopes of seeing her again during the voyage were abandoned. This, however, did not discourage Cook from pursuing his researches in the South Pacific, in which he intended to occupy the whole of the ensuing summer, while his officers and crew expressed themselves willing to accompany him even without their consort, wherever he might think fit to go.

On the morning of the 26th of November, the *Resolution* took her departure from Cape Palliser, and steered south inclining to the east. Heavy gales were soon met with, and on the morning of the 12th of December, in latitude 62° 10′ s. and longitude 172° w., the first iceberg was seen, as also were many antarctic birds, while the explorers were greeted with a fresh gale and thick haze and snow, a great sea rolling up from the north-west and south-west, at the same time showing that there was no continent in that direction, unless at a great distance. Two days afterwards more large ice islands and loose ice were encountered; and with strong gales of wind, a heavy sea, dense snowstorms and fogs, surrounded by masses of floating ice, the ship pursued her course to the east. Christmas day was calm, and with a hundred ice islands in sight, the ship was allowed to drift quietly on. Providentially the weather was clear, with a light air, and as there was continued daylight, she was prevented from falling aboard any of the masses of ice. Had it been blowing, and as foggy as on the preceding days, a miracle alone could have saved her from being dashed to pieces. A full description of this part of the voyage would be tedious. Especially so must the reality have been to the voyagers; and before long all began to feel the effects of the bitter weather to which they were exposed. Cook himself was dangerously ill, though he concealed his malady from the crew.

On the 30th of January, at four in the morning, the clouds over the horizon were perceived to be of an unusual snow-white brightness, denoting a wide extent of ice. By eight the ship was close to its edge, when, from the mast head, it was seen to extend to the brink of the southern horizon, as well as to the east and west, while ninety-seven ice mountains were counted rising out of it. To penetrate this field was hopeless, and at length the captain, to the satisfaction of all on board, announced his intention of proceeding in search of the island of Juan Fernandez, said to have been discovered a century before in latitude 38°, and failing to find it, to look for Easter Island, or Davis Land, which had been unsuccessfully sought for by Byron, Carteret and Bougainville. After this he purposed getting within the tropic, and had thoughts of running as far west as the Tierra Austral del Spiritu Santo of Quiros. In vain the island of Juan Fernandez was looked for in the latitude in which it was supposed to lie, and the conclusion arrived at was that though such an island might be in existence, it could occupy but a small space in the ocean.

The captain was now again taken ill of what he calls a bilious cholic, which was so severe as to confine him to his bed, the charge of the ship devolving on Mr. Cooper. Mr. Patten, the surgeon, proved not only a skilful physician, but an affectionate friend. A favourite dog belonging to Mr. Forster, fell a sacrifice, it being killed and made into soup for the captain; there being no other fresh meat in the ship. A few fish were afterwards caught, which were very acceptable to him.

Early on the morning of the 11th of March, 1774, land was seen about twelve leagues distant, which, to the joy of all on board, ultimately proved to be the long sought for Easter Island. On getting near the coast, off a sandy beach, two men in a canoe came off, and after sending up, by a rope, a bunch of plantains they returned to shore. This showed the good disposition of the islanders, and gave the voyagers hopes of obtaining refreshments. A better anchorage than this part of the coast afforded having been found, the ship brought up here. On the English landing, a few potatoes, plantains and sugar-canes were brought to them; but the natives were such expert thieves that those on board could scarcely keep their hats on their heads or anything in their pockets. A supply of potatoes was obtained, indeed this appeared to be the chief production of the island. The natives had been digging them up as fast as they could from a field close to the landing-place, till a person arrived, who appeared to be the rightful owner, and who drove all the rest away.

As Captain Cook was unable to walk any distance, he sent Lieutenants Pickersgill and Edgecombe, with a party of men armed, to explore the country. They were at first pressed on by a crowd of the natives, till a man appeared, tattooed and painted, who drove them away, and then hoisting a piece of white cloth on a spear, marched forward at the head of the party. A considerable portion of the island was barren and stony, but in other parts were plantations of potatoes, plantains, and sugar-canes. Water was very scarce, and hardly drinkable. Some huts were found, the owners of which came out with roasted potatoes and sugar-canes, and as the party marched in single file on account of the narrow path, gave some to each man as he passed by. They distributed water in the same manner. On the east side, near the sea, three ruinous platforms of stone were met with, on each of which had stood four large statues; but most of them had fallen down and been broken. Mr. Wales measured an entire one, and found it to be fifteen feet in length, and six feet across the shoulders. On the head of each statue was a large cylinder of a red coloured stone. One of these cylinders, which was measured, was fifty-two inches high, and sixty-six in diameter. There were others, however, very much larger. Some of them were perfectly round, others had a cavity worked out, in the upper edge, for a quarter of the way round.

The opposite side of the island to this, to which their guide conducted them, was full of these gigantic statues, some placed in groups, on masonry, others single, fixed only in the earth. The latter were much larger than the others. One which had fallen down was twenty-seven feet high, and eight feet across the shoulders; and yet this was much shorter than one they found standing—its shade being sufficient to shelter their party of nearly thirty persons from the rays of the sun at about two o'clock. Near this place was a hill, from which a view of the whole island was obtained. Not a creek large enough even for a boat was seen, nor any indication of fresh water. In a small hollow on the highest part of the island several cylinders were found, and Mr. Wales was of opinion that the quarry had been at that spot, and that after the cylinders had been formed they were rolled down the hill. There must have been great difficulty in raising them to the heads of the statues. It was conjectured that this was done by raising a mound round each statue and rolling up the stone on it, the mound being afterwards removed. It must have required a considerable amount of mechanical knowledge to bring the statues from the quarry, and to place them upright. The natives knew nothing whatever as to the origin of the statues, nor did they look on them with any respect, nor indeed seem interested in any way in them. No quadrupeds were seen on the island, but few birds, and only two sorts of low shrubs.

The party were greatly inconvenienced in their walk by the attempts of the natives to steal from them, and at length one man, who ran off with a bagful of provisions, was fired upon with small shot and wounded slightly. He dropped the bag, and seemed in no way offended at the treatment he received. The people carried short clubs and also spears with flint heads. The dress of the chiefs consisted of two pieces of cloth, one round the waist, and the other thrown over the shoulders; but many were almost naked. The men wore their hair and beards short, with a fillet ornamented with feathers round the head; while the women wore the hair long, and had straw caps shaped like a Scotch bonnet on their heads. Their habitations were low huts, built with sticks, bent overhead, and joined together so as to form an arch. The longest seen was sixty feet long, and only four or five wide. Their canoes were very poor, owing to the want of materials, and very few were seen. Captain Cook considered that there were about six or seven hundred inhabitants on the island. In colour, features, and language they were similar to the inhabitants of the islands to the west, so that it was evident they had sprung from the same race.

The *Resolution* left Easter Island on the 16th of March, and stood north-west-by-north, and north-north-west, for the Marquesas, with a fine easterly gale. Having reached the latitude of the group, the course was changed to west. On the 5th of April first one island, and then others in succession were seen; and the explorers were satisfied that they had reached the Marquesas, discovered by the Spaniards in 1595. The first island seen was called Hood's Island, after the midshipman who discovered it, and the others were St. Pedro, Dominica, and St. Christina. The ship, after being nearly driven on the rocks, brought up in port in the last-mentioned island. Directly afterwards, thirty or forty natives came off in ten or twelve canoes, in the bow of each of which a heap of stones was observed, while all the men had slings fastened to their hands. It required some address to get them alongside, but at last a hatchet and some spike-nails induced the people in one canoe to venture under the quarter galley. The rest then followed, exchanging bread-fruit and fish for small nails. At sunset they all returned to the shore. The next morning the natives returned in greater numbers, with plantains, bread-fruit, and a pig; but soon showed themselves ready to cheat, and to be expert thieves. Captain Cook was going into the boat to look for a convenient place to moor the ship, when, seeing too many natives on board, he warned one of the officers on deck, saying that something would be stolen. Just then he was told that an iron stanchion had been carried off from the opposite gangway. He therefore ordered the officer to fire over the canoe till he could get round in the boat, but to be careful not to kill any one. But the noise made by the natives prevented this last warning from being heard, and at the third shot the unhappy thief was killed. Two other natives who were in the canoe leaped overboard, but soon got in again and threw away the stanchion. One of them sat baling the blood and water out of the canoe, uttering a kind of hysteric laugh, while the other, a youth of fifteen, looked at the dead body with a serious and dejected countenance. The latter was found to be the son of the man who had been killed. Immediately on this, the natives took to flight, but on being followed by the captain into the bay, the people in one canoe were persuaded to come alongside the boat, and to receive some nails. This restored their confidence in some degree, but soon afterwards they attempted to carry off the buoy of the kedge anchor. A musket shot on this was fired at them, but it fell short, and they

MARQUESAS ISLANDER.

took no notice of it; but a second bullet passing over them, they immediately let go the buoy and made for the shore.

The natives undoubtedly were bold fellows, for notwithstanding the effects of the firearms which they had witnessed, before long some more ventured off. One of them appeared to be a person of consequence. His dress was similar to that of the chiefs of Otaheite. Round his head was a fillet with the tail feathers of birds fixed in it, and standing upright. He also wore ornaments of feathers round his legs and arms. The women wore a petticoat of native cloth, and a broad fillet made of the fibre of the cocoa-nut husk, with a piece of mother-of-pearl shell the size of a tea-saucer in front. On either side were other ornaments of tortoise-shell and mother-of-pearl, with feathers in the upper part. The chief brought a pig, and was persuaded to come up the side, but soon went away.

The party from the *Resolution* who went on shore were received with courtesy by the natives; the captain was disappointed in not obtaining the number of pigs he had expected. Some of the young officers, it seemed, gave away thoughtlessly several articles which the natives valued more than the nails, and thus spoilt the trade. Among those highly-coveted objects were some of the red feathers obtained at Tonga.

The productions of the Marquesas Islands were similar to those of Otaheite; the habitations were of a like character, but not so well built, and the habits of the people were not so cleanly. The people were considered the handsomest that had been met with during the whole voyage. The men were generally tattooed, but the women and children, who were not so, were thought to be as fair as many Europeans. Hogs were the only quadrupeds, and cocks and hens the only tame fowls seen; and these were not procured in any great number. Notwithstanding the length of time the crew had been at sea previous to their arrival at the

Marquesas, yet owing to the abundant supply of antiscorbutic food, and the watchful care of the surgeon, there was not a man seriously ill on board. Captain Cook therefore determined to proceed on his voyage without further delay.

The *Resolution* therefore left the Marquesas on the 12th of April, 1774; and ten days afterwards she reached Otaheite, and anchored once more in Matavai Bay. In the course of this passage several low coral islands or islets had been passed, and one of them had been visited. This was the island of Tioakea, first of all discovered by Captain Byron, and formed one of a group, called St. George's Islands. After passing these the *Resolution* had fallen in with four other small islands, not set down in any chart; and these Captain Cook had named Palliser's Isles, in honour of his particular friend, Sir Hugh Palliser.

Captain Cook's object in visiting Matavai Bay was that Mr. Wales, the astronomer, might correct the chronometers of the ship by a known longitude. The first thing done, therefore, was to erect tents, and to land the instruments required in this operation.

As soon as the arrival of the voyagers was known, many of their old friends paid them a visit, expressing great joy at seeing them. Among others came Otoo, the king, with several chiefs, and a train of attendants, who brought with them a dozen large hogs, and a quantity of fruit, which made them very welcome. A supply of red parrots' feathers having been collected at Tonga, these were shown to the natives, and took their fancy to such a degree that the principal people of both sexes brought hogs, fruit, and everything the island afforded, in order to obtain them. So exhausted was his stock-in-trade, that had it not been for these feathers, Cook says he should have found it difficult to supply his ship with the necessary refreshments. He had intended remaining here only long enough to allow Mr. Wales to take the observations

VALLEY OF AKAOUI, MARQUESAS ISLANDS.

he desired, but he found so great an improvement in the state of the country, and provisions so abundant, that he resolved at once to repair and refit his ship.

When Captain Cook on one occasion went to Opparree to pay King Otoo a visit, a formidable fleet of three hundred double war canoes was found drawn up along the beach, while a number of armed men were seen on the shore. What could be the object of this armament it was difficult to conjecture. The Englishmen, however, on landing were received with great courtesy; but Otoo was not to be found, and, greatly disappointed, they returned on board. At length they were told that this fleet was part of an armament intended to be sent against Eimeo, whose chief had declared himself independent of Otaheite.

The chief next in consequence to Otoo was Towha, who seemed to be a very sensible man, and most friendly to the English. He showed it on a trying occasion. A native had been caught stealing a water-cask, and having been kept in irons on board, was returned on shore to be flogged. Otoo, his sister, and others, begged that the man might be set at liberty; but Cook explained that as he flogged any of his people who stole from them, or behaved ill in any way, so in justice, and to preserve peace between them, he must punish any natives who behaved ill to him. The sentence was carried out, the natives looking on. On the culprit being set at liberty, the people were going away, when Towha called them back and addressed them, recapitulating what had been said to Otoo, condemning their present bad habits, and advising a reformation in future. The gracefulness of action, and the attention with which he was heard, showed that he was no mean orator. After this the marines went through their exercises and loaded and fired in volleys, to the utter amazement of the natives, especially of those who had seen nothing of the kind before.

The next morning a small portion of the fleet of war canoes was observed exercising, and Mr. Hodges had the opportunity of sketching them. The largest had about thirty rowers, the smaller only eighteen. The warriors stood on the stage, and encouraged the rowers, or paddlers rather, to exert themselves. Some youths were seated high up on the carved stem above the steersman, with white wands in their hands, apparently to look out and give notice of what they saw. The warriors were completely equipped for war, and the quantity and weight of cloth they had on them made it difficult to conceive how they could stand up under it when fighting. A large quantity was wrapped round their heads as turbans or helmets, to guard them from the blows of their enemies. The turbans of some of the warriors were surmounted by small bunches of shrubs covered with white feathers, intended as ornaments. On returning to the shore all the rowers leaped out the moment the canoe touched the ground, and with the assistance of those on shore, hauled it up on the beach. Each man then walked off with his paddle, and so rapidly was everything done, that in less than five minutes there was no sign of the canoes having been lately afloat. Afterwards, at the dockyard of King Otoo, among many large canoes, two were seen in the course of building, a hundred and eight feet long. They were to be united so as to form one double canoe; the largest, Cook says, he had seen in those seas.

On another occasion, an example was given of the way the warriors, in attacking a place, are thrown on shore. Four or more canoes were lashed side by side, and then each division paddled in so judiciously that they formed one unbroken line along the shore. To do this they were directed by a man who stood in the fore part of the centre vessel, with a long wand in his hand, directing all their movements. The fleet was attended by some small double canoes, called marais. On the fore part of each was a sort of bed

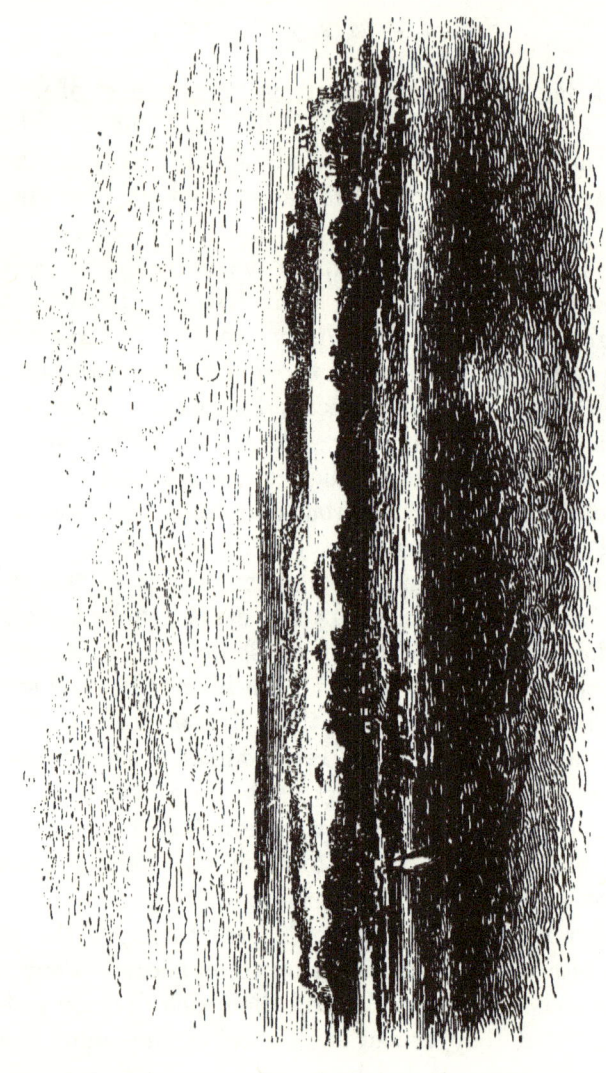

CORAL ISLAND, NAMED WHITSUNDAY ISLAND, IN THE PACIFIC OCEAN.

place with one division, capable of holding the body of a man, intended for the reception of any chief who might be killed in battle. Cook estimated, from the number of canoes he saw furnished by each district, that the whole island could raise and equip one thousand seven hundred and twenty war canoes, requiring sixty-eight thousand men, calculating forty for each canoe. As these would not amount to a third of the number of people in the island, he considered that it could not contain less than two hundred and four thousand inhabitants. He was convinced, from the vast swarms of people he met wherever he went, that this estimate was not too great. This is possible; but war, disease, and vicious habits had fearfully decreased the population before Christianity was established among them.

Otoo and his chiefs at first appeared very anxious that Captain Cook should accompany them in their proposed expedition, and they begged him to help them against their enemies. This he very properly declined doing, but would have been glad to have accompanied them to witness the mode in which they carried on their naval operations. It would have been more in accordance with the character of a Christian people had the English tried to reconcile the contending parties, and to prove to them the advantages and blessings of peace. But such a thought does not appear to have entered the mind of the sagacious navigator, or of his companions.

Cook's endeavours to benefit the islanders in other respects appeared likely to be successful. Two goats had been left by Captain Furneaux. They had had two kids, now nearly full grown, and the mother was also again with kid. The animals were in excellent condition, and the people seemed very fond of them. One of two sheep had, however, died, but twenty cats were given to the natives, though it is difficult to understand how they were likely to prove useful, unless mice had threatened to overrun the island.

During this visit a man from a distant part of the island made off with a musket and effected his escape. The dread of the consequences to themselves caused Otoo and several other chiefs to run away and hide themselves, and the people were afraid to bring down provisions to the ship. After a considerable amount of negotiations, and the delay of nine days, the muskets and some other articles which had been stolen were, by the intervention of the chiefs, brought back to the tents, and confidence was restored.

Preparations were now made for leaving Otaheite. On the 11th of May a large supply of fruit arrived from all parts, some of it sent by Towha, the admiral of the fleet, with orders to his servants to receive nothing in return. However, the captain thought fit to send an equivalent present by Oedidee. That young native had come to the resolution of remaining at Otaheite, but was persuaded to go on in the ship to Ulietea, his native island. Nothing but Captain Cook's warning that it was very probable he would be unable to return to the Pacific would have induced him to leave the ship, so great was his affection for the English, and his desire to visit their country.

On the 12th old Oberea, who had been supposed by Captain Wallis to be the queen of the island, came on board, and brought a present of pigs and fruit, and soon afterwards Otoo appeared with a great retinue, and a large quantity of provisions. Handsome presents were made in return, and the visitors were entertained in the evening with fireworks. A succession of broadsides from the great guns on another occasion must have still more astonished the natives.

Captain Cook waited in vain for the sailing of the fleet on the proposed warlike expedition. It was evident that the chiefs considered, since they could not obtain the assistance of the English, that they should be more at liberty to act if left alone, and therefore, as long as the *Resolution* remained, they continued to make excuses for not setting out. Otoo's large canoe had been called at Cook's request the Britannia, and he had presented to the king a grappling iron, a rope, and an English jack and pendant for her.

Several natives were anxious to accompany Captain Cook, but he firmly resisted all their solicitations, from motives of humanity, knowing the great probability that they would never return to their native land. At length, on the 14th of May, 1774, the anchor was hove up, and the ship proceeded out of the harbour, Otoo remaining in his canoe alongside till the ship was under sail. At that juncture, all the boats being hoisted in, a gunner's mate, a good swimmer, slipped overboard, hoping to reach the shore and to remain behind. He was, however, seen before he got clear of the ship; a boat was lowered and he was brought back. He was an Irishman by birth, but he had been long absent from home, and he was without any tie of kindred; Captain Cook says that he could not be surprised at his wish to remain where he could enjoy not only all the necessaries, but all the luxuries of life, in ease and plenty; and that had he asked permission to remain it might perhaps have been granted. He had formerly been in the Dutch service, and had come on board the *Endeavour* at Batavia during the former voyage.

On the 15th the *Resolution* anchored in O'Wharre Harbour, in the island of Huaheine, and immediately old Oree, the chief, and several natives, came on board, when the former presented a hog and some other articles with the usual forms. A friendly intercourse was kept up with Oree the whole time of the visit, but several of the officers and men were robbed on shore. There appeared to exist a gang of banditti who set their chief at defiance and robbed everyone they met. Captain Cook, however, landed, and quietly took possession of a house with two chiefs in it, who were kept as hostages till the articles were returned. On another occasion, at the request of Oree, he, with a strong party of armed men, landed, and went in pursuit of the thieves; but Oedidee, who was with them, became alarmed, and warned the captain that they were being led into an ambush to be destroyed. From the strict discipline, however, kept up by the party this (even should the natives have intended treachery) was rendered impossible. In spite of these drawbacks, the people brought cocoa-nuts and other fruits, and two young chiefs presented to the captain a pig, a dog, and some young plantain trees, the usual peace offerings. Notwithstanding this good feeling, he caused several volleys to be fired to show the natives the power and effect of musketry, for the young officers and others who went on shore shooting with muskets were so very inexpert in their use that they had brought firearms somewhat into contempt.

On the 21st a fleet of sixty canoes was seen steering for Ulietea. The people on board them were *Eareeoies*, going to visit their brethren in the neighbouring islands. They formed a sort of secret society, and seemed to have customs which they would not explain. Infanticide appeared to be almost universal among them, and they had many other practices of a most abominable character. Cava drinking and acting plays seemed to be the principal amusements of the chiefs of this island.

Early on the morning of the 23rd the ship put to sea. The good old chief Oree was the last man who left her. When told by the captain that he should see him no more, he wept, and said, "Let your sons come, we will treat them well."

The next day, it having been calm all night, the *Resolution* reached Ulietea. While warping into a secure berth the captain's old friend, Oreo, with several other persons, came off, bringing presents. On returning the visit, the captain and his companions were met at the door of the house by five old women, who had been cutting their heads with sharks' teeth, and now, while the blood was streaming down their faces, insisted on saluting their visitors. Directly afterwards they went out, washed themselves, and returned, appearing as cheerful as any of the company. A large number of people had collected on shore near the ship; they were said to be *Eareeoies,* and they continued feasting for several days. There, as at the other islands, plays were acted for the amusement of the visitors.

Ulietea was Oedidee's native island, and here he took leave of his English friends, whom he left "with a regret fully demonstrative of his esteem and affection; nor could anything have torn him from them but the fear of never returning." The captain declares that he had not words to describe the anguish of this young man when he went away. "He looked up at the ship, burst into tears, and then sank down into the canoe."

This young South Sea islander is described as "a youth of good parts, and of a docile, gentle, and humane disposition," and as one who would have been—physically at least—a better specimen of the people than Omai. It is to be feared, that he returned to his home, after his lengthened cruise with his English patrons, without having received any real benefit from the intercourse. So far as can be learned, "no man had cared for his soul."

After leaving Ulietea the *Resolution* proceeded westward on her voyage, being cautiously navigated at night, and having all sails set in the daytime. The first land seen was Howe Island, previously discovered by Captain Wallis, the next was an island before unknown, to which was given the name of Palmerston.

On the 20th of June more land was in sight. This proved to be an island about eleven leagues in circuit, and standing well out of the sea, having deep water close into its shores. As this island was perceived to be inhabited, Captain Cook was induced to go on shore with a party of explorers, and endeavoured to open communication with the natives. They were found, however, to be fierce and intractable, furiously attacking the visitors with stones and darts. Two or three muskets discharged in the air did not hinder them from advancing still nearer, and one of them threw a long dart or spear which na.rowly missed the captain, passing close over his shoulder. The boldness and fury of this man nearly cost him his life, for, aroused by the instinct of self-preservation, and probably also by momentary anger, Captain Cook raised a musket he carried, and pointing it at his assailant, who was only a few paces off, he pulled the trigger. Happily the weapon missed fire, and the English commander was spared the after remorse of needless bloodshed, for the explorers, or the invaders and intruders, as the natives considered them, reached their boat, and afterwards their ship, unharmed.

POLYNESIAN SCENE.

In consequence of the apparent disposition and the behaviour of the people, the island received from Cook the name of Savage Island, a name it still bears, although the inhabitants no longer merit the appellation of Savage Islanders.

After leaving this island the ship's course was west-south-west, and on the 25th of June, a string of islands was seen ahead when the wind dropped. The next morning more islands were seen and soundings found. The islands in sight proved to be those of the Tonga group to which Cook had given the name of the Friendly Islands. A canoe came boldly off, and the people in her pointed out Anamocka, or Rotterdam, towards which the ship proceeded, and anchored on the north side of the island. The natives came off in their canoes in great numbers, and exchanged yams and shaddocks for nails and old rags; but, as usual, some began to pilfer; and one man got hold of the lead-line, which he would not relinquish till fired at.

On the captain and some of the officers going on shore they were received with great courtesy by the natives, who assisted in filling the water casks and rolling them down to the beach, contented with a few nails as payment. When, however, the surgeon was afterwards out shooting by himself, having been left on shore, a fellow seized his fowling-piece and made off with it. Afterwards, when the watering party were on shore, Mr. Clerke's gun was snatched from him and several of the cooper's tools were carried off. This style of proceeding, if allowed, would have hazarded the safety of all on board; the captain, therefore, who had been summoned, sent off for the marines, while two or three guns were fired from the ship to alarm Mr. Forster who was on shore. Several of the natives remained, who acted with their usual courtesy, and long before the marines arrived Mr. Clerke's gun was brought back. As the other was not restored, two large double sailing canoes were seized by the marines on their landing; and one man, making resistance, was fired at with small shot. This showed the natives that the English were in earnest, and the musket was returned; but an adze had also been carried off, and it was insisted that this also should be brought back. The chiefs thought that the captain wanted the man who had been wounded, and whom they said was dead. Soon afterwards he was brought up, stretched out on a board, and apparently lifeless. Captain Cook was very much shocked at first, till examining the body he found that the man was alive and only slightly hurt. His wounds were dressed by the surgeon, who soon afterwards arrived, and a poultice of sugar cane was applied to prevent inflammation. A present recompensed to some extent what the poor man suffered. No person of any consequence was seen by the voyagers while they remained here. Several lofty islands were seen in the group—among them Amattagoa whose summit was veiled in clouds, and was rightly supposed to be a volcano. Many of the islands in the South Sea are volcanic, and in some of them the volcanoes are in full activity. That of Kilanea in the Sandwich Islands often presents a spectacle of awful fury and grandeur.

After leaving the Friendly Islands and calling, on the 1st of July, at Turtle Island, a brisk gale carried the ship on for some distance, till, on the 15th, high land was seen to the south-west. This was the Australis del Espirito Santo of Quiros; it also went by the name of the Great Cyclades. After exploring the coast for some days the captain came to an anchor in a harbour in the island of Mallicollo, where one of his objects was to open friendly communication with the natives.

A number of these came off, some in canoes, others swimming. They exchanged arrows tipped with bone for pieces of cloth, while two who ventured on deck received presents. The next morning so many made their appearance, and with such increased confidence, that after a large number had boarded the ship it was found necessary to refuse admittance to others. Upon this, one of the repulsed natives threatened to shoot a boat-keeper in one of the boats. In the confusion that ensued, Captain Cook came on deck, when the savage turned his arrow towards him. Upon this the captain, who had a gun in his hand loaded with small shot,

CRATER OF KILANEA, SANDWICH ISLANDS.

fired at his assailant, who, being but slightly wounded, still kept his bow bent in a threatening attitude. Receiving the contents of a second musket, however, he dropped his bow and paddled off with all speed.

By this time others of the natives had begun to discharge their arrows; neither did a musket fired over their heads frighten them. It was not till they heard the thunder of a four-pounder, that they were seriously alarmed; then the natives on deck and in the cabin leaped overboard, and, with those in the canoes, made their escape as fast as they could. Directly after the gun was fired drums were heard beating on shore, probably to summon the people to arms.

The next day the captain landed with a green branch in his hand, and was met by a chief who also carried one, and these being exchanged, a friendly intercourse was established. The English made signs that they wished to cut down wood, and permission was granted to them by the natives to do so. These people, however, set no value on nails or anything their visitors possessed. They seemed unwilling that any one should advance beyond the beach, and were only anxious to get rid of the strangers. When the English left the shore the natives retired in different directions. In the afternoon a man was seen to bring to the beach a buoy which had been taken in the night from the kedge anchor. On a boat being sent it was at once put on board, the man walking off without saying a word, and this was the only thing which was stolen while the ship lay there. Some houses, similar to those of the Friendly Islands were seen, with plantations of cocoa-nuts, plantains, yams, and bread-fruit, and a number of pigs were running about.

Other parts of the shore were visited, but the people kept aloof; and not till the ship was under weigh did they come off, showing then every disposition to trade, and acting with scrupulous honesty. Sometimes, for instance, they had received articles, and not having given anything in return, their canoes being shoved off by their companions, they used every exertion to get back to the ship. They were the most ugly, ill-proportioned people the explorers had yet seen; dark-coloured and rather diminutive, with long heads, flat faces, and monkey-like countenances. Their hair was black or brown, short and curly, but not so soft or woolly as that of a negro. Their beards were strong, crisp, and bushy. A belt round the middle curiously contracted that part of the body, while, with the exception of a wrapper between the legs, they went naked. The women wore a petticoat, and a bag over their shoulders in which the children were carried; but none came near the ship. A piece of white stone an inch and a half long, with a slight curve in it, was worn in a hole made through the nose. Their arms were clubs, spears, and bows and arrows. Some of the officers were very nearly poisoned by eating portions of two reddish fish, the size of large bream, caught with hook and line. They were seized with violent pains in the head and bones, attended by a scorching heat all over the body, and a numbness of the joints. A pig and dog died from eating the remainder. It was a week or ten days before the officers quite recovered. The crews of Quiros had suffered in the same way. He had named the fish Porgos.

A number of islands were now passed, to which the names of Montagu, Sandwich, Hinchinbrook, and Shepherd, were given; the ship continuing along the coast to the south-east.

On the 3rd of August the *Resolution* approached another island, and anchored about a mile from the shore, when several natives attempted to swim off to her, but a boat being lowered they returned. The next morning the captain went off to the shore in search of wood and water, with presents which he distributed among some people who appeared on the rocks which line the

ATTACKED BY THE SAVAGES.

coast. In return they offered, as he supposed with a friendly feeling, to drag the boat through the surf on shore; but he declined the offer, wishing to have a better place to land at. This he found on a sandy beach, in a bay where he could land without wetting his feet. To this spot crowds followed him, headed by a chief, who made them form a semicircle, while with only a green branch in his hand, Cook stepped on shore. The chief was loaded with presents, which he received courteously, and when, by signs, water and fruit were asked for he immediately sent for some. Still as all the people were armed with clubs, spears, bows and arrows, the captain was suspicious of their intentions, and kept his eye on the chief. Again signs were made by the natives that they would haul the boat up, and just then the chief disappeared among the crowd. On this Cook stepped back into the boat, making signs that he would soon return. The islanders, however, had no intention of allowing him to depart, so while some of them laid hold of the gang board, and attempted to drag up the boat on to the beach, others snatched at the oars and tried to wrest them away from the sailors. In this predicament, and seeing that neither expostulations nor menaces were of any avail, the captain raised his musket, pointed it at the chief, who had again made his appearance, and pulled the trigger; but, as on a former occasion, the piece missed fire, or only flashed in the pan. The savages then began throwing stones and darts, and shooting their arrows. The captain now felt compelled to order his men to fire. The first discharge threw the savages into confusion; but even a second was hardly sufficient to drive them off the beach; and they then retired behind trees and bushes popping out every now and then to throw a dart. Four lay to all appearance dead; but two managed to crawl behind the bushes. Happily half the muskets missed fire, or more would have been wounded. One of the boat's crew was badly wounded in the cheek by a dart, and an arrow shot from a distance struck Mr. Gilbert. The skirmish ended by the English making good their retreat.

On the arrival of the party on board, the ship was got under weigh and stood closer in shore; and presently two of the natives appeared with two oars which had been lost in the scuffle. In a fit of exasperation, probably, on account of the treatment he had received, and of mortification at his partial defeat, Captain Cook ordered a round shot to be fired at the men, which, though it proved harmless, had the effect of driving the men away. They left the oars, however, leaning against some bushes.

The whole of this unhappy affair seems to have been a series of misunderstandings. At least it is not difficult to conceive that the natives were, at first, friendly disposed; that their offer to haul the boat upon the beach may have been dictated by kind motives, and that their subsequent conduct arose from what they might have conceived to be the suspicious actions of their strange and uninvited visitors. As to their being armed, and declining to lay down their arms, it is to be remembered that the English had arms also, which they did not lay down. It certainly does not seem improbable that if the chief of these poor barbarians and the English captain could have interchanged a few words, intelligible on both sides, and so convinced each other of their honest intentions and wishes, the subsequent fracas might have been prevented; but this, of course, was out of the question. It is to be feared, too, that the superiority over all uncivilized nations which the English voyagers proudly felt themselves to possess, gave an air of contemptuous defiance to their actions which the natives might resent. The firing of that last shot was not unlikely (together with the previous scuffle) to provoke feelings of deep enmity, and not only to rankle in the minds and memories of those present, but to be handed down by tradition to the next generation, and the next after that, so as to keep up both detestation of all white men, and dread of their future visits.

These remarks are not uncalled for, nor will they be considered as without point when the name of the island is given:— ERROMANGA: a name full of painful associations to all who take an interest in missionary enterprise, and in the advancement, by human instrumentality, of the kingdom of the Redeemer. It was here that, sixty-six years afterwards, the valuable life of one of the foremost in the rank of modern Christian missionaries, John Williams was sacrificed to the hatred of the whites of which we have just spoken. The proximate incentive to the murder was revenge for some ill treatment the natives had shortly before received, from a white man, a sandal wood trader; but it is probable that the commencement of their strong dislike to strangers may be traced to the visit of the *Resolution* to their native island, in 1774.

After leaving Erromanga the ship steered for another island, which proved to be Tanna, being directed at night by a great light which was seen at the east end of it, and which in the morning was discovered to be that of a volcano in full activity. A harbour was found, and two boats well armed, were sent in to sound. Here the ship anchored. A number of armed natives were seen on shore, and soon they began to come off, some swimming, others in canoes. Some cocoa-nuts were thrown into one of the boats, and cloths and other articles were given in return. This induced more to venture alongside, when they proved themselves to be most daring thieves; some attempting to knock off the rings from the rudder, others tried to tear away the fly of the ensign, and a bold effort was made to run away with the buoys. A musketoon fired over their heads had the effect of driving them off. Even here there was an exception to the rule. An old man continually came off to the ship with fruit, evidently trying to ingratiate himself with the

Missing Page

The watering party meanwhile filled the casks; but still the lower orders were very troublesome. Some buckshot fired at a man at last brought them to order, and now everything seemed to go on pleasantly. Paowang even brought an axe and several other articles which had been left on shore; indeed Cook's demeanour seemed to have won the respect of the savages, and it was no longer necessary to mark a barrier line, as they did not press near the tents nor incommode the English when at work. Yet savages they were, for they acknowledged voluntarily that they were cannibals, and asked their visitors if they also did not eat the flesh of their enemies. Yet they could have no excuse for the practice, as their island abounded with pigs, and fruit of all sorts.

All this time the English were constantly on their guard; still they ran no little risk, as they made some excursions up the country, when they were threatened by parties of natives, who however retired when they turned towards the harbour. It is manifest however, that the natives were not badly disposed, but were influenced by the very natural feeling of jealousy at seeing strangers, whose object they could not comprehend, attempting to penetrate their country. It would have been difficult to convince untutored savages, who had been peppered with duck shot, and fired at with bullets and cannon balls, that their white visitors were influenced by the purest feelings of philanthropy, and a disinterested desire to do them good. Fortunately the muskets supplied to the *Resolution* must have been kept in very bad order, as they missed fire as often as they went off, or more lives of savages would have been sacrificed. There is no doubt, as has already been intimated, that Captain Cook had no delight in exercising cruelty towards the natives of the places he visited; and believed that he acted in self-defence, when he, as he would have said, was unfortunately called upon to wound and perhaps to slay them. It may be added also, that he frequently had great trouble in restraining the ardour of his officers, who were not troubled with so nice a conscience as the captain's regarding the lives of savages.

On one occasion for instance, some native boys (little mischievous urchins, no doubt,) who had got into a thicket near where a party were cutting wood, and had thrown stones, were fired at by some of the petty officers. The captain was very much displeased at so wanton a use being made of fire-arms, and took measures, as he thought, to prevent it for the future: but not long afterwards, to his horror, he saw a sentry level his musket, and before he could cry out, the soldier had fired and shot a native dead. The marine's only excuse was that he saw a native bending his bow, an act they often performed without intending to shoot. After all, the sentry did not kill the man who bent the bow, but another who was standing near.

Among the excursions made by the officers was one towards the volcano, which however they could not reach. It was in such furious eruption that the air was filled with dust and ashes, and when it rained they were covered with mud. On their way they passed a spot emitting columns of smoke, and near the harbour hot springs were discovered, a thermometer placed in one of them rose to 170°.

Although the people of this island had no notion of the use of iron, they were not so savage as at first appeared; their plantations were carefully cultivated, and produced sugar-canes and yams, bread-fruit, plantains, and cocoa-nuts. They had, however, one of the chief characteristics of savages—the women carried all the burdens, and were compelled to do every description of hard work. Though dark, they had not the peculiarities of the negro race, but they made themselves darker than they were by painting their skins. They differed in many respects from the inhabitants of the neighbouring islands both in appearance and language. Their dwellings were of some size, but had no walls, being merely roofs—looking like those of English barns taken off their walls and placed on the ground. Their canoes were tolerably well constructed, but though their shores abounded with fish they had no notion of catching them with nets or lines, the only way being to spear them as they swam by.

On the morning of the 20th of August, the ship left Resolution Harbour * in Tanna, and continued the survey along the coasts of this extensive group of islands. A large number of natives were seen at the south-west side of Mallicolla, and on the opposite shore a brief communication was held with apparently another race of people, who came off in numerous small outrigger canoes. Though gifts were handed to them they could not be induced to come up the side, or even to take hold of a rope.

The scenery of the coast in all directions was much admired; the vegetation was most luxuriant, every hill was chequered with plantations, and every valley was watered by a sparkling stream. The survey of the group being at length completed, the *Resolution* stood away towards New Zealand. The supposed continent of Quiros had dwindled into a small island, and as Captain Cook took his departure from the south-west point in latitude 15° 40′, longitude 165° 59′, he named it Cape Lisbourne. The *Resolution* continued her course to the south-west, from the 1st of September till the 4th, when land was discovered bearing south-south-west, and extending round for some leagues. Breakers were seen half way between the ship and the shore, and inside them were several canoes, evidently coming off, but as night fell they returned. The night was spent in standing off and on the land, and the next morning the boats having discovered a channel through the reef, the ship stood in and came to anchor. She was immediately surrounded by a number of natives, who came off in eighteen

* So called by Captain Cook, because the *Resolution* had anchored there.

canoes. They were entirely unarmed, and apparently well disposed. Some presents were thrown to them for which they offered two stale fish in return, and confidence being established, numbers crowded on board. Some were asked into the cabin to dinner. They showed however no curiosity to taste the pea-soup, salt beef, or pork, but eat some yams.

Except a curious wrapper generally in use, these people were entirely naked. They seemed intelligent, and examined with considerable interest the goats, hogs, dogs, and cats on board, which it was evident they had never before seen. They valued spike nails and cloth of all colours, but red cloth they preferred. A young chief was seen in one of the canoes, but did not come on board. After dinner, Captain Cook, accompanied by a native, landed with two armed boats' crews. The beach was thronged with people, and the native pointed out those to whom presents should be given, mostly old men, among them was the chief Teabooma, who soon calling for silence, addressed the people, apparently in favour of the strangers. All the chiefs in succession made speeches, the old men giving a grunt and a nod of approbation at the end of each sentence. The captain kept his eyes on the people all the time, and was completely convinced of their good intentions. Having made signs that water was wanted, his native friend conducted them along the coast lined with mangroves, to a creek, on going up which, above the mangroves, a straggling village appeared; the ground around being laid out in well cultivated plantations of sugar-canes, plantains, yams, and other roots, watered by rills conducted from the main stream, whose source was in the hills. Here was an abundance of fresh water. Among other things some roots were seen baking in an earthern jar, holding from six to eight gallons, apparently manufactured by the natives. On their way Mr. Forster shot a duck, which the native begged to have that he might explain to his countrymen how it was killed. The party returned on board at sunset, convinced that they were not likely to obtain provisions at the place, as it did not appear to produce more than the inhabitants themselves required, although it was clear that they were ready to give what they could, for a more obliging, civil, pleasant people had not been met with during the voyage. Hundreds came on board the ship, but not a theft was committed. One of them who had attached himself to Captain Cook brought some roots; a few of the others had weapons, such as clubs and darts, which they willingly exchanged for nails and pieces of cloth. A present had been made up for Teabooma, who, however, slipped out of the ship and lost it. A good watering place was found not far off up a creek; but as only a small boat could enter it, the casks were rolled over the beach, and put on board the launch. Plenty of fuel could also be procured.

An excursion on shore gave the explorers a better idea of the island than they could otherwise have possessed. They were accompanied by several natives, the numbers increasing as they advanced, till they had a large *cortège*. Reaching the summit of a rocky hill, the sea was observed in two places on the opposite side between the heights, thus enabling them to calculate the width of the island. Below them was a large valley, through which ran a river, on whose banks were several villages and plantations, while the flat land which lay along the shore appeared to great advantage; the winding streams running through it, the plantations, the little straggling villages, the variety in the woods, the shoals on the coast, with the blue sea, and the white breakers, made up a very beautiful and picturesque scene. The country in general bore a strong resemblance to parts of New Holland, under the same latitude, several of its natural productions appeared to be the same, while the forests, as in that country, were without underwood. The general aspect of the island was, however, that of a dreary waste; the sides of the mountains and other places being of hard rock, or of a thin soil baked by the sun. Even these unpromising spots were, however, covered with a coarse grass, which though of no use, as there were no cattle to feed on it, would afford pasture to numberless sheep if they were to be introduced into the island. There was a good supply of fish on the coast; but one day a somewhat ugly looking one being dressed for supper, the captain and the two Mr. Forsters though they did but taste the liver and roe, were seized with a numbness and weakness over their limbs. An emetic and a sudorific con-

NATIVE HUT, EXTERIOR.

siderably relieved them by the morning, but a pig which ate the fish died. A native who had sold the fish did not warn the buyer, though its poisonous character seems to have been known to the people, for on seeing the skin hanging up the next morning, they expressed their utmost abhorrence of it, and intimated that it was not fit to eat.

The captain was anxious to benefit the people as far as his short stay would allow, he therefore presented a dog and a bitch to Teabooma, who seemed delighted with the gift—indeed he could scarcely suppose that the animals were for him. A

NATIVE HUT, INTERIOR.

boar and a sow were also intended for him, but as he was not then to be found they were given to another chief, or head man, and his family, who promised to take care of them. These people had made some advance out of the purely savage state. Their dwellings were circular, very thickly thatched, something like a bee-hive, and very close and warm. Many had two fire-places, and some had two storeys, spread with mats and grass. As the entrance was very small, and there was no other outlet for the smoke the heat was intolerable. It was strange that natives of so hot a climate should delight in all the extra heat they could get. Outside the huts were little pyramids, five together. On the point of the pyramids the clay pots, in which they cooked their food, were placed, not upright, but on the sides, the fire being lighted beneath. The canoes of the islanders were large, but rude and clumsy in build; and they constructed double canoes formed of the trunks of two trees fastened together, much in the fashion of the other double canoes of the Pacific. They had sometimes one and sometimes two lateen sails composed of pieces of matting, the ropes being made of the coarse filaments of the plantain tree. When they could not sail they were propelled by sculls, the handles of which rose, nearly upright, four feet above the deck.

On standing down the coast, some objects were seen, which the scientific gentlemen insisted were basaltic pillars, like those of the Giant's Causeway in Ireland, contrary to the opinion of the captain, who held that they were trees of a peculiar growth. An island was discovered to the south of the large island, and the name of the Isle of Pines was given to it, on account of the number of tall trees growing thereon, and which the philosophers still maintained were basaltic pillars. It was not without some difficulty that, at length, the ship got near enough to the Isle of Pines to enable the captain, with a party of officers, to land on one of the islets connected with it. The objects observed were found to be a species of spruce pine, admirably fitted for masts and spars. After dinner, therefore, two boats went on shore with the carpenter and his crew, and as many spars as were required were cut down. It was of this tree that the natives made their canoes. The island on which the party landed was called Botany Island.

The *Resolution* got under weigh on the 1st of October. Soon afterwards a gale sprang up, which, in spite of all the exertions which could be made, rendered the further survey of the group impossible. She therefore bore away for New Zealand.

New Caledonia, thus discovered, Captain Cook considered to be, with the exception of New Zealand, the largest island in the South Pacific Ocean, being about eighty-seven leagues long, extending from the north-west to south-east, that is from latitude 19° 37' to 22° 30' s, and from longitude 163° 37' to 167° 14' E, although its width is nowhere very considerable.

The ship stood on about west-south-west till the 10th of October, when land was discovered—an island of good height, five leagues in circuit, to which, as a compliment to the family of Howard, the name of Norfolk Island was given. The ship stood in, when after dinner, two boats landed without difficulty behind some large rocks. The island

CABBAGE PALM.

was found to be uninhabited, and probably no human being had ever before set foot on its shore. Many trees and plants common in New Zealand were observed, especially the flax plant, which here appeared to be more luxuriant than in any part of that country. A spruce pine also grew in abundance, and to a great size, and there were also found a number of cabbage palms. They had large pinnated leaves, and the cabbage is properly speaking the bud of the tree. Each tree produces but one crown, which grows out of the stem, and by cutting this out the tree is destroyed. As many as could be collected were carried on board, and proved very welcome. The voyage to New Zealand was then continued.

On the 17th of October, Mount Egmont was seen, and the next day the ship anchored at the entrance of Ship Cove, a strong wind preventing her getting in. The day after she warped up, and being moored, the usual preparations were made for carrying on operations on shore. The forge was set up, and coopers' and sail-makers' tents were erected. For several days no natives appeared. The gardens were visited, and several of the plants were in a flourishing condition. When the natives did appear their conduct was very strange. At first they kept at a distance, with their weapons in their hands; but when they recognised Captain Cook and his officers, they danced and skipped about like mad men, though even then they would not let any of their women come near.

Several of them talked about killing, but their language was so imperfectly understood that no meaning could at first be gathered from what they said. The following story was made out, however, before long: the natives said that a ship like the *Resolution* had been lost in the Strait, and that some of the people got on shore, when the natives stole their clothes, for which several were shot; that afterwards, when the sailors could fire no longer, the natives rushed in and killed them with their clubs and spears, and ate them. The narrators declared that they themselves had no hand in the matter, which occurred at some distance along the coast.

Friendly relations were at once established with the natives the English had first met, who brought a good supply of fish, which they willingly exchanged for Otaheite cloth. Cook's training in the merchant service had given him some useful notions with regard to mercantile principles, and in many other cases as well as in this, he purchased articles with the view of taking them to another market, where their value would be increased. Still, though Cook was trying to do the natives all the good in his power, it was evident that they were shy of the English. Their more intimate friends at last acknowledged that the *Adventure* had been there, and though the captain's mind was relieved with regard to her, he still feared that some disaster had occurred to another vessel along the coast. He probably was as usual on his guard, and careful in preventing any causes of dispute between his people and the natives, or he himself might have had to experience the effects of New Zealand treachery.

On the 10th of November, the *Resolution* left Queen Charlotte's Sound for the last time, and steered south-by-east, with a fine wind, Cook's intention being to get into latitude 54° or 55°, and to cross the ocean nearly in those parallels, thus to pass over those parts which were left unexplored the previous summer.

On the evening of the 17th of December, the west coast of Terra del Fuego near the entrance of the Straits of Magalhaens, was made; and now Captain Cook says that he had done with the South Pacific, but he had a sound ship and a healthy crew and he resolved to accomplish some more work before returning home. Among other things he made a survey of the coasts he was now on. Nothing could be more desolate than those shores. They seemed entirely composed of rocky mountains, without the least

NATIVES OF TERRA DEL FUEGO.

appearance of vegetation, the mountains terminating in horrible precipices, while their craggy summits shot up to a vast height. The mountains seen inland were covered with snow, but those nearer the sea coasts were free from it. The former were supposed to belong to the mainland of Terra del Fuego, while the latter were probably islands.

The ship at length was brought to an anchor, on the 20th of December, in one of the numerous harbours in which the otherwise inhospitable looking coast abounds. This was called Christmas Sound, as the ship remained at anchor during Christmas day. An abundance of wild fowl were shot here, so that the Christmas fare consisted of roast and boiled geese, goose pie, goose stew, and goose in every form which could be thought of, accompanied in the cabin by some Madeira, the only article of their provisions which had improved by keeping.

Some natives made their appearance here in nine canoes. They were a little, ugly, half-starved, beardless race. They were almost naked, their clothing being merely two or three seal-skins, sewed together to form a cloak reaching to the knee. Most of them had only one seal skin, and the women had a sort of apron, but in other respects were clothed like the men. Some young children were seen entirely naked, so that they must be inured to cold and hardships from their infancy. They had with them bows and arrows, and darts, or rather harpoons, made of bone fitted to a staff. These were probably intended to kill fish and seals, or perhaps whales, as the Esquimaux do. That they were accustomed to the use of train oil the noses of the officers had powerful evidence; indeed it was far from pleasant to approach them. Their canoes were made of bark, and in each was a fire, round which the women and children huddled. There was also a large seal skin, perhaps to form a covering to a hut on shore. As these people seemed well acquainted with Europeans, it was considered probable that they moved during the winter more to the northward. They called themselves Pecheras, at least that word was continually in their mouths. "Of all the people I have ever seen, these Pecheras are the most wretched," says Cook; "they are doomed to live in one of the most inhospitable climates in the world, without having sagacity enough to provide themselves with such conveniences as might render life in some measure more comfortable." Yet, unattractive as were these people, they had souls as precious in the sight of a loving Saviour as those of the more intelligent and attractive inhabitants of Otaheite. It was in the attempt to carry the glad tidings of salvation to people such as these that the noble-minded Captain Allan Gardiner lost his life; and it is for the sake of people sunk as low as were these in the scale of humanity, that missionaries are labouring in many other parts of the earth.

A good supply of wood and water having been obtained at Christmas Sound, the *Resolution* got under weigh again on the 28th, and steered towards Cape Horn, which she rounded the next morning. She now steered E. by N. ½ E. for the Straits of Le Maire, with a view of looking into Success Bay, to ascertain if the *Adventure* had been there. A boat, commanded by Lieutenant Pickersgill, was sent on shore, but no traces of her were found. A notice, however, was left nailed to a tree, in case Captain Furneaux should afterwards touch there. Some natives appeared, who behaved very courteously to Lieutenant Pickersgill, and made signs to him to bring in the ship. The bay was full of whales and seals, indeed great numbers had been seen in the straits. At last the *Resolution* came to an anchor near an island, on which seals had been observed. After dinner three boats were hoisted out and landed with a large party of men, some to kill seals, or sea-lions, and others to kill or catch birds, fish, or whatever came in their way. The sea-lions, with which the island was covered, were so unaccustomed to the sight of man that they did not attempt to escape, and were knocked on the head with sticks and clubs. The only danger was by getting between them and the water, when as they came floundering on, they were likely to knock down and rush over any one thus placed. A large supply of sea-lions, bears, geese, and ducks, was soon obtained. The old lions were killed solely for the sake of their blubber, from which oil was extracted, for their flesh was abominable, but that of the cubs was considered very good, and even that of the lionesses was not amiss.

Once more, on the 3rd of January, 1775, the *Resolution* was at sea, steering an easterly course in search of land said to exist in about the latitude 53° or 54°. At nine o'clock on the morning of the 13th land was seen by a man named Willis. At first it was taken for an iceberg, but on their drawing nearer the appearance changed, and soundings being found, with a muddy bottom, at 175 fathoms, there was no doubt that it was really land, and the name of the discoverer was given to it. Passing between Willis Island and another islet, called Bird Island, land was seen extending for a considerable distance. The ship ranged along it, about a league from the shore, for part of two days, till an inlet appeared towards which the ship steered. Instead, however, of the ship going in, a boat was hoisted out, and the captain with Mr. Forster and others, embarked in her to survey the bay. They landed in three different places, displayed the British flag, and took possession of the country in His Majesty's name, under a discharge of small arms.

The appearance of the territory thus added to the dominion of Great Britain, was not attractive. The head of the bay as well as two portions on either side, consisted of perpendicular ice cliffs of considerable height. Pieces were continually breaking off and floating out to sea, and even while they were in the bay huge masses fell which made a noise like the discharge of cannon. The inner parts of the country were not less savage and horrible. Wild rocks raised their lofty summits till they were lost in the clouds, and even the valleys were covered with everlasting snow. Not a tree was to be seen, nor even a shrub big enough to make a toothpick. The only vegetation met with was a coarse, strong-bladed grass growing in tufts, wild burnet, and a plant like moss, which sprang from the rocks.

Seals or sea-bears were pretty numerous, and so were penguins; some very large, weighing from twenty-nine to thirty-eight pounds, were brought on board. At first it was hoped that the land now discovered was part of a great continent, but by going partly round it, it was discovered to be an island of about seventy leagues in circuit, and the name of the Isle of Georgia was given to it. It seemed to answer very little purpose, for though the island lies between the latitudes of 54° and 55°, the whole coast was a mass of ice and snow even in the middle of summer. "The disappointment I felt did not, I must confess, affect me much," says Cook, "for to judge of the bulk by the sample it would not be worth the discovery." Various other islets and rocks were seen, when, believing that no other discovery of importance would be made thereabouts, on the 25th of January the *Resolution* continued her course, steering east-south-east.

On the 31st, several islands, and a considerable extent of land were discovered, to which the name of Sandwich Land, or Southern Thule was given, as it was the most southern land then known. It showed a surface of great height, everywhere covered with snow. While the *Resolution* was close in with this coast, the wind fell, and left her to the mercy of a great westerly swell, which set right upon the shore. A line of two hundred fathoms found no bottom. The weather became hazy, the coast could not be seen. A most fearful wreck now seemed inevitable, when the fog cleared away, and a point (Cape Bristol) appeared bearing east-south-east, beyond which no land could be seen. This discovery relieved the explorers from the dread of being carried by the swell on to one of the most horrible coasts in the world. After undergoing this, and similar fearful risks, it was scarcely necessary for Cook to make any apology for leaving this inhospitable region, and proceeding in search of the long-sought-for Cape Circumcision. He sailed over and round the spot where it was said to lie, and became thoroughly convinced that no cape, indeed no land, lies thereabouts. He was soon sure that if there was land it would only be a small island, from the long southerly swell which was found in that latitude.

What we are most struck with is the hardihood and fine seamanship displayed by Captain Cook and his officers in this run across the Antarctic Ocean. It was the summer season, and the nights were short; but they had to encounter storms and bitter cold, ice and snow and hail, with the risk, at any moment, of running on an iceberg, or some hidden rock; but still greater was the risk when such inhospitable shores as those of Terra del Fuego or Staten Island, or the Isle of Georgia or Southern Thule, were to be explored.

A course was now steered for the Cape of Good Hope, greatly to the delight of all on board. On the 16th of March, two sail were seen in the north-west, standing westward, one of them under Dutch colours, a sign that they were once more approaching civilized regions. In the evening land was seen. In pursuance of his instructions, the captain now demanded of the officers and petty officers the log books and journals which they had kept, and which were sealed up for the inspection of the Admiralty. The officers and men were also especially charged not to say where they had been, until they had received the permission of the Lords of the Admiralty.

Several other ships were now met with, one of which proved to be the *True Briton*, Captain Broadly, from China, bound direct home. With that liberality for which commanders of East India Company's ships were famed, Captain Broadly sent on board the *Resolution* a present of a supply of fresh provisions, tea, and other articles, which were most acceptable. A heavy gale kept the *Resolution* from entering the harbour. At length, however, on Wednesday, the 22nd of March according to the ship's reckoning, but with the people on shore Tuesday the 21st, she anchored in Table Bay. Finding an East India Company's ship homeward bound, Captain Cook sent by her a copy of his journal, charts, and other drawings, to reduce the risk of the result of his enterprise being lost. He also found here a letter from Captain Furneaux, from which the mysterious conduct of the natives of Queen Charlotte's Sound was completely explained. It was as follows:— On the 17th of December, 1773, the large cutter with ten men, under charge of Mr. Rowe, a midshipman, had been sent on shore to gather greens for the ship's company, with orders to return that evening. On their non-appearance, another boat was sent under the command of Lieutenant Barney, when the mutilated remains of the cutter's crew were discovered, some parts scattered about on the beach, and others carefully packed, with fern leaves, in baskets, evidently intended for the oven. It was clear that some quarrel had arisen, and that after the unfortunate men had discharged their muskets they had been clubbed by the natives. It was afterwards discovered, by the acknowledgment of the natives, that they themselves had been the aggressors, having stolen some of the seamen's clothes, and that then they pretended to make up the quarrel; but that finding the party seated at dinner, and utterly unsuspicious of evil, they had rushed down on them and killed them all. After this misfortune the *Adventure* sailed for the Cape of Good Hope and thence returned to England.

Captain Cook speaks of the great courtesy and kindness he received from the Dutch authorities, as well as from the residents;

CAPE TOWN, TABLE BAY, AND MOUNTAIN.

and of the abundance of good provisions which he obtained. On the 27th of April, the repairs of the ship being completed, the *Resolution* sailed in company with the *Dutton*, East Indiaman, for St. Helena, and was saluted with thirteen guns. She was also saluted by a Spanish and Danish Indiaman as she passed them—she of course returning the salutes.

At daylight, on the 15th of May, the island of St. Helena was sighted. It, at that time, belonged to the East India Company, and was laid out chiefly in pasture, in order that their ships might here obtain supplies of fresh meat.

The *Resolution* anchored off Ascension on the 28th of May, and found some vessels from America come to load with turtle. A good supply was taken on board, and on the 31st she again sailed. On the 9th of June the island of Fernando de Moronha was sighted, and was found to be in possession of the Portuguese. Without anchoring, the *Resolution* continued her course for the Azores, at one of which, Fayal, she anchored on the 13th of July. Among several vessels there, was one belonging to the place which had taken in a cargo of provisions at the Amazon, for the Cape de Verde Islands; but had been unable to find them, a specimen of Portuguese navigation, not at all singular even in later days. The *Resolution* sailed on the 19th, passing the island of Terceira, and on the 29th made the land near Plymouth, and the next morning anchored at Spithead. The same day Captain Cook landed at Portsmouth, with Messrs Wales, Forster and Hodges, and set off for London. He had been absent from England three years and eighteen days, and during that time had lost but four men, and only one of them by sickness. This was owing, under Providence, to the very great care taken of the health of the people. All means were used to induce the crew to keep their persons, hammocks, bedding, and clothes, clean and dry. The ship once or twice a week, was aired with fires, and when this could not be done she was smoked with gunpowder, mixed with vinegar and water. There was frequently a fire in an iron pot at the bottom of the well. The ship's coppers were kept carefully clean, fresh water being taken on board whenever practicable. For remedies against scurvy, the sweet wort was proved to be most valuable. At the slightest appearance of the disease, two to three pints a day were given to each man. A pound of sour-krout was supplied to each man twice a week at sea. Preparations of potatoes, lemons, and oranges, were served out with good effect. Sugar was found useful, as was wheaten flour, while oatmeal and oil were considered to promote the scurvy—such oil, at least, as was served to the navy. Olive oil would probably have had a different effect. Captain Cook thus concludes his journal of the voyage: "But whatever may be the public judgment about other matters, it is with real satisfaction, and without claiming any merit but that of attention to my duty, that I can conclude this account with an observation which facts enable me to make, that our having discovered the possibility of preserving health amongst a numerous ship's company for such a length of time, in such varieties of climate and amidst such continued hardships and fatigues, will make this voyage remarkable in the opinion of every benevolent person, when the disputes about a southern continent shall have ceased to engage the attention, and to divide the judgment of philosophers."

In concluding this account of Captain Cook's second voyage round the world, it is well, while admitting the value of the discoveries made, and admiring the perseverance and general prudence and kindness of the discoverer, to express deep regret that the scrupulous and unremitting care exercised over the physical health of the crew, was not, with equal assiduity and anxiety manifested in respect of their spiritual health. Those were not the days in which the souls of sailors were much cared for; but it may be supposed that the character of this expedition, together with the

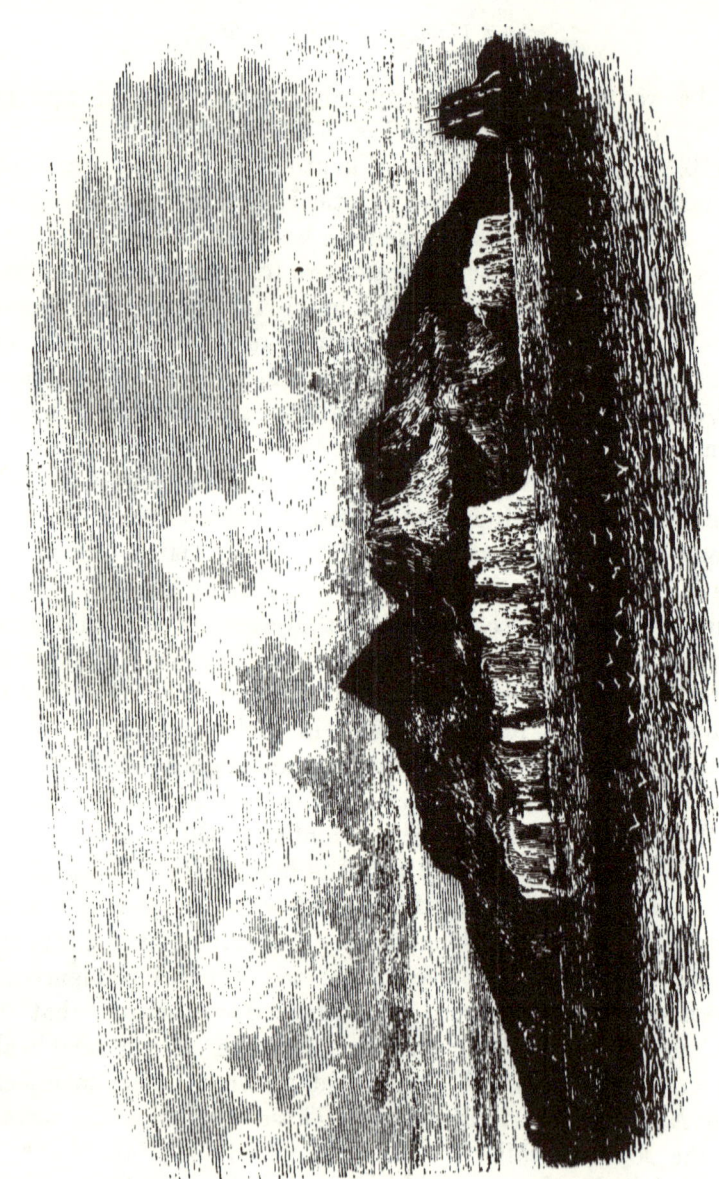

ISLAND OF ASCENSION.

unusual number of educated gentlemen on board, furnished facilities for Christian exertion, which certainly were not improved. So far, indeed, as the existing records of this voyage inform us, we are led to the conclusion that instead of setting an example of morality and virtue to the ignorant heathen they visited, it would, in many instances, have been better for the heathen, had they never known these so-called Christians.

AUSTRALIAN BOWER BIRD.

CHAPTER IV.

THIRD VOYAGE OF DISCOVERY.

From July 1776, *to October* 1778.

It will be remembered that Captain Cook landed in England on the 30th of July, 1775. He at once received well-merited acknowledgments of the services he had rendered to his country. On the 9th of August he received post rank; and three days afterwards was nominated a captain in Greenwich Hospital, an appointment that would have enabled him to spend the remainder of his days in honourable retirement. In February of the following year, he was elected a Fellow of the Royal Society; and on the evening of his admission, the 7th of March, a paper was read, in which he gave a full account of the various means he had adopted for the preservation of the health of his crew.

The importance of this paper, and the way in which it was received, will be best understood by those who have read accounts of Lord Anson's and other voyages, where the scurvy made fearful havoc among the ship's companies. In consequence of this paper, it was resolved by Sir John Pringle, the president of the council of the Society, to bestow on Captain Cook the gold medal known as the Copley annual medal, for the best experimental paper of the year. Cook was already on his third voyage before the medal was bestowed, though he was aware of the honour intended him; and his wife had the pleasure of receiving it.

Sir John Pringle's words are worthy of repetition. Having

pointed out the means by which Captain Cook, with a company of a hundred and eighteen men, performed a voyage of three years and eighteen days, in all climates, with the loss of only one man from sickness, he proceeds, "I would now enquire of those most conversant in the study of the bills of mortality, whether, in the most healthful climate, and in the best conditions of life, they have ever found so small a number of deaths within that space of time. How great and agreeable then must our surprise be, after perusing the histories of long navigations in former days, when so many perished by marine diseases, to find the air of the sea acquitted of all malignity; and, in fine, that a voyage round the world may be undertaken with less danger, perhaps, to health than a common tour in Europe." He concludes, "For if Rome decreed the civic crown to him who saved the life of a single citizen, what wreaths are due to that man who, having himself saved many, perpetuates in your Transactions the means by which Britain may now, on the most distant voyages, preserve numbers of her intrepid sons, her mariners, who braving every danger, have so liberally contributed to the fame, to the opulence, and to the maritime empire of their country."

This address ought to be read by all British ship-owners and ship-masters. They possess ample means of preventing the approach of the scurvy, and yet numerous vessels even at the present day return home with a portion of their crews suffering from that fearful scourge. The masters must exert themselves, must take some trouble in the matter, no doubt; but if they will not do so, if they will not take an interest in the welfare of their men, they are unfit to command ships; they are a disgrace to their honourable profession.

Among those who reached England in the *Adventure* with Captain Furneaux, was Omai, the native of Ulietea. Captain

Cook did not approve at the time of the selection Captain Furneaux had made, as Omai did not belong to the chiefs, nor to the priestly class, while in appearance and intelligence he was inferior to many of his countrymen. Oedidee, who had been received on board the *Resolution,* had, it will be remembered, been left behind at Ulietea, Cook fearing that he might have no other opportunity of restoring the youth to his native island. Both seem to have been inferior to Tupia, who died at Batavia. However, Omai, as the first native of the South Sea Islands who had been seen in England, was made a great deal of by people of all ranks. He was introduced to George the Third, who settled on him a pension while he remained in England. He had his portrait painted by Sir Joshua Reynolds, and Cowper mentions him in one of his poems, while he was constantly in the society of Dr. Johnson, Madame D'Arblay, Sir Joseph Banks, Dr. Burney, Lord Sandwich, Lord Mulgrave, Granville Sharpe, and many other illustrious persons. The power of imitation is strong among his people, and he therefore very quickly copied the manners of the people with whom he associated, and became, in appearance, a polished gentleman.

He very slowly acquired a knowledge of English, indeed, he always required the aid of signs and gestures to express himself.

In vain was much trouble expended in trying to teach him to write, by Mr. Sharp, who also endeavoured with no better success to instruct him in the principles of Christianity. Such was Omai, a dark-minded savage, amidst civilization and enlightenment. His great desire seems to have been to obtain the means of successfully waging war with the men of Bolabola, of expelling them from Ulietea, and of regaining possession of his hereditary property. It is with regret that we read this account of the miserable Omai, when we reflect how eagerly and how thoroughly many of his fellow-islanders in after years imbibed the principles of the Christian faith, and how stedfastly they have held to them, in all simplicity and purity. Had Omai—like the Ethiopian eunuch of other days—but embraced with all his heart the truths of the gospel, and returned to his native land, carrying with him the glad tidings of salvation to his benighted countrymen, the light of the knowledge of the glory of God might have been spread throughout the islands of the Pacific even then.

For two centuries a strong desire had existed in England, among people interested in navigation, to discover a passage by the north-west, round the coast of North America into the Pacific, so that China and Japan and the East Indies might be reached by a route shorter than that by the Cape of Good Hope. All the early expeditions had been undertaken by private enterprise, to encourage which, an Act of Parliament was passed in 1745, securing a reward of 20,000*l.* to any ship belonging to any of His Majesty's subjects, which should discover the passage. Often was the attempt made by numerous bold adventurers, from Frobisher in 1576, onwards to the time of which we are writing. In the middle of the century, public interest was again awakened by the exertions of Mr. Dobbs, who was strongly impressed with the belief that a north-west passage could be found. Captain Middleton was sent out by Government in 1741, and Captains Smith and Moore in 1746. In 1773, at the instigation of the Hon. Daines Barrington, an influential member of the Royal Society, Lord Sandwich sent out Captain Phipps (afterwards Lord Mulgrave), with the *Racehorse* and *Carcase*. Captain Lutwidge commanded the latter vessel, and had on board a young boy—Nelson, the future naval hero. Captain Phipps returned, unable to penetrate the wall of ice which barred his progress.

Still, that a passage existed and might be found, was the belief of many enlightened men, and the Admiralty came to the resolution of sending out another expedition, better prepared than former ones to encounter the difficulties to be met with. Lord Sandwich very naturally desired to have Captain Cook's opinion on the subject, and his lordship accordingly invited him to meet Sir Hugh Palliser, Mr. Stephens, and others at dinner, where it might freely be discussed.

The importance and grandeur of the undertaking, and, should it be successful, the great advantage it would be to navigation and science, thus completing the circuit of discoveries made by Cook, were particularly dwelt on. When it came to the point of fixing on a fit person to recommend to His Majesty to command the proposed expedition, Captain Cook started to his feet, and declared that he himself was ready to take the command.

This was probably what Lord Sandwich desired; Cook's offer was eagerly accepted, and he was appointed to the command of the expedition on the 10th of February, 1776. It was arranged that, on his return to England, he should be restored to his post at Greenwich. An Act was also at once passed, by which the officers and ship's company of any of His Majesty's ships discovering a north-west passage would be able to claim the reward of 20,000*l.* offered in 1745 only to persons not in the royal navy. The usual plan of search was to be reversed, and instead of commencing on the Atlantic side of America, and endeavouring to penetrate into the Pacific, the expedition was to proceed round Cape Horn, and then sailing north, attempt to work its way through Behring's Straits eastward into the Atlantic.

Two vessels were fixed on for the intended service, the *Resolution* and the *Discovery*. The command of the former was given to Captain Cook, with Mr. Gore as his first lieutenant, and of the other to Captain Clerke, while Lieutenant King went out again as second lieutenant of the *Resolution*. He had undertaken to make the necessary astronomical and nautical observations during the voyage in conjunction with his captain, and for this purpose various instruments were intrusted to him.

Mr. Bayley was again appointed as astronomer, to sail on board Captain Clerke's ship, while Mr. Anderson, the surgeon of the *Resolution*, took charge of the department of natural history. An artist, Mr. Webber, was selected to sail on board the *Resolution*, and to make sketches of any scenes of interest which might be met with.

Every care and attention was paid to the fitting out of the ships, and some months passed before they were ready for sea. The officers of the *Resolution* were John Gore, James King, and John Williamson, lieutenants; William Bligh, master; William Anderson, surgeon; Molesworth Philips, lieutenant Royal Marines: those of the *Discovery* were, James Burney, John Rickman, lieutenants; Thomas Edgar, master; John Law, surgeon. The latter vessel, which had been purchased into the service, was of three hundred tons burden.

An ample supply of all the articles which past experience had shown were likely to preserve the health of the crews was put on board these vessels, as well as an abundance of warm clothing. By desire of the king, several useful animals, which were to be left at the Society or other islands for the benefit of the natives, were embarked, with fodder for their support. There were two cows and their calves, a bull, and several sheep. Others were to be purchased at the Cape. The captain was also furnished with a large variety of European garden seeds, for distribution among the inhabitants of newly-discovered islands. He received, besides, by order of the Board of Admiralty, many articles calculated to improve the condition of the natives of the islands of the Pacific, while, for the purposes of traffic, a large assortment of iron tools, trinkets, and other articles, was sent on board. Nothing indeed was omitted which it was thought likely would benefit the people to be visited, or would promote the success of the voyage. As it was not probable that another opportunity would occur of restoring Omai to his native island, it was settled that he should return in the *Resolution*. It was supposed that this semi-civilized and still heathen savage had become so impressed with the grandeur and power of England, and so grateful for the patronage he had enjoyed, and the presents he had received, that he would (as a writer of the day expresses it) "be rendered an instrument of conveying to the inhabitants of the Pacific Ocean the most exalted ideas of the greatness and generosity of the British nation." How completely these hopes were disappointed the following narrative will show; nor should we be surprised at this, when we recollect how entirely superficial were all poor Omai's accomplishments. He appears to have learned to play very well at chess; but that seems to have been the only science in which he attained anything like proficiency. The truth is, he had been made a lion of, and had been courted and petted by the rank and fashion of the day. It would not have been surprising if his head had been turned. Possibly, a man of superior mind or quicker sensibilities might have been powerfully affected by the same amount of flattery. On being told that he was to go, he could scarcely refrain from tears when he spoke of parting from his English friends, but his eyes immediately sparkled with pleasure when his native islands were mentioned.

Captain Cook received the secret instructions for his guidance on the 6th July, 1776. His chief object was to find a passage from the Pacific into the Atlantic. He was to leave the Cape of Good Hope early in November, and first to search for certain islands said to have been seen by the French, south of the Mauritius. He was not to spend much time in looking for them, nor in examining them if found, but to proceed to Otaheite, touching at New Zealand, should he consider it necessary to refresh his crews. Thence he was to proceed direct to the coast of New Albion, avoiding, if possible, any Spanish settlements; or should it be necessary to touch at any, to take great care not to excite the jealousy or ill-will of the Spaniards. Arrived in the frozen ocean, he was to examine all channels and inlets likely to lead eastward, and to take possession of any territory on which he might land not before discovered, with the consent of the natives, in the name of the king of Great Britain. He was to winter at the Russian settlement of St. Peter and St. Paul in Kamschatka, and to return in the spring to the north. Each ship was supplied with a small vessel in frame, which was to be set up if necessary to prosecute the search for a passage along the northern coast of America.

Although numerous expeditions have since been sent out, they have mostly commenced their operations on the Atlantic side of America; and it is remarkable that the only successful one, that of Captain M'Clure in the *Investigator*, and Captain Collinson in the *Enterprise*, in the years 1850-53, entered the frozen sea on the Pacific side.* Captain M'Clure had, however, to abandon his ship, and to make the voyage over the ice, till he could join one of the ships sent up Baffin's Bay to his relief, while Captain Collinson, getting his ship free from the ice, returned westward by the way he had come. The question of a north-west passage was thus solved in the affirmative; but, unless in some very exceptional case, it is shown to be impracticable and useless for all commercial purposes. It is easy to conceive what would have been the fate of Cook's ships had they proceeded eastward, and there become beset by the ice.

* It should be mentioned that Lieutenant Pickersgill was sent out in 1776 with directions to explore the coast of Baffin's Bay, and that in the next year Lieutenant Young was commissioned not only to examine the western parts of that bay, but to endeavour to find a passage on that side from the Atlantic to the Pacific

Captain Cook, with Omai in his company, joined his ship on the 24th of June, 1776, at Sheerness, and immediately sailed for Plymouth. He did not leave that port till the 11th of July, and, owing to contrary winds, did not take his departure from the Scilly Isles till the 16th.

The *Discovery* remained at Plymouth, Captain Clerke not having yet arrived on board. He was directed to proceed, as soon as he was ready for sea, to the Cape of Good Hope, there to join the *Resolution*. Captain Cook touched at Teneriffe, where he found an abundance of supplies, and sailed again on the 4th of August. On the evening of the 10th, Bonavista, one of the Cape de Verd Islands, was seen bearing south, little more than a league off, though at the time it was supposed that the ship was at a much greater distance from the land. Just then breakers were discovered directly under her lee, and for a few minutes she was in great danger. She happily just weathered them, and stood for Porto Praya, where it was expected the *Discovery* might be. As she was not there, the *Resolution* did not go in, but continued her course to the Cape. On the 1st of September the line was crossed, and the usual ceremonies were observed; on the 18th of October the ship anchored in Table Bay. Here arrangements were at once made to obtain a supply of fresh bread and other provisions which, as soon as ready, were conveyed on board, while the tents were set up on shore, and astronomical observations diligently carried on. Meantime the ship was caulked, which she much required. On the evening of the 31st a fearful gale tore the tents to pieces, and some of the instruments narrowly escaped serious injury. No communication with the *Resolution* was possible for those on shore.

Ocean. Both officers returned without effecting anything. The first was severely censured for his conduct; but we who know the difficulties he would have had to encounter may readily excuse him.

She was the only ship in the harbour which rode out the gale without dragging her anchors.

On the 10th November the *Discovery* entered the bay. She had sailed on the 1st of August, and would have come in a week sooner, but had been blown off the coast by the late gale. She also required caulking, which detained the expedition some time.

On the 30th of November the two ships sailed together. The *Resolution* had now on board, in addition to her former stock of animals, two bulls and two heifers, two horses and two mares, two rams, several ewes and goats, and some rabbits and poultry—all of them intended for New Zealand, Otaheite, and the neighbouring islands, or other places where there might be a prospect of their proving useful. The course steered was about south-east. Before long a heavy squall carried away the *Resolution's* mizen-topmast; and a mountainous sea made the ship roll so much that it was with difficulty the animals on board could be preserved. Owing to this and to the cold several goats and sheep died.

On the 12th of December two islands were seen about five leagues apart. These, with four others which lie in the same latitude, about nine degrees of longitude more to the east, were discovered by two French navigators in 1772. Cook now bestowed the name of Prince Edward's Island on the two he had just discovered, and those of the French officers on the four others. They were mostly covered with snow, and where the ground seemed free from it, lichens or a coarse grass was the only herbage.

On leaving Prince Edward's Island a course was shaped to fall in with Kerguelen's Land. On the evening of the 24th, an island of considerable height, and the next day other islands, were seen. As the ships ranged along the coast, a terrific sea rolled in on the shore, placing them in great danger, and both had considerable difficulty in weathering the points and reefs they met with. Though it was midsummer, the weather was as cold as it is generally during the winter in the British Channel. At last a harbour was discovered, into which the ships beat and found good anchorage, an abundance of water, innumerable penguins and other birds, as also seals, which were so unacquainted with human beings that they allowed themselves to be knocked on the head without attempting to escape. The casks were immediately landed to be filled up with water, while a supply of seals was secured for the sake of their oil. Not a tree nor shrub was to be found in this inhospitable region. A bottle was brought to Captain Cook containing a document left by Kerguelen, who had discovered this land at the end of 1773, and had taken possession of it in the name of the king of France. The harbour in which the ships lay was called Christmas Harbour, in commemoration of the day on which they entered it. The ships left this harbour on the morning of the 28th, and continued to range along the coast, in order to discover its position and extent. They brought up in another harbour just in time to escape a heavy gale, and then proceeded to the south, towards Cape George, to determine the shape of the land. On finally leaving it on the 30th December the ships steered east-by-north for New Zealand. Captain Cook came to the conclusion that the land he had just left was a large island, seventy or eighty miles from north to south, and a much greater distance from east to west. Captain Furneaux had in 1773 passed across the meridian of this land, only seventeen leagues to the south of Cape George, thus settling the point of its being an island.

It seems to have been a mistake to send the ships into these inclement regions with cattle on board, as many died; among them two young bulls and a heifer, two rams, and several more of the goats.

The weather continued so thick that for many days together the ships did not see each other, though, by constantly firing guns, they managed to keep in company. At length Captain Cook determined to put into Adventure Bay, in Van Diemen's Land, where Captain Furneaux had touched on the former voyage. The land was made on the 24th of January, and on the 26th the ships brought up in the bay. They expected to obtain a supply of wood for fuel, and of grass for the cattle, of which they stood greatly in need. A supply of fish was caught, and plenty of grass brought on board. While the party on shore were cutting wood some natives appeared. They came forward with perfect confidence, only one having a lance in his hand. They were entirely without clothes, their skin and hair black, their stature about the ordinary height, their figures rather slender. Their features were not disagreeable, as they had neither very thick lips nor flat noses, while their eyes and teeth were good. Most of them had their heads and beards smeared with a red ointment, while some had their faces painted with the same composition. They seemed indifferent to all the presents offered them; even bread and fish they threw away, till some birds were given them, at which they expressed their satisfaction.

A boar and sow had been landed for the purpose of being left in the woods, but no sooner did the natives see them than they seized them by the ears, evidently with the intention of carrying them off and killing them. Captain Cook, wishing to know the use of the stick one of them carried, the native set up a mark and threw his stick at it. He missed it, however, so often that Omai, to show the superiority of the white men's arms, fired his musket. This very naturally made the whole party run off, and drop some axes and other things which had been given to them. They ran towards where the *Adventure's* people were cutting wood, when the officer, not knowing their intention, fired a musket over their heads, which sent them off altogether. The boar and sow were carried to a thick wood at the head of the bay, where it was hoped that they would conceal themselves and escape the natives; but some cattle which it had been intended to leave there were returned on board, as it was clear that the natives would immediately kill them.

A calm kept the ships in harbour, and the next day, notwithstanding the fright which the natives had received, a party of twenty or more, men and boys, made their appearance. Among them was one terribly deformed, who seemed to be the acknowledged wit of the party, as he and his friends laughed heartily at the remarks he made, and seemed surprised that the English did not do the same. Their language was different from that of the tribes met with in the north. Some of these people had bands of fur passed several times round their necks, and others of kangaroo skin round their ancles. They seemed to be unacquainted with fishing, by the way they looked at the English fishhooks, and their rejection of the fish offered them, though near their fires quantities of mussel shells were found, showing that they lived partly on shell-fish. Their habitations were mere sheds of sticks covered with bark, and there were indications of their taking up their abodes in trees hollowed out by fire or decay. From the marks of fires it was evident that they cooked their food, but they did not appear to have the slightest notion of cultivating the land. The people here described have disappeared from the face of the earth. The last remnant, who had become exceedingly ferocious and mischievous, were collected and carried to an island in Bass's Straits, where they were allowed to roam at large, it having been found impossible to tame them. It is believed that they finally died out. Mr. Anderson records the beauty of the scenery and of the climate, though he remarks that not one single natural production could be found fit for the food of man.

The ships left Adventure Bay on the 30th of January, when, soon afterwards, the mercury in the barometer fell, and a furious gale began to blow from the south. At the same time the heat became almost insupportable, the mercury in the thermometer rising from 70° to near 90°. This high temperature, however, did not last long.

On the 12th of February the ships anchored in Queen Charlotte's Sound. That no time might be lost, the tents for the observatory with the usual guard, and the water casks, were landed; and operations were immediately commenced. Before long several canoes came alongside, but few of the people in them would venture on board, the greater part being evidently afraid that the English would punish them for their murder of the *Adventure's* people. Captain Cook recognised several of those with whom he was well acquainted during his former visits. They must also have seen Omai, and remembered that he was on board the *Adventure* at the time, and thus known that Captain Cook could no longer have been ignorant of what had occurred. He, however, did his best to make them understand that he was not come to punish them for that act, and that he wished to be friends with them as before. In consequence of this, the natives very soon laid aside restraint and distrust. After the fearful experience he had had of their treachery, however, the captain took extra precaution to prevent a surprise. While the people were engaged in their various occupations on shore, a guard was posted for their protection, while all the men worked with their arms by their sides, Mr. King and two or three petty officers being constantly with them. No boat was sent to a distance unless well armed, and under charge of an officer who could be depended on. Captain Cook thinks that the precautions were probably unnecessary, though he felt it his duty to take them. The natives showed no fear, and came and built their huts close to the ship, and many employed themselves in fishing, exchanging the fish they caught for the usual articles of barter.

Besides the natives who settled near them, chiefs from other parts frequently visited the ship. Among them came a chief called Kahoora, who was pointed out as the leader of those who attacked the crew of the *Adventure's* boat, and was said actually to have killed Mr. Rowe, the officer in command. Greatly to the surprise of the natives, as also to that of Omai, who entreated that he might at once be killed, Captain Cook declined seizing him, saying that he had granted an amnesty, and that no one should be punished. Kahoora, trusting to the captain's promise, came frequently on board, though, by thus doing, he placed himself entirely in the hands of the English. Once only, when Omai accused him in the cabin of having killed Mr. Rowe, he hung down his head and folded his arms, expecting instant death; but was soon reassured by the captain, who told him that he wished to forget the circumstance, though should a similar one occur, the natives must expect the fearful vengeance of the English. He says that had he listened to the suggestions and requests of the chiefs and others to kill their enemies, he should soon have extirpated the whole race. In no country could life be much more insecure. Tribes and even families living in the same neighbourhood were constantly fighting with each other, and war was carried on with the utmost cruelty and ferocity. If a man was unable to revenge an injury inflicted on himself or any member of his family, it was the duty of his son to take up the quarrel, and often many years elapsed before an opportunity occurred of wreaking his long-delayed vengeance. When such an opportunity arrived, he and his companions stole on their unsuspecting enemies in the night, and if they found them unguarded they killed every one indiscriminately, not even sparing women or children. When the massacre was completed, they either made a horrid banquet of the slain on the spot, or carried off as many dead bodies as they could, and devoured them at home, with acts of brutality too shocking to be described. As they never gave quarter nor took

Ferocity of New Zealanders.

prisoners, the defeated party could only save their lives by flight. More powerful chiefs made war in the same barbarous way on a larger scale, and depopulated whole districts if the people offended them. On the introduction of firearms the bloody work went on with still greater rapidity. In the time of George IV. a chief who was taken to England and received at Buckingham Palace, and was looked upon as a highly civilized person, on his return exchanged at Sydney all the articles which had been given him for firearms and ammunition, and immediately commenced a war of extermination against all the surrounding tribes, and feasted without scruple on the bodies of his foes. It is not surprising that, under such circumstances, two-thirds of the inhabitants of New Zealand have been, within the last century, swept away by warfare.

NEW ZEALAND IDOL.

The process of extermination had, indeed, commenced long before Cook visited those shores, and it would probably ere now have completed its ravages had not the Christian church been roused to a sense of its responsibilities, and conveyed to New Zealand, as to other lands, the knowledge of Him who teaches us by His Word and Spirit to love our enemies, to bless those who curse us, and to do good to those who despitefully use us and persecute us.

The wandering propensities of the New Zealanders were shown by the desire expressed by several youths, of embarking on board the ships. One named Taweiharooa, eighteen years of age, the son of a dead chief, was selected to accompany Omai who had been desirous of having a companion. That Taweiharooa might be sent off in a way becoming his rank, a boy Kokoa of about ten years of age, to act as his servant, was presented by his own father with as much indifference as he would have parted with a dog. It was clearly explained to the youths that they would probably never return to their native country, but, as Cook observes, so great was the insecurity of life in New Zealand at that time, that he felt no compunction in the matter, as the lads could scarcely fail to improve their lot by the change.

The ships left Queen Charlotte's Sound on the 25th of February. No sooner had they lost sight of land than the New Zealand adventurers were seized with sea sickness, which, giving a turn to their thoughts, made them bitterly lament what they had done, while they expressed their feelings in a sort of song which they continued to sing till they got better. By degrees their lamentations ceased, and in a short time their native country and friends seemed to be forgotten, and they appeared as firmly attached to their new friends as if they had been born among them.

On the 29th of March, 1777, the *Discovery* made the signal of land in the north-east. It was soon found to be an island of no great extent, and the night was spent standing off and on, in the hope that the next day a landing place might be found. No landing nor anchorage, however, appeared practicable, on account of the heavy surf which broke everywhere, either against the island or the reef which surrounded it. Before long a number of people appeared on the shore, or wading to the reef, most of them nearly naked except the usual girdle, brandishing spears and clubs. Some of them had mantles of native cloth over their shoulders, and turbans or wrappers round their heads. After a time a canoe was launched, and came off with two natives to the ship. When presents were offered, they asked for some for their Eatooa before they would accept any for themselves. Omai spoke to them in the tongue of Otaheite, which they perfectly understood. The principal man said that his name was Monrooa, and that the island was called Mangaia. His colour was that of most southern Europeans; he was stout and well made, and his features were agreeable.

The other man was not so good looking. Both of them had strong straight black hair, tied at the crown of the head. They wore sandals to protect their feet from the coral rocks.

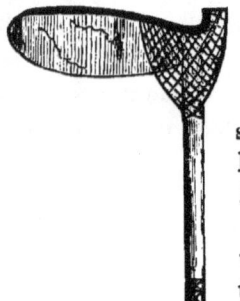

AXE LEFT BY COOK AT MANGAIA.

The men would not venture on board, but when the boats were lowered and stood towards the shore to find a landing place, Monrooa stepped into Captain Cook's of his own accord, and took his seat by his side. No landing could be found without the risk of swamping the boats; they therefore returned, and Monrooa came on board. He was evidently too anxious about his safety to ask questions. At last he stumbled over one of the goats, when he enquired eagerly of Omai what strange bird that was? The boat conveyed him just outside the surf, when he leaped overboard and swam through it; his countrymen being seen eagerly gathering round him to receive accounts of what he had seen. Cook says he left that fine island with regret, as it seemed capable of supplying all their wants.*

Mangaia was left on the 30th of March, and the next day at noon two islands were seen, a large and a small one. The following day the shore of the larger island was reached, and boats at once put off to try and find a landing place. At the same time,

* Amongst the presents left by Cook at Mangaia was an axe, roughly-fashioned on the ship's arrival out of a piece of iron. It is still treasured in the island as a relic of his visit.

several canoes came from the shore with one man in each. The natives stepped on board without showing fear, but seemed to value very little any of the gifts bestowed on them. After the first party had gone, a man arrived in a canoe, bringing a bunch of plantains as a present to Captain Cook, whose name he had learned from Omai. This present had been sent by the principal chief. The bearer went away well contented with an axe and a piece of red cloth. Not long after a double canoe approached the *Resolution* with twelve men in her, who chanted in chorus, and when their song was finished they came alongside and asked for the chief. On the captain's showing himself, a pig and some cocoa-nuts were handed up the side, and the natives coming on board presented some pieces of matting in addition. Though the natives expressed surprise at some of the things they saw, nothing seemed to fix their attention. They were afraid of the horses and cows, and inquired when they saw the goats, as the native of Mangaia had done, what sort of birds they were.

The following day Mr. Gore and Mr. Burney, with Mr. Anderson and Omai, went on shore in hope of obtaining food for the cattle. The boats approached the surf, when some canoes came off and took the party through it. The day passed on, and as they did not return, Captain Cook became somewhat uneasy; his only comfort being that the natives continued to come off to the ship as before, bringing cocoa-nuts, and taking anything given them in return. Late in the day the boats returned; it then appeared that the party had been conducted, amid a vast crowd, up an avenue of cocoa-palms till they reached a body of men drawn up in two rows, armed with clubs resting on their shoulders. In the middle row was a chief, sitting cross-legged on the ground, and having bunches of red feathers in his ears. They were then introduced to two other chiefs, one, though a young man, excessively corpulent, also distinguished by the red feathers, and they were then entertained by a dance performed by twenty girls all of whom wore red feathers. The dancers did not leave the spot where they stood, for though their feet moved up and down, the dance consisted of various motions of the body and hands. The visitors were next entertained by a sham fight between the men armed with clubs. They now found themselves separated from each other, and pressed on by the crowd, while they had their pockets picked of every article they possessed, the chiefs not interfering. Their position was sufficiently embarrassing, for whenever they tried to get back to the boats they were stopped. Omai meantime, who was by himself, surrounded by a crowd of natives and equally anxious with the rest, described in exaggerated terms the power of the English guns, which he affirmed could blow the whole island to pieces. He had some cartridges in his pocket, and to prove his assertion, he let several of them off together. The sudden flash and report seem to have produced a great effect on the minds of the natives, as the party were sent off with a large supply of cooked plantains as a gift, and a bag containing a pistol which Mr. Anderson particularly required, was restored.

Omai found on this island three of his own countrymen who had arrived there eleven years before in a canoe. They were the survivors of a party of twenty persons who had been driven before the wind from Otaheite, distant at least two hundred leagues. They declined a passage offered to them to return to their native island. The circumstance was interesting as giving an example of the way the islands of the Pacific have been peopled. The name of this island was Wateeoo. The language was equally well understood by Omai and the two New Zealanders.

Though the visit was an interesting one, the chief object in calling off the island (that of procuring provender for the cattle), was not attained, as nothing was sent off. From the small island which had been seen three days before, and to which the ships now steered, all that was required was obtained, consisting of grass and leaves of young cocoa trees and of the pandanus. Though the island, called Ota Kootaia, was uninhabited, still as it was occasionally visited by the natives of the neighbouring island, Mr. King left an axe and some nails in payment for what he took away.

Captain Cook next sailed for Hervey Island, which he had supposed when he discovered it in 1773 to be uninhabited. As he now approached, however, a number of canoes came off, but the people on board behaved in a very wild and disorderly manner. They were of a darker colour than the neighbouring islanders, and of a fiercer expression of countenance. As no anchorage was found for the ships, they stood away for Palmerston's Island, which was found to be thickly covered with cocoa-nut trees, pandanus, cabbage palm, and grass. The ships stood off and on for three days, while four or five boats' crews were busily employed in cutting food for the cattle, and in collecting two thousand cocoa-nuts for the crews of the two ships. On leaving Palmerston's Island a course was steered for Annamook, and on the night between the 24th and 25th April, Savage Island was passed.

On the evening of the 28th the ships anchored off Komango, and the next morning canoes came off with all sorts of provisions. Mr. King who went on shore was treated very civilly by the inhabitants, and by two chiefs, Taipa and Toobou. As it was important to find a good harbour, and no other after two days search having been discovered, Captain Cook came to anchor in the spot where he had been three years before. Here the chief Toobou received him, and offered a boat, and also a house to serve as a tent; at the same time he promptly selected a spot where the observatories might be set up, and other arrangements made. He conducted the captain and Omai to his house. Round it was a fine grass plot, which he explained was for the purpose of enabling people to clean their feet before entering the house. The floor was covered with mats, and no carpet in an English drawing-room could be kept cleaner. Taipa, the chief who had been among the first to introduce himself, that he might be close to his new friends, had a house brought on men's shoulders full a quarter of a mile, and placed near the shed they occupied. The greatest man, however, had not as yet appeared, and on the 6th of May a chief arrived, it was understood, from Tongataboo, who was introduced by Taipa as Feenou, king of all the Friendly Islands. That he was of great power there could be no doubt, as the natives ordered out to meet him bowed their heads as low as his feet, the soles of which they touched first with the palm and then with the back of each hand. He appeared to be about thirty years of age, tall but thin, and had more of the European features than any native of the South Seas yet met with. He showed his power by recovering a large axe which had been stolen out of the ship. The people of these islands were great thieves, even the chiefs stole. One was caught, when he was sentenced to receive a dozen lashes, and was not set free till he had paid a hog for his liberty. This put a stop to the practice among the chiefs. At Feenou's invitation, Captain Cook agreed to go to Hapaee. During the passage the great chief came on board and remained all day, but in the evening took his departure with Omai, while the ship remained under sail in a somewhat perilous position, no anchorage having been found. Several times during the day the smoke from the burning mountain of Toofoa was seen; at night the flames were observed bursting forth, but to no great height.

Hapaee consists of four islands of inconsiderable elevation. Immediately the ships came to an anchor on the 17th they were crowded with natives, who brought off all sorts of provisions. A house had been brought down to the beach, and on Captain Cook's going on shore, he and Omai, with Feenou, took their seats within it, the other chiefs and people forming a circle outside.

Feenou then directed Taipa to proclaim to the people that the strangers were going to remain five days, and that they were to bring hogs, fowls, and fruit to the ships; that they were not to steal, but to behave in every way politely and courteously. After this, it was suggested by Taipa that a present should be made to Earoupa, the chief of the island.

Omai seems to have been greatly taken with Feenou, and scarcely ever quitted him. The next day this chief came off, requesting the captain's presence on shore, when a hundred men appeared, laden with bread-fruit, plantains, yams, cocoa-nuts, and sugar-canes, with several pigs and fowls, and two turtles, which were deposited in two heaps, Earoupa seating himself near one heap, and another chief near the other. A number of men then appeared, armed with clubs made out of the green branches of the cocoa-nut tree. They formed two parties, and numerous single combats took place, the victors being highly applauded by the spectators. These were succeeded by wrestling and boxing matches, much in the English fashion. In the latter several young women took part. One of the first pair gave in within a minute, but the second fought on till separated by two old women. The greatest good humour prevailed, however, though many severe blows were received. Feenou now explained that one-third of the presents were for Omai, and the others for Captain Cook, who made the handsomest returns he could. There was enough to fill four boats; indeed, no chief in any part had ever made a present at all equal to it.

At the desire of the chief, the marines were exercised on shore, and in return a sort of dance was performed by a hundred and five men, who had each a paddle in his hand. Nothing could exceed the beautiful precision, and the variety of graceful movements of the performers. When it grew dark, their visitors greatly pleased the natives by a display of fireworks. After this the people collected in an open space among the trees, where a circle was formed by lights, and just outside the circle a number of dances were performed, some by men and others by women, many of the principal people taking a part. The performances appear to have been very graceful and perfect in every way, the natives evidently priding themselves on them.

Making an excursion on shore, Captain Cook formed a high opinion of the state of cultivation of Lifooga. On his return on board, he found a large double canoe, with the silent chief who had been met with at Tongataboo, and was supposed to be the king of the island. Feenou was on board, but neither great man took the slightest notice of each other. Feenou now announced that business required his absence, and begged Captain Cook to await his return. He had not been gone long when a large sailing-canoe arrived, in which was a person named Poulaho, and whom the natives on board affirmed to be the real king of Tongataboo, and of all the neighbouring islands. He was a sensible, sedate man, enormously fat, and about forty years of age. He was of course invited into the cabin, but his attendants observed that that could not be. On this, the captain sent Omai to say that he would give directions that no one should approach the part of the deck above the cabin. The king, however, settled the question by going below without making any stipulation. Omai seemed much disappointed at discovering that the chief he had taken to be king was no king after all. Feenou was, however, a very powerful chief; generalissimo of the army, and head of the police of all the islands; so that he was held in general awe.

The king was much pleased with the presents he received, and when he went on shore, ordered two more hogs to be sent off, in addition to two he had brought with him. On landing, he was taken up to the house erected for his accommodation, on a board resembling a hand-barrow. On Feenou's return he looked rather confused on finding that the king had paid the voyagers a visit; and he then acknowledged who and what he really was. After this, on one occasion Poulaho and Feenou accompanied the captain on board. Feenou, however, did not presume to sit with the king, but, saluting his foot with head and hands, retired out of the cabin. It appeared, indeed, that he declined to eat and drink in the royal presence, though there were persons of much inferior rank who did so.

At the request of Poulaho the captain paid a visit to Tongataboo, where his ships were in considerable danger of driving on a low, sandy island, but escaped. At Tongataboo the English were entertained much in the same way that they had been at Hapaee.

The king had a son, Fattafaihe, to whom great respect was paid. His mother was the daughter of an old chief of large possessions and great influence, called Mareewagee, and Feenou was his son. That chief was therefore brother-in-law to the king, and uncle to the heir-apparent.

On the 19th of June, Captain Cook invited the chiefs and others to a meeting, that he might present them with the animals he proposed to leave on the island. To the king, Poulaho, he gave a young English bull and cow; to Mareewagee, a Cape ram and two ewes; and to Feenou, a horse and mare; and he instructed Omai to explain their use, and that they must be careful not to injure them, but to let them increase till they had stocked the island. Some goats and rabbits were also added. It soon appeared, however, that the chiefs were dissatisfied with this allotment, and early next morning it was found that a kid and two turkey cocks were missing. On this, the captain put a guard over the king, Feenou, and some other chiefs, whom he found in the house which the English occupied on shore; and told them that they should not be liberated till the animals and other articles lately stolen had been restored. On the captain inviting them to go on board to dinner they readily consented. Some objected to the king's going, but he jumped up and said that he would be the first to go. They were kept on board till four, and on their return on shore the kid and one of the turkey cocks was brought back, and the other was promised the next day. After this, a party of officers from both ships made an excursion into the interior with muskets and ammunition, and a number of articles for barter, but the natives stripped them of everything. The officers made application through Omai for restitution; and this caused the king, Feenou, and other chiefs hastily to go off. Omai, however, persuaded Feenou that nothing would be done to them, when he, and afterwards the king, returned and were apparently on as good terms as ever.

Captain Cook even ventured to attend a grand ceremony held for the purpose of introducing the young prince to certain royal privileges, the principal of which was to be that of eating in the society of his father. There seemed to be great distinctions of rank among the people. There were some who had greater honour shown to them than even to the king himself. His father had an elder sister of equal rank with himself, and she married a chief who came from Fejee. By him she had a son, the silent chief Latoolibooloo, who was looked upon as a madman, and two daughters. The king met one of these women on board the *Resolution*, and would not venture to eat in her presence. On afterwards encountering Latoolibooloo, the king bent down and touched the silent prince's feet with the back and palms of his hands, as he was accustomed to be treated by his subjects.

Captain Cook here observed the taboo system. If applied to places, they may not be entered or approached; if to persons, they may not be touched, or may not feed themselves; if to things, they may not be touched. The system, however, did not appear to be rigidly observed in Tonga as in some other groups of the Pacific.

With regard to the religion of the people, Captain Cook gained very little information, and Omai, who seems to have been especially dull of apprehension, and never to have made inquiries of his own accord, was very little able to help him. That great cruelty was exercised by those in authority was evident by two or three occurrences witnessed by the English. On one occasion, when Feenou was on board the *Resolution*, an inferior chief ordered all the people to retire from the post occupied on shore by the English. Some ventured to return, when the chief took up a stick and beat them most unmercifully. He struck one man with so much violence on the side of the face that the blood gushed out of his mouth and nostrils, and after lying for some time motionless, he was removed in convulsions. The chief laughed when told that he had killed the man, and seemed perfectly indifferent to the matter.

All classes, from the highest to the lowest, were found to be thieves; and when the chiefs themselves did not steal, they employed their servants to pilfer for them. To check this propensity, Captain Clerke suggested a plan which was adopted with good effect. Whenever any of the lower orders were caught stealing, he had their heads completely shaved, so that they became objects of ridicule to their countrymen, and did not again venture on board the ships.

It appeared that the larger portion of the land belonged to certain great chiefs; and that the inferior chiefs held their estates under them, while the mass of the population were mere serfs who tilled the soil for their masters, and received but a scanty remuneration for their labour.

Captain Cook heard of the Fejee Islands, distant about three days' sail; and of the savage and cannibal propensities of the inhabitants, some of whom he saw at Tonga. The inhabitants of Tonga held them in great dread, on account of their prowess in

A STORM IN THE FOREST.

war, and always endeavoured to keep on friendly terms with them. He concluded that the Friendly Islanders had not, till lately, kept up any intercourse with those of Fejee, because dogs, which are very common in the latter group, had only been introduced into Tonga since his last visit, and to none of the other islands.

All was ready for sailing, when the king invited Captain Cook and his officers to the ceremony which has already been mentioned, and which took place at Mooa where the king resided. During it they had to sit, as did the natives, with their shoulders bare, their hair hanging down loose, their eyes cast down, and their hands locked together. None but the principal people and those who assisted at the celebration were allowed to be present. These circumstances, Captain Cook says, were sufficient evidence to him that the people considered themselves as acting under the immediate inspection of a Supreme Being. He was told that in about three months, there would be performed on the same account, a far grander solemnity, on which occasion, not only the tribute of Tongataboo, but that of Hapaee, Vavaoo, and of all the other islands, would be brought to the chief, and ten human beings from among the inferior sort of people would be sacrificed to add to its dignity: "a significant instance," Captain Cook remarks, "of the influence of gloomy and ignorant superstition over the minds of one of the most benevolent and humane nations upon earth." King Poulaho warmly pressed his guests to remain that they might witness a funeral ceremony, which was to take place the next day.

During their stay in the island they had suffered from a succession of violent storms. The wind raged fearfully amongst the forest trees, the rain fell in torrents, the lightning flashed, and the thunder pealed with an awful fury of which we, in these more temperate regions, have little idea. Now, however, the wind had become fair and moderate, Captain Cook and his officers therefore hurried on board, and as soon as possible the ships got under weigh. As, however, they could not get to sea before it was dark, they had to bring up for the night under Tongataboo. The next day they reached Eooa, where the English were well received by Captain Cook's former acquaintance, the chief of the island, Taoofa, or, as he then called him, Tioony. An abundant supply of yams and a few hogs were obtained, and the ram and two ewes of the Cape of Good Hope breed of sheep were intrusted to the chief, who seemed proud of his charge.

Captain Cook made an excursion into the interior, and, as he surveyed, from an elevation to which he had ascended, the delightful prospect before him, "I could not," he says, "help flattering myself with the pleasing idea that some future navigator may, from the same station, behold these meadows stocked with cattle brought to these islands by the ships of England; and that the completion of this high benevolent purpose, independently of all other considerations, would sufficiently mark to posterity that our voyages had not been useless to the general interests of humanity." The great navigator here gives utterance to the genuine feelings of his heart, for such were undoubtedly the principles which animated him. He little dreamed that those friendly natives, of whom he had thought so highly, and whom he had praised as among the most humane people on earth, had, headed by Feenou, laid a plot for his destruction and that of all his followers. Providentially, the conspirators could not agree as to the mode of proceeding; but all were equally eager to possess themselves of the stores of wealth the ships were supposed to contain. Probably Feenou's pretended friendship for the foolish Omai was in the hope that he would then have a ready tool in his hands. He had offered to make Omai a great chief if he would remain in Tonga, but Cook advised him not to accept the offer.

Captain Cook had settled to sail on the 15th of July, but,

pressed by Taoofa, who promised more presents, he consented to remain a couple of days. During this period, a seaman was surrounded by a number of people, and being knocked down, had every particle of clothing torn from his back; but by seizing on a couple of canoes and a fat hog the English obtained the restoration of some of the articles.

The captain kept to his purpose of sailing, but when still not far from the land, a canoe with four men came off, saying that orders had been sent to the people of Eooa to supply the ships with fat hogs, and that if they would return to their former station, the king and a number of chiefs would, in a couple of days, be with them. As, however, there was an abundant supply of provisions on board, Captain Cook declined the offer and continued his course.

It is scarcely necessary to remind the reader that more fearful massacres of the crews of various ships were perpetrated by the inhabitants of these islands than by any other natives of the Pacific, from the time of the visit just recorded, till they were formed into a civilized community under their present government.

After the ships had left the Tonga group they did not see land till the 8th of August, when they fell in with a small island having on it hills of considerable elevation, covered with grass: tall trees and numerous plantations on a border of flat land ran quite round it, edged with a white sand beach. A number of people were on the shore, and two canoes came off with a dozen men in them, but could not be persuaded by all Omai's eloquence to venture along side. They spoke the language of Otaheite, and called their island Toobouai. It was at this island that Christian and the mutineers of the *Bounty* tried to form a settlement in 1789. It is the scene also of Lord Byron's poem of "the Island," though he altered the name to Toobouia. Some of the people were dressed in native cloth, but the great mass had only girdles. One continued to blow a conch-shell most of the time the ships lay off their island, while his companions made signs, inviting the strangers to land. It is worthy of remark that no weapons were seen among them.

On the 12th, Maitea was seen, and soon after Otaheite hove in sight, and the next day the ships anchored in the Bay of Oheitepeha. Some common people came off in canoes, but Omai took no notice of them, and they did not seem to recognise him as a countryman. At length, his brother-in-law Ootee appeared; but there was no exhibition of regard or affection till Omai took the other into the cabin and showed him the drawers in which he kept his red feathers. This instantly changed the face of affairs, and Ootee begged that they might be *tayos*, and change names.

Soon after the ships anchored Omai's sister came on board, and the meeting was marked with expressions of the most tender affection, evidently not feigned. Afterwards on going on shore with Captain Cook, Omai met a sister of his mother. "She threw herself at his feet, and bedewed them plentifully with tears of joy," says the captain; adding, "I left him with the old lady in the midst of a number of people who had gathered round him."

Cook found that since his last visit, two Spanish ships had twice visited the bay; that a house had been built, and that several persons had been left in the interval, of whom some had died, and the rest went away when the ships came back. They had presented the islanders with a bull, some hogs and goats, and dogs; and had taken away four people, two of whom died and two came back from a place which Cook conjectured to be Lima. The house which stood close to the beach, was made of planks, and as these were all numbered, they had evidently been brought ready to be set up. It was divided into two small rooms, and, in the inner one, were a bedstead, a table, a bench, some old hats, and other trifles, of which the natives seemed to be very careful, as also of the house itself, which had suffered no hurt from the weather,—a shed having been built over it. There were scuttles all round which served as air-holes, and perhaps they were intended to fire from with musketry, should it have become necessary. At a little distance from the front stood a wooden cross, on the transverse part of which was only the inscription, *Christus vincit*, and on the perpendicular part *Carolus III. imperat* 1774. On the other side of the post Cook preserved the memory of the prior visits of the English by inscribing, *Georgius tertius Rex*, Annis 1767, 1769–1773, 1774 and 1777. The natives pointed out the grave of the commodore of the two ships who died there during their first visit.

The expeditions of the Spaniards to Otaheite and the neighbouring islands, had been undertaken in consequence of the jealousy of the Spanish Government at the visits of the English to the South Seas. The first was under the command of Don Domingo Bonechea, in the *Aguila* frigate, in 1772. He gave so favourable a report of the islands that he was again sent out in 1774, having on board two monks of the order of St. Francis, a linguist, a portable house, sheep, cattle, and implements. Having landed them at Oheitepeha Bay, as soon as the house was up he set sail to make further discoveries. He then returned to the Bay, and six days afterwards died, and was buried with becoming ceremonies at the foot of the cross, which was erected with great pomp amid the chanting of masses, and the discharges of musketry.

In 1775, a third visit was paid by the *Aguila*, sent from Callao, to ascertain the fate of the missionaries. They were found to be utterly disappointed, and determined to abandon their task, having made no progress in the conversion of the natives; and were so alarmed at the human sacrifices constantly taking place, that they would only consent to remain under the protection of a Spanish garrison.

In God's providence the people of Otaheite were destined to

receive from Protestant missionaries a simpler and purer faith than that taught by the priests of Rome. To that faith they have held fast, in spite of all the efforts and machinations of the Romanists.

While in this bay, as an abundant supply of cocoa-nuts could be obtained, Captain Cook proposed to his crew that, as it was important they should economize their spirits, they should give up their grog except on Saturday nights, and drink cocoa-nut milk instead. To this, without a moment's hesitation they consented, as did Captain Clerke's crew. On their first arrival in this place, red feathers were looked on as of great value, but as everybody had them on board they soon became a drug in the market. Poor Omai began very soon to exhibit his want of judgment. He had prepared a crown or cap of yellow and red feathers for Otoo the king of all the islands, which the captain recommended him to present himself. Instead of so doing, his vanity induced him to exhibit it before Waheiadooa, the chief of that part, who thereupon kept the crown himself and sent only a few tufts to the king.

TROPICAL VEGETATION

On the 23rd of August the ships moved to Matavai Bay. The following morning the captain landed with Omai and several officers, to pay his respects to the king, who was attended by his father, his two brothers, three sisters, and a large number of people. Omai, who was becomingly dressed, kneeled and embraced the king's legs, but very little notice was taken of him. He made the king a present of some red feathers and three yards of gold cloth; and the captain gave him a suit of fine linen, a gold-laced hat, some more red feathers, and some tools. Captain Cook's wish had been to leave Omai with Otoo, as he thought of landing all his animals here, and supposed that Omai would assist in looking after them, and show their various uses. He therefore encouraged the friendship of Omai with the chiefs, even though it might have depended much on his supposed wealth. Omai, however, rejecting his kind friend's advice, conducted himself in so imprudent a manner, that he soon lost the friendship of Otoo and of every other person of note in Otaheite. He associated with none but vagabonds and strangers, whose sole object was to plunder him; and had not the captain interfered, they would not have left him a single article worth carrying from the island. Of course this drew on him the ill-will of the chiefs, who found that they could not procure such valuable presents as Omai bestowed on the lowest of the people, his companions.

After dinner the captain and a party of officers accompanied Otoo to Oparre, taking with them the poultry with which they were to stock the island. They consisted of a peacock and hen, a turkey-cock and hen, one gander and three geese, and a drake and four ducks; all left with the king. A gander was found there, left by Captain Wallis, several goats, and a fine Spanish bull, which was kept tied to a tree near Otoo's house. Three cows and a bull, some sheep, and the horse and mare were also landed, greatly to the captain's satisfaction, and to that of everybody else on board probably, when it is considered the care and attention it must have required to keep them alive for so many months. A piece of ground was also cleared for a garden, and in it among other things, were planted several shaddock trees, which had been brought from the Friendly Islands, two pine-apple plants, some melons, and potatoes. The Spaniards had left a vine which flourished, but before the grapes were ripe the natives tasted them, and finding them sour nearly destroyed it. It was, however, pruned, and cuttings were taken from it, and the natives were advised to wait till the fruit was ripe another season.

The youth, called Oedidee, whose real name was Heete-heete, who had been seven months with Captain Cook, was here met with. The captain gave him a chest of tools, and some clothes had been sent out for his use; but after a few days he declined wearing them. One of the natives who had been on board one of the Spanish ships, had also resumed his native garments, and "perhaps," Captain Cook observes, "Omai, who has almost entirely assumed English manners, will do the same."

While the ships lay at Matavai, news was brought that the people of Eimeo had revolted, and it was resolved to send Towha with a fleet against them. Before the fleet could sail it was necessary that a grand human sacrifice should be offered. The unhappy victim—one of the common people—had already been knocked on the head for the purpose. Captain Cook, wishing to ascertain the truth of the accounts he had received, accompanied Otoo to witness the ceremony, and with him Mr. Anderson and Mr. Webber, followed by Omai in a canoe. Every facility was given them for witnessing the barbarous and disgusting rite. The English were allowed to examine the victim, who was a man of middle age, and had been killed by a blow on the right temple. Forty-nine skulls were counted in one heap, which, as they had suffered little change by the weather, had belonged to people evidently not long killed.

On the captain's return he met Towha, who became very angry

because he positively refused to assist him in his proposed expedition.

Omai gave an entertainment on shore about this time, at which the king condescended to attend; and the following day a party dined with their old shipmate, Oedidee; among other dishes admirably dressed was a hog weighing about thirty pounds, which an hour or two before was alive. Some fireworks let off before a large concourse of people frightened some of them so much that they could scarcely be kept together. On the return of Otoo on the 13th of September, from assisting at another human sacrifice, the two captains mounted the two horses, and took a ride round the plains of Matavai, to the astonishment of a large number of people. The ride was repeated every day, and seemed to convey to the natives a better idea of the greatness of the English, than any of the other novelties brought to them by their European visitors.

Most of the chiefs and other people of importance who were known to the English during their former visit were still alive, and as the island had enjoyed the blessings of peace, it seemed to be in a very flourishing condition. Omai received here one present from Towha in return for the many he had given away: this was a handsome double canoe, ready for sea; but when he exhibited himself on board in a suit of chain armour, so unpopular had he become, that the people would not look at him. He had all along entertained the idea that Captain Cook would take him back to Ulietea, and reinstate him by force of arms, on his father's property. This made him refuse to remain at Otaheite.

On leaving that island on the 30th of September, the ships proceeded to Eimeo. Omai, in his canoe, had arrived some time before. An excellent harbour was found, in which the ships lay close to the shore. The *Resolution* was much infested by rats, and as an expedient to get rid of them, she was hauled as close in with the shore as the depth of water would allow, and some stout hawsers were fastened to the trees to afford them a bridge to cross over. The natives would scarcely have thanked their visitors for the gifts intended for them; but whether any rats were thus got rid of is not known. The natives managed, however, to carry off a goat, which, as it was of value for the purpose of stocking other islands, it was necessary to recover. This, however, was not done till several canoes and some houses had been burned.

The island is described as rising in one hill, with very little level ground, and the people, especially the women, were said to be inferior in appearance to those of the neighbouring islands. Another day's sail brought the ships to the entrance of the harbour of Owharre, on the west side of the island of Huaheine. As Omai refused to attempt the recovery of his property in Ulietea except by force of arms, Captain Cook determined to leave him here, making the best terms with the chief that he could. The English were received on shore by a large concourse of people, many of whom appeared to be people of consequence; the king was, however, only a child. It is painful to read the following account given of the meeting: "Omai began with making his offering to the gods, consisting of red feathers, cloth, etc. Then followed another offering, which was to be given to the gods by the chief: each article was laid before a priest, who presented it with a prayer dictated by Omai, who did not forget his friends in England nor those who had brought him safely back. The King of England, Lord Sandwich, Cook and Clerke, were mentioned in every one of them." Finally the chief agreed to give Omai a piece of ground, extending about two hundred yards along the shores of the harbour, and reaching to the foot of the hill. Here observatories were set up, and the carpenters of both ships were set to work to build a house for Omai, in which he might secure his European commodities. At the same time some hands were employed on shore, making a garden for his use, planting shaddocks, vines, pine-apples, melons, and other seeds, many of which were in a flourishing state before the English left the island. Omai here found a brother, a sister, and a brother-in-law; but they were not people capable of affording him any protection. Cook therefore advised him to make handsome presents to some of the chiefs, that they might be induced to protect him. To increase his security, Captain Cook took every opportunity of impressing on the inhabitants, that he purposed returning, and that should he not find Omai in the state of security in which he left him, his enemies might expect to feel the weight of his resentment.

On the 22nd a man found means of carrying off a sextant from Mr. Bayley's observatory. Omai fixed on the culprit, who was a Bolabola man, a hardened scoundrel. He confessed that he had taken the instrument, and would show where it was. This did not save him however from having his head and beard shaved, and both his ears cut off, as a terror to the rest.

Omai's house being nearly finished on the 26th, many of his movables were carried on shore. Among a variety of other useless articles, was a box of toys, which seemed greatly to please the multitude; but his plates, dishes, mugs, and glasses, he saw would be of no use to him, and he therefore exchanged them with the crew for hatchets and other iron tools. He is said to have had an electrical machine, a portable organ, a coat of mail and a helmet. He had also a musket and bayonet, a fowling-piece, two pair of pistols, and two or three swords or cutlasses. The possession of these made him quite happy, though Cook was of opinion that he would have been better without them. A horse and mare, a boar and two sows, and a goat with kid, were likewise given to him.

The following inscription was cut on the outside of Omai's house:—

Georgius Tertius, Rex, 2 *Novembris,* 1777.

Naves. { *Resolution, Jac. Cook, Pr.*
Discovery, Car. Clerke, Pr.

T

On bidding his friends farewell Omai sustained himself with firmness, till he came to Captain Cook, when his utmost efforts failed to conceal his tears, and he wept all the time of going on shore. Even at last he would have remained on board the *Resolution*. The two New Zealand youths were very anxious to remain with the English, and the youngest, who was a witty smart boy, and consequently much noticed, had to be carried on shore by force.

Deep interest was often expressed in England as to the fate of the "gentle savage" who had been brought from the South Seas, and so soon learned the manners of civilized life. Had he devoted his talents to the instruction of his countrymen, and raised their condition to a state somewhat resembling that he had seen existing in England?

Many years passed before the truth was known, and yet who that has read the account given of him by Cook, and remembers that he remained to the last a dark idolater, could have expected otherwise from him? Mr. Ellis in his "Polynesian Researches" gives the account:—

"Soon after the departure of his friends he assumed the native dress, and at the same time gave himself up to the vices, indolence, and barbarism of his countrymen. The only use he made of the horses left with him was to ride about the country for the purpose of astonishing or frightening the more ignorant natives; and so far from lamenting the barbarous condition of the people, and endeavouring to raise them in the social scale, his great delight consisted in exhibiting the superiority which his English weapons enabled him to assume. As his fire-arms, especially, had rendered him a powerful subject, he married the daughter of a chief who made himself king; and was invested with the high title of *Paari* (wise and instructed). He had now gained the position his philosophical friends in England had desired for him, and had a favourable opportunity of acquiring the title of his country's benefactor, which they had hoped he would deserve. But how did he employ his advantages?

"From thenceforth," adds the narrator, "he continued the inglorious tool of the king's cruel and wanton humour, assisting him with his musket in time of war, and, in peace, frequently amusing the monarch by shooting at his subjects at a distance, or gratifying his revenge by despatching with a pistol those who had incurred his wrath.

"He died within three years after his celebrated voyage, and the New Zealanders did not long survive him. His name is now rarely mentioned except with contempt or execration. The site of his dwelling is, by the natives, still called Beritain (Britain); and amid the ruins of the garden they show a dark and glossy-leaved shaddock tree which they love to tell was planted by the hands of Cook. The horses which he left did not long survive; but the breeds of goats and pigs yet remain; many of the trinkets, part of the armour, and some of the cutlasses, are also preserved; and the numerous coloured engravings of a large quarto Bible, are objects of general attraction.

"There is perhaps no place in the island to which greater interest is attached; for besides its association with the name just mentioned, on this spot was reared the first building in which the true God was publicly worshipped in Huaheine; and here also was erected the first school for the instruction of the benighted inhabitants in the knowledge of letters and the principles of Christianity."

On leaving Huaheine, the ships stood over to Ulietea, and the following day, the 3rd of November, entered the harbour of Ohamaneno. Here they hauled close in with the shore, and made another attempt to get rid of their troublesome guests, the rats. The captain's old friend, Oreo, chief of the island, and his son-in-law, Pootoe, at once came off to visit him; the visit was returned, and amicable relations were soon established. In spite of this, however, thefts were continually committed; and other circumstances arose which seemed to threaten a rupture of this friendship.

One of these events was the desertion of a marine who, being on duty, went off, carrying his arms with him. Captain Cook, with a few of his people, instantly pursued the man, fearing that he would have escaped to the mountains. He was soon discovered, however, among the natives, who readily delivered him up to the captain. But a more serious case of desertion took place a few days afterwards—that of a midshipman and a seaman. The captain, thereupon, set off with two armed boats, but could not find the fugitives, hearing only that they had gone over to the neighbouring island of Bolabola.

The next morning, the chief, his son and daughter, and his son-in-law, came on board the *Resolution;* and the three last-mentioned were invited to the *Discovery,* with a view to their detention there, till the deserters should be brought back—an act of high-handed injustice of which, one would suppose, no amount of condescension and familiarity on the part of the English was likely to efface the remembrance.

At any rate, the step thus taken caused great consternation among the natives, many of whom, including many women, came off in canoes under the stern of the ship, and bewailed the captivity of the king's daughter. Oreo, on his part, quickly aroused himself, and sent off canoes to Bolabola and elsewhere, to find the fugitives. The natives, in the meantime, in a spirit of natural retaliation, formed a plan for seizing Captain Cook while bathing, as was his custom every morning. Failing in this, they attempted to make prisoners of Captain Clerke and Mr. Gore. News indeed was brought off to the ships that they had been captured; and Mr. King, with several armed boats, was immediately despatched to rescue them, when it was found that they had escaped the plot, probably owing their safety to the fact that Captain Clerke carried a pistol in his hand. Oreo must have been aware of the plot, for he more than once asked Captain Cook why he did not go and bathe as usual.

The chief at length set out for Bolabola, it being arranged that the ships should follow; but a strong wind kept them in harbour, and the next day he returned with the two deserters, who had gone from Bolabola to the small island of Toobaee, where they were taken by the father of Pootoe. The three captives were then released. Before leaving the island, Captain Cook presented Oreo with an English boar and sow, and two goats. Oreo and several chiefs took a passage on board the English ships to Bolabola, which was reached the day after they left Ulietea. A large concourse of people, with the great chief, Opoony, in their midst, were ready to receive the English.

One object Captain Cook had in putting in here was to obtain one of the anchors which M. Bourgainville had lost at Otaheite, and which, having been taken up by the people there, had been sent as a present to Opoony. That chief, with remarkable honesty, positively refused to accept any present till the anchor had been seen, not believing it worth what was offered. Cook's object was to manufacture it into tools and nails, of which he had run short. He insisted on his presents being taken, and was glad to get the old iron for the object he had in view. Very many years afterwards the missionary Williams was in the same manner thankful to find an old anchor, out of which he manufactured the iron work required for the missionary vessel he was building, *The Messenger of Peace.*

As a ram had before been conveyed to the island, the captain made a present of a ewe to Opoony, hoping thus that the island might be stocked in time with a breed of sheep.

He now prepared to take his departure for the north; and as this was the last visit paid by Cook to these islands, his opinion may be quoted, that it would have been better for the people of the Pacific Islands had they never been discovered by Europeans, than once having become acquainted with them and their goods, to be afterwards left to their own resources. "When their iron tools are worn out, and the use of their stone ones is forgotten, how are they to get others?" he asks; and adds, "it is incumbent therefore on Europeans to visit them once in three or four years, in order to supply them with those conveniences which we have introduced to them."

The minds of those enlightened and civilized visitors were occupied with the glory of their achievements as discoverers of hitherto unknown lands; their remaining thoughts, which they would have called patriotic, were principally occupied with the question how these discoveries might be turned to account for the profit and honour of England; and if a nook remained for a benevolent wish for "the savages," the wish was limited to the improvement of their material condition. Otherwise, as the English discoverer found them, so he was willing that they should remain; satisfied with the idea that he had increased the productive powers of the different lands he visited.

Thus also, in the case of the wretched Omai, whose end we have seen. It seems scarcely to have entered the minds of those who, in England, petted and spoiled him, that he had a soul as valuable, or rather as invaluable, as theirs; and that he needed, as all need, the transforming influences of Divine grace, to make him a future blessing, instead of a curse, to his poor countrymen. We are told, indeed, of his being slow to receive Christian instruction; and we read also that, among his goods and chattels collected in England, he had a large quarto Bible, with coloured engravings— a book, however, which was a sealed book to him and his countrymen.

The ships now stood north; and, on December 24th, discovered an uninhabited island, with a lagoon. It was hoped that turtle would abound here; they therefore came to an anchor. The voyagers were not disappointed, and a considerable number were taken. Two men while thus employed lost themselves in different parts of the island, and as there was not a drop of water to be found they suffered greatly from thirst, especially one who would not drink turtles' blood. They were both happily recovered. The telescopes were landed, and on the 30th of December an eclipse of the sun was observed. Not a trace of any inhabitants having ever been on the island could be discovered. There were about thirty cocoa-nut trees, but the fruit was of an inferior quality. Three hundred turtle were taken, and as many fish as could be consumed; but not a drop of fresh water could be found. As Christmas was spent here, the name of Christmas Island was given to the new discovery. It lies in latitude 1° 41' north, and longitude 157° 15' east. Some cocoa-nuts and yams were planted on the island, and some melon seeds; while a bottle was deposited with the names of the ships and the date of the visit. The ships sailed thence on the 2nd of January, 1778, and proceeded northward. The wind blew faint at first and then freshened, and the albatross with other birds were seen increasing in number; all indications of land being near, though none was seen till the 18th, when first one high island and then another hove in sight. On the 19th the first seen bore east, several leagues distant, and being to windward could not be approached. On standing towards the other, a third island was discovered in the direction of west-north-west. At first it was doubtful whether the islands were inhabited, but that question was soon solved by the appearance of several canoes, which came alongside; but the people in them would not at first venture on board, though they willingly exchanged a few fish and some sweet potatoes for nails and other articles offered them.

They spoke the language of Otaheite and of the other islands lately visited. They were of a brown colour, of an ordinary size, and the cast of their features was not unlike that of Europeans. Some wore their hair long, others short, but all had stained it of a brown colour. Some were slightly tattooed, and all wore the usual girdle, stained red, white, and black. As the ships sailed

THE ALBATROSS.

along the coast looking for a harbour numerous villages were observed, with plantations of sugar-canes and plantains, while vast numbers of people crowded the shore or collected in elevated places to watch the ships.

The next day, the ships again standing in, several natives ventured on board, and showed by the wild looks and gestures with which they regarded everything on board that they had never before been visited by Europeans. They knew the value of iron, however, when they saw it, and it was supposed that they had gained their knowledge of it from the fact that the masts and spars of a ship with iron attached, and casks with iron hoops, had been cast on their shore. They soon proved themselves to be daring thieves, and, unhappily, a boat being sent on shore, on their attempting to seize the oars they were fired at, and one man was killed. Of this circumstance Captain Cook was not informed at the time.

As soon as Captain Cook landed the people assembled fell flat on their faces; nor would they rise till by expressive gestures he urged them to do so. He understood that this was the way they paid respect to their own great chiefs. Having arranged about getting a supply of water, he walked with Messrs. Anderson and Wilder into the country, to visit an obelisk of wicker-work, fifty feet high, standing in a morai. A native had been selected as a guide, and wherever they went the people fell prostrate before the captain. The morai was similar to those seen at Otaheite. In and about it were a number of idols, one having on its head what resembled an ancient helmet. They ascertained, without doubt, that human sacrifices were offered up at these morais. On the wicker-work were pieces of grey cloth, such as was generally offered to idols, and a piece of which had been pressed on the captain on landing. The next day, among other articles brought off, were some beautiful cloaks of red and other feathers, and helmets and caps of the same.

Captain Cook in his journal expresses his belief that the people were cannibals. This arose from seeing a man on board who had a piece of salted meat done up in a cloth, and which he said that he ate to do him good. It seems to have been highly dried and seasoned, and to have been taken as a stimulant.

The natives called their island Atooi, and Captain Cook gave the name of the Sandwich Islands to the whole group. The friendly disposition of the natives was shown on all occasions, especially when three boats went on shore and, bad weather coming on, were detained for several days. Five islands were seen on this occasion, and were distinguished by the names of Woahoo, Atooi, Oneeheow, Oreehoua, and Tahoora. The islands were mostly high, well watered, and apparently thickly populated.

It was found that the taboo existed with even greater vigour than at Tongataboo, for the people constantly asked, with signs of fear, whether anything they desired to see, and the English were unwilling to show, was taboo, or, as they pronounced the word, tafoo.

On the 2nd of February, 1778, the ships left the Sandwich Islands, and stood towards the coast of America.

On the 7th of March, early in the morning, the long-looked-for coast of New Albion, so called by Sir Francis Drake, hove in sight. The ships stood along the coast, now off and now on again, with uncertain weather, till at length, on the 29th of March, an inlet appeared in latitude 49° 15' north, and longitude 126° 35' east. The ships sailed up this inlet for several miles, when they cast anchor. Natives came off in three canoes, shaped like Norway yawls. Having drawn near, a person stood up in one of them and invited the strangers, in a speech and by gesture, to land, at the same time strewing handfuls of red feathers towards them, while his companions threw red dust in the same way. The next day a large number of people came off, who all behaved in the most peaceable manner, and offered for sale a number of skins of bears, foxes, wolves, deer, racoon, pole cats, martins, and sea otters. The difficulty was to find articles to exchange for these really valuable commodities, for the natives would receive nothing but metal, and at last insisted on having brass. To supply them whole suits of clothes were stripped of their buttons, bureaus of their handles, and copper kettles, tin canisters, and candle-sticks went to wreck. The ships required a great deal of repairs, and even some fresh masts, and for this purpose they were hauled close into the shore and securely moored. The natives called this inlet Nootka Sound, but Captain Cook gave it the name of King George's Sound.

Two persons were on board the ships at this time whose names afterwards became well known; Mr. Vancouver, then a midshipman of the *Resolution*, who afterwards, as Captain Vancouver, made many important discoveries on the coast then visited, and gave his name to a valuable island, now a colony of Great Britain; and Corporal Ledyard, whose travels in Siberia were of a very extraordinary character.

The clothing of the people of Nootka Sound consisted of a dress of flax, fringed with fur, and reaching to the feet; and over it a cloak of the same substance, with a hole cut in it, through which the head was thrust, and which hung down over the shoulders and arms as low as the waist. The head was covered with a hat like a truncated cone of matting, with a knob or tassel at the top, and strung under the chin. A large cloak of bear or wolf skin was occasionally worn over all. They also at times wore wooden masks. Their habitations were made of planks loosely put together, about seven or eight feet in height in front, and higher at the back. Several families resided in each, with a very slight division between them. Each had its own bench, and in the centre was the fire, without hearth or chimney. At the ends were seen trunks of trees, carved into hideous images, and rudely painted, supposed to be their gods; though but little veneration was paid them. Two silver spoons of old Spanish manufacture were obtained here from a native, who wore them as ornaments round his neck.

The progress of the ships along this coast can be but briefly described. Although the mercury in the barometer fell very rapidly, Captain Cook was so anxious to put to sea, that he kept to his purpose of sailing on the 26th of April. A perfect hurricane came on ere long, in which the *Resolution* sprang a serious leak. When the weather moderated, one pump kept it under. The ships proceeded along the coast, and several islands and headlands were seen and named.

The voyagers landed at several places, and had some intercourse with the natives. One inlet, where the ships brought up, was named Prince William's Sound. Here the natives made a daring attempt to plunder the *Discovery*, a mob of them getting on board, evidently under the impression that she was feebly guarded. But before they had time to carry out their nefarious design, the crew came on deck with their cutlasses, and the plunderers went off in their canoes.

Captain Cook, believing that it was too late in the year to do anything of importance in the way of fresh discoveries, resolved to return to the south, and wait at the Sandwich Islands till the next season.

From Prince William's Sound, the ships proceeded along the coast, steering south-west, and passing many more capes till the mouth of a large river was found, up which they sailed. A volcano was here seen, emitting smoke, but no fire.

A number of natives, of no very prepossessing appearance now came off the banks of the river to the ships, and a considerable quantity of skins were obtained from them. It was held by some on board that this river might be a strait, leading to Hudson's Bay; and to settle this question, Captain Cook sailed up it nearly seventy leagues from its mouth, at which distance it still seemed to be a river, and nothing more, upon which the explorers returned. On the 1st of June, Lieutenant King was sent on shore to display the royal flag, and to take possession of the country, as in former instances, in the name of the king of Great Britain. In describing this inlet, Captain Cook left a blank in the chart, and, therefore, the Earl of Sandwich directed that it should be called Cook's Inlet.

Leaving Prince William's Sound, the next place reached was the island of Oonolaschka. Here, at different times, some canoes came off with natives, who had bows of the European fashion, and delivered two Russian letters, the purport of which could not be understood.

During the stay of the ships at this island, a canoe was upset, and the occupant, a fine young man, was brought on board the *Resolution*, when, without hesitation, he entered the captain's cabin, and exchanged his wet garments for a European suit of clothes, which he put on with perfect ease.

Soon after this, the expedition suffered a very great loss in the death of Mr. Anderson, the surgeon of the *Resolution*, who had long been suffering from consumption. The ships were proceeding northward at the time, along the coast of Asia, but were compelled to return on account of the shallowness of the water. An island, in sight, was called Anderson's Island, to perpetuate the memory of that gentleman.

On the 9th, the ships anchored under a point of land, to which the name of Cape Prince of Wales was given, and which was considered the most western point of America. It is only thirteen leagues distant from the eastern cape of Siberia. Thence they stood over to the coast of Siberia to the country of Tschutski. Again sailing, the ships steered to the east, and on the 18th, fell in with the ice, which, in latitude 70° 44', was as compact as a wall, and ten or twelve feet high, being much higher farther to the north. It was covered with sea-horses, a number of which were caught, and, in spite of the prejudices of some of the crew, were found to be superior to salt pork. Cook continued to traverse the arctic sea beyond Behring's Straits in various directions, till the

29th, when the ice beginning to form rapidly, he abandoned all hope of attaining his object that year.

On the 3rd of October, the ships anchored in the harbour of Samganoodha, in the island of Oonolaschka. The carpenters at once set to work to repair the ships. While they lay here, each of the captains received the present of a well-known Russian dish. It consisted of a salmon, highly seasoned, and baked in a coating of rye bread like a loaf. The loaves were accompanied by notes in Russian. A few bottles of rum, wine, and porter, were sent in return by Corporal Ledyard, who was directed to make the Russians understand that the strangers were English and their friends; and to gain all the information in his power. On the 14th a visit was received from a Russian of considerable ability. Cook intrusted to his care a letter and chart for the Lords Commissioners of the Admiralty, which were duly delivered. The natives of this island were the best behaved and most peaceably disposed of any yet met with, while not one of them was found guilty of an act of dishonesty. They were, however, far from moral in their conduct.

Samganoodha Harbour was left on the 26th of October, and the ships proceeded south towards the Sandwich Islands. Cook's intention was to spend the winter there, and to return to Kamtschatka by the middle of May. In case of separation, he directed Captain Clerke to meet him at the Sandwich Islands, for the first place of rendezvous, and the harbour of Petropaulowska in Kamtschatka for the second. The rigging of the ships had now become very bad; on board the *Discovery* the maintack gave way, killed one man, and wounded the boatswain and two others.

On the 25th of November one of the Sandwich Islands, called by the natives Mowee, hove in sight. Several canoes came off, belonging to a chief named Terreeoboo; but as another island was discovered, called Owhyhee,* which it was found possible to fetch,

* Now altered in spelling to Hawaii.

Discovery of Owhyhee.

the ships stood towards it, and their visitors accordingly left them. On the morning of the 2nd of December, the summits of the mountains of Owhyhee were seen covered with snow. On the evening, an eclipse of the moon was observed. For several weeks the ships continued plying round the island, bartering with the natives, who came off with hogs, fowls, fruit and roots. On the 16th of January, 1779, a bay being discovered, the masters

KARAKAKOOA BAY, OWHYHEE.

were sent in to examine it, and having reported favourably, the ships on the next day came to an anchor in Karakakooa Bay.

The ships were crowded with visitors, but not a single person had a weapon of any sort. There must have been at least a thousand about the two ships, and one of them took the rudder out of a boat and made off with it. Cook ordered some muskets and four-pounders to be fired over the canoe which was escaping. The multitude, however, seemed more surprised than frightened.

Besides those who had come off in canoes, the shore of the bay was covered with spectators, and many hundreds were swimming round the ships like shoals of fish. Few of the voyagers now regretted that they had been unable to find a north-west passage home in the summer, as they "thus had it in their power to revisit the Sandwich Islands, and to enrich the voyage with a discovery which, though the last, seemed in many respects to be the most important that had hitherto been made by Europeans throughout the extent of the Pacific Ocean."

This paragraph concludes Captain Cook's journal; they were probably the last words he ever wrote. Captain King is our chief authority for the remaining transactions of the voyage.

Among the chiefs who attached themselves to the English was a young man named Pareea, who introduced himself as an officer of the king of the island, then gone on a military expedition to Mowee. That he had great influence among his people was evident, for so large a number of people had collected on one side of the *Discovery*, that they made her heel over. Captain Cook pointed out the fact to him, and he immediately cleared the ship. Another chief, the next day, cleared the *Resolution* in the same way; and one man loitering behind, he took him up in his arms and threw him into the sea. They brought on board a third chief, once a warrior, now a priest, named Koah, a little old man of emaciated figure, his red eyes and scaly skin showing that he was a hard drinker of cava. Not far from the shore was a temple or morai. It was a square, solid pile of stones, about forty yards long, twenty broad, and fourteen in height. The top was flat and well-paved, and surrounded by a wooden rail, on which were fixed the skulls of the victims sacrificed on the death of their chiefs. At one end was a kind of scaffold, and on the opposite side towards the sea, two small houses with a covered communication. At the entrance were two large wooden images with features violently

DIAMOND HEAD CRATER, HONOLULU, OWHYHEE.

distorted, and on the head of which was a large piece of carved wood of a conical form inverted. The lower part was without form, and wrapped round with red cloth. Not far off, in a retired grove by the side of a pool, was a collection of huts, inhabited by priests who attended this temple, of which Koah was the chief. There were two villages on the shores of the bay, one on the north point, called Kowrooa, and at the bottom of the bay one still larger, called Kakooa.

Our narrative is now drawing near to the tragic scene which terminated both the labours and life of Captain James Cook. But, to understand what led to that event, a preliminary explanation must be given.

The natives of Owhyhee had a legend to the effect that a certain god, Rono or Orono, formerly lived near Karakakooa Bay, and that, having killed his wife in a fit of jealousy, remorse drove him from the island. He set sail in a strangely shaped canoe, promising that he would return on a floating island, furnished with all that man could desire. When, therefore, the English ships appeared, their commander was supposed to be the long-absent Rono, come to restore peace and prosperity to the country.

The priest Koah, having dined on board the *Resolution*, accompanied Captain Cook and Mr. King on shore—Mr. King being taken for the son of the former. They were met by four men, having wands tipped with dogs' hair, and who shouted a short sentence in which the word Orono was plainly distinguishable, and frequently repeated. During this progress, the crowd either rushed away as in fear, or fell prostrate on the ground around the party. Koah led the way into the morai, and, chanting a hymn, took the captain to a sort of altar on which were arranged twelve idols, in a semicircle, while on a table before the centre one, which nearly resembled the idols of Otaheite, lay a putrid hog. A tall young man with a beard, Kaireekeea by name, having presented

Cook to the idols, old Koah put the putrid hog to his nose, and then let it drop. At this time a procession approached, bearing a hog and red cloth. Kaireekeea went forward to meet them, when they all prostrated themselves. The hog then was offered to the captain by Koah, who wound the red cloth round him. Chanting followed. Captain Cook meanwhile had considerable difficulty in keeping his seat upon the rotten scaffolding. They then descended, and as Koah passed the images, he snapped his fingers at them, and said something in a sneering tone. He, however, prostrated himself before the centre figure and kissed it, and induced the captain to do the same. The captain and Mr. King were then led to another division of the morai, where in a sunk space, three or four feet deep, they took their seats between two wooden idols, Koah holding up one of the captain's arms, and King the other. While here, another procession arrived with a baked hog and vegetables. Cook put an end to the ceremony as soon as he could, and returned on board.

No doubt the proceedings of the old priest and the people were in some measure incomprehensible to Captain Cook, but it is certain that, in bearing a prominent part in the mummery just narrated, he must have been aware that he was encouraging heathen idolatry and hero-worship in its grossest forms. It is not to be supposed that he was acquainted with the legend of Rono; but the conduct of the people must have shown him their utter debasement, and he can scarcely have failed to perceive that by submitting to their ceremonies and taking a part in them, he was lowering himself to their level.

It is probable that Captain Cook expected, by yielding to the superstitions of the natives, to obtain greater facilities for trading, and keeping up amicable relations with them. If so, the subsequent events prove how baseless were these anticipations, while the reader will scarcely fail to be reminded of the striking

Scripture narrative of the king of whom the people shouted, "It is the voice of a god, and not of a man;" and who "gave not God the glory."

The day following that on which the events described took place, Mr. King, with a company of marines, landed, and erected an observatory near the morai, the ground being marked off by the priests. For some unknown reason—but one probably connected with the previous exhibition—the entire bay was tabooed for a day or two: and no canoes ventured off with provisions. The priests, however, sent to the observatory, and also to the ships, a regular supply of hogs and vegetables for Orono, as if they were discharging a religious duty; and would take nothing in return. Whenever, too, after this, Captain Cook went on shore, he was attended by one of the priests, who gave notice to the people to prostrate themselves; and inferior chiefs often requested to be allowed to make offerings of hogs, which they did with evident marks of fear in their countenances.

On the 24th of January, 1779, the bay was again tabooed on account of the arrival of the King Terreeoboo, who soon came off privately in a canoe, with his wife and children. He was found to be the same infirm old man who had come on board the *Resolution* when the ships were off Mowee. The next day the king came off in state, on board a large canoe, attended by two others.

In the first he himself came, dressed, as were his attendant chiefs, in rich feathered cloaks, and armed with long spears and helmets. In the second, were Kaoo, the chief of the priests, and his brethren, with idols of wicker-work of gigantic size, covered with feathers of different colours and red cloth. Their eyes were large pearl oysters, with a black mark fixed in the centre; while their mouths were marked with double rows of dogs' fangs. The whole had a most hideous appearance. In a third canoe were hogs and vegetables. The visitors, however, did not go on board, but, inviting the captain on shore, returned. Mr. King, who was at the observatory, ordered out the guard to receive the party. The king then threw a superb cloak over the captain's shoulders, and placed a helmet on his head: he then spread at his feet six other cloaks, all exceedingly beautiful; and his attendants brought four hogs and sugar-canes and bread-fruit and cocoa-nuts. The ceremony was concluded by the king exchanging names with Cook.

An old seaman greatly attached to Captain Cook died here, and was buried in the morai with the usual funeral service read over him; but the priests thought that they ought to do their part, and threw a dead hog and plantains into the grave, and for several nights sacrificed hogs and chanted their hymns.

When the ships were about to sail, a magnificent present of provisions was made to the captain; and Terreeoboo and Kaoo waited on him and entreated that he would leave his supposed son, Mr. King, behind. On the 4th of February the ship sailed, but met with very bad weather. During it they picked up two canoes, driven off the land, the people in them nearly exhausted. In this gale also the *Resolution* sprung her foremast, and fearing that, should the weather continue, another harbour might not be found, Cook returned, on the 10th of the month, to Karakakooa Bay.

It was observed by some of the explorers, on this occasion, that the conduct of the natives had now undergone an ominous change. The bay was found to be under taboo, and several circumstances occurred which gave evidence that, from some cause or other, the English were regarded by the natives with suspicion. And this breach was unhappily widened by some of the common causes of dispute. For instance,—some people from the island visiting the *Discovery*, after the taboo was removed, went off with several articles they had stolen, whereupon the ship opened fire on the fugitives, and a chief on shore was killed. The stolen articles were soon returned, but an officer commanding a party on shore, not knowing this, seized a canoe belonging to Pareea. In a squabble which ensued that chief was knocked down. Captain Cook, also, not knowing that the articles had been brought back, followed the supposed thieves for several miles into the interior, when, on its getting dark, he returned unmolested on board.

The next morning, the *Discovery's* cutter was found to have been carried off, and Captain Cook resolved to seize the king and hold him captive till the boat was returned. For this purpose, loading his double-barrelled gun, he went on shore with Mr. Phillips and nine marines. Mr. King ordered the marines to remain within the tents; to load their pieces with ball; and not to quit their arms. He then went up to the huts of the priests, and endeavoured to quiet their alarm, assuring them that no one would be hurt. Captain Cook, meantime, proceeded to the king's house, and found him just awake. He easily persuaded the old man to come on board with two of his sons; but as they were embarking one of his wives came down and entreated him not to go off.

A vast number of people now began to collect, armed with all sorts of weapons and their war mats. Captain Cook held the king's hand, and pressed him to come on, but finding that the lives of many natives might be sacrificed if he persisted in the attempt, he abandoned it, and only now thought of how he might best draw off his party. Unfortunately, the boats stationed in the bay had fired at some canoes trying to get out, and killed a chief of the first rank. This news quickly reached the hostile natives. Mr. Phillips, on this, withdrew his men to some rocks close to the water side.

The natives now began to throw stones, and one man especially, threatened the captain with his dagger. In defence he fired. As the barrel was only loaded with small shot it killed no one. The other barrel had a ball in it, with which a man was killed. By this time the marines had begun to fire, and the captain turned round, either to order them to cease, or to direct the boats to come in, when a tall man struck him on the back with a long club, and he fell forward on his hands and knees, letting his fowling-piece drop. A chief with a long dagger now plunged it into his back; he fell under the water, and the natives who crowded round prevented him from rising. Nothing more was seen of him. All was now horror and confusion. The natives pressed on the marines, four of whom were killed before they could reach the boats, and another who could not swim remained struggling in the water, when Lieutenant Phillips, with heroic gallantry, leaped overboard, and, though badly wounded himself, brought the man safely on board the pinnace. Though the boats still kept up a hot fire, the chiefs were seen plunging their daggers in the body of Cook, seemingly with the idea that they were consecrated by the death of so great a man. It was said that old Koah, who had been long suspected, had been seen going about with a dagger hid under his cloak for the purpose, it was supposed, of killing Captain Cook or some of his officers.

All this time, Lieutenant King with a party of men, had remained on shore, at the observatory near the morai. Before long the natives began to attack them, but met with so warm a reception that they willingly agreed to a truce. As soon as the murderers of Cook had retired, a party of young midshipmen pulled to the shore in a skiff, where they saw the bodies of the marines lying without sign of life; but the danger of landing was too great to be risked.

Mr. King went on shore, to try and negotiate for the body of Cook. On the 15th, a man who had been his constant attendant came off with some human flesh, saying that the rest had been burnt; but that the head, and bones, and hands, were in possession of the king. The natives even now would not believe that Rono was killed. When they saw him fall, they cried out, "This is not

Rono!" Others inquired when he would come back, and whether he would punish them. An order had been given to fire some houses, but unfortunately the flames communicated to the priests' dwellings, all of which were consumed, though they had been the best friends to the English. Several people were shot attempting to escape. On the 18th, King Terreeoboo sent a chief with presents to sue for peace; and on the 20th, the hands, and various parts of the body of Cook were brought on board, wrapped in a quantity of fine cloth, and covered with a cloak of black and white feathers. The feet and other parts were returned the next day, and being placed in a coffin, they were committed to the deep with the usual naval honours.

We may imagine the feelings of the members of the expedition as they witnessed the ceremony, and thought that he who had been so long their chief, and who had led them successfully through so many dangers, was no more. The officers might have felt many vain regrets; they might have asked themselves whether all had been done that could have been done to save the valuable life which had been so cruelly sacrificed, and whether the object which had been attempted was adequate to the risk that had been run. So furious was the rage of the crews of the two ships, that they almost mutinied against their officers, when prevented from going on shore as they desired, to wreak their vengeance on the heads of the natives. It is remarkable that Captain Clerke had received orders to go on shore and seize the king; but, suffering from the consumption which was rapidly hurrying him to his grave, he was too weak to leave his cabin; and on hearing this, Cook immediately exclaimed that he would go himself.

Captain Cook was in the fifty-first year of his age when he was thus suddenly cut off. He was a man of great intelligence, perseverance, energy, and determination. He possessed a calm judgment, and cool courage under the most trying difficulties. As a seaman, he was probably unsurpassed. By employing every moment he could snatch from his professional duties, with the aid of such books as came to his hand, he made himself a good mathematician and a first-rate astronomer, while few officers of his day could have equalled him as a marine surveyor and draughtsman. All subsequent navigators who have visited the regions he traversed have borne evidence to the great accuracy of his surveys, and the exactness with which he laid down on his charts the numerous lands he discovered.

Various opinions have been expressed as to Captain Cook's temper. That he was at times hasty and irritable, there seems to be no doubt; but this fault was greatly counterbalanced by his kind-hearted and humane disposition. He seems to have had the power of attracting both officers and men to his person; hence many who had accompanied him in his first voyage volunteered to serve under him again in his subsequent expeditions. At the same time, he was stern and determined, though always just; and he considered it his duty, when necessary, to carry out to the full the rigid discipline of the navy in those days. He was a kind and affectionate husband and father, and it is said that his portrait at Greenwich Hospital, from which numerous copies have been made, does not convey a satisfactory idea of the ordinary expression of his countenance. It was painted at the earnest desire of Sir Joseph Banks, by Sir Nathaniel Dance, just before Cook left England on his last expedition, and as the mind of the navigator was probably far away on board his vessels, the grave and preoccupied expression which the portrait exhibits is fully accounted for.

His ability as a seaman, and his calmness in danger, inspired the most perfect confidence in all who served under him, so that in times of the greatest trial he could always reckon on being implicitly obeyed; it is said that, placing reliance on his officers, after he had given his directions, he would retire to rest and sleep as soundly as though no danger were near. Such is the character drawn of the great navigator by those who knew him;

CAPTAIN COOK. FROM THE PORTRAIT BY DANCE.

but we shall form a more just estimate of him if we consider the work he accomplished. We have only to compare a chart of the Pacific before Cook's time, and to note the wide blanks and the erroneous position of lands, with one drawn from his surveys, to see at a glance the extent of his discoveries: but a still higher estimation will be formed of them if we judge of them by their value to the present generation. Let us consider the importance of his admirable survey of the whole eastern coast of New Holland, showing its vast size and insular character. Not less important was his survey of the island of New Zealand, which with New Holland, or Australia, are now among the most valuable possessions of the British crown. He discovered New Caledonia, and surveyed most of the islands of the New Hebrides, and other islands in the Austral Ocean. He made known to the world the larger portion of the Friendly Islands, or Tonga group, as also of the Marquesas. Nothing can surpass the general accuracy of his description of the habits and customs of the inhabitants of Otaheite. He completed the discovery and survey of the Society Islands. He was successful in his search for Easter, or Davis Island, which had in vain been looked for by several previous navigators. He visited the groups of the Low, or Coral Archipelago, and discovered the numerous separate islands of Norfolk, Botany, Palmerston, Hervey, Savage, Mangaia, Watceoo, Otakootaia, Turtle, Toobouai, and Christmas. His most important discovery was his last—that of the Sandwich Islands—since become an independent and semi-civilized kingdom. He sailed along the North American coast, where, from unavoidable circumstances, his surveys were less accurate than usual. They were, however, completed many years after by his follower, Captain Vancouver. He ascertained the breadth of the strait between America and Asia to be eighteen leagues, a point left unsettled by Behring, and many years passed before any navigator penetrated farther to the north than he had done. His explorations in the Antarctic Ocean showed a hardihood and determination seldom surpassed. He brought to light Sandwich Land, settled the position of Kerguelen's Land, as also the Isle

Grande of La Roche, while he made a survey, long unsurpassed, of the southern shores of Terra del Fuego. Such is a rough and rapid sketch of the discoveries made by Cook during his three voyages; but what he, with justice, chiefly prided himself on, was the means by which he successfully maintained his crews in perfect health during his second and third voyages; and it is satisfactory to know that his successor in the command of the expedition, by following his system, brought home his ships' companies with few or no sick among them.*

As soon as the remains of Captain Cook had been committed to the deep, the taboo which had been placed on the bay by the chief Eappo was removed at the request of Captain Clerke, who said that, as the Orono was buried, the remembrance of what had passed was buried with him. As soon as it was known that the people might bring their provisions as usual, the ships were surrounded by canoes, and many chiefs came on board, expressing great sorrow at what had happened, and their satisfaction at the reconciliation which had taken place. Several friends who did not come themselves sent presents of large hogs and other provisions. Among the rest came the treacherous old Koah; but he was refused admittance.

Captain Clerke was anxious to visit the islands to leeward before the news of the events which had occurred at Owhyhee could reach them, and a bad effect be produced. He therefore gave orders to unmoor, and every preparation was made for quitting the bay. In the evening all the natives were sent on shore, and Eappo and the friendly Kaireekeea took an affectionate farewell. As the ships stood out of the bay, the natives collected in great

* A promotion of officers necessarily followed the death of Captain Cook. Captain Clerke, having succeeded to the command of the expedition, removed to the *Resolution*. By him, Mr. Gore was appointed captain of the *Discovery*, and the rest of the lieutenants obtained an addition of rank in their proper order.

numbers on the shore, and received the last farewells of the English with every mark of affection and good will.

The first island visited was that of Woahoo, which was found to be high and picturesque and thickly populated; the next was the island of Atooi. A party was here sent on shore to fill the casks with water, when the natives collected in great numbers, threatening to attack them, and it was with difficulty that they were enabled to reach the boats and return on board ship. The next day, however, some chiefs arrived on the spot; and the day after Mr. King, who commanded the party, going on shore, found the whole distance to the watering place marked with little white flags, and the English were not in the slightest degree molested. While the ships were at this island it was ascertained that some goats which were left there at the first visit of the English soon increased in number, and had bidden fair to stock the island, when a quarrel took place about them, and the animals were killed. A contest between two tribes or families was still going on about the matter, in which several people had lost their lives.

It was now the 12th of March, and preparations were made for quitting the islands and proceeding on the search for a passage through Behring's Straits into the Atlantic. There was, from the first, very little prospect of its success. Captain Clerke was sinking rapidly with consumption, and every one but himself knew that his days were numbered. Still, in spite of his weakness, he kept up his spirits in a wonderful manner, and though fully aware that the cold climate he was going to encounter would prove injurious to his health, this did not prevent him from attempting to carry out the instructions of his late chief to the utmost of his power.

On the 15th of March, the ships left the Sandwich group and steered for the harbour of St. Peter and St. Paul. The ships encountered very severe weather on approaching the coast of Siberia. The rigging and decks were so completely coated with ice that it was not without great difficulty the ropes could be handled; and the crew sensibly felt the change from the warm temperature to which they had been so long accustomed. To add to their difficulties, the *Resolution* sprang a serious leak, and split her second suit of sails. As the decks below were deluged with water, the only place in which the sail makers could work was in the cabin of their dying captain. At length, on the 28th of April, the harbour of St. Peter and St. Paul was reached. The town was found to consist of about thirty miserable log huts and small conical buildings raised on poles. The commandant was a sergeant, with a few men under him. The appearance of the expedition at first caused great consternation among the inhabitants. This arose from the circumstance that the celebrated Polish exile Beniowski had, a short time before, made his escape from Bolcheretsk with a couple of vessels and a considerable number of men. It was supposed that the exploring squadron was in some way connected with him. Another opinion was that the strangers were French, at that time enemies of the Russians. Fortunately, a German of the name of Port was at the place, and as Mr. Webber spoke German well, the intercommunication was speedily established, and as soon as the Russians were convinced that their visitors were English, nothing could exceed their kindness and hospitality. As provisions were, however, very dear here, Captain Clerke despatched Captain Gore and Mr. King, with Mr. Webber and the German, to visit Major Behm, the governor of Bolcheretsk, in order to obtain a supply through him. They travelled partly in boats and canoes, and partly in sleighs drawn by dogs, and were well wrapped up in skins to protect them from the cold. On their arrival at Bolcheretsk, they were received with the greatest kindness and hospitality by Major Behm and the officers of the garrison. These kind-hearted and liberal men would not allow the English to pay for such stores as the town could produce. Among other things, they presented the ships' companies with three bags of tobacco of a hundred weight each, and loaf sugar for the officers, while Madame Behm sent several delicacies to poor Captain Clerke. Major Behm accompanied the English officers to the ships, and made arrangements that stores should be sent from Okotsk to meet them on their return, should they fail to discover the passage of which they were in search. It is worthy of remark that when the English seamen received the tobacco which had been sent them from Bolcheretsk, they begged that their own allowance of grog might be stopped, and that it might be presented to the Russian garrison, who they understood were in want of spirits. Knowing the value a sailor sets on his grog, the feeling of gratitude which prompted the proposal will be the better appreciated. The generous Russian would however accept but a very small portion of what was offered. As Major Behm was on the point of returning to St. Petersburg, Captain Clerke, feeling sure that he was a man of the strictest honour, resolved to entrust him with a copy of the journal of the voyage, and an account of all transactions up to the arrival of the ships in the harbour of St. Peter and St. Paul. Mr. Bayley and Mr. King also sent home an account of all the astronomical and other scientific observations made during the voyage. These were duly delivered within a few months from the time of their being entrusted to Major Behm.

It is remarkable that on the arrival of the expedition in the harbour of St. Peter and St. Paul, the whole Russian garrison of the place were found to be suffering more or less from scurvy, many of the men being in the last stage of that disease. They were immediately placed under the care of the English surgeons, and by a free use of sour-kraut and sweet-wort they nearly all quickly recovered. Through the exertions of Major Behm a supply of rye-flour was furnished to the ships, and a bullock was sent on board, which was served out to the men on Sunday. It was the first fresh beef they had tasted since leaving the Cape of Good Hope, two years and a half before. Twenty head of cattle were afterwards sent on board, with other supplies, and the English themselves caught with their nets an abundance of fine fish.

On the 12th of June the ships were unmoored for the purpose of putting to sea, but it was not till the 16th that they were able to get clear of the bay. The eruption of a neighbouring volcano took place at this time, which covered the decks with cinders and small stones. From the first the ships encountered bad weather. The intense cold severely tried the crews. The men had taken no care of their fur jackets and other warm clothing, but they had been collected by their officers and cased up in casks to be produced when most required.

The expedition passed through Behring's Straits on the 5th of July, and having run along the coast of Asia, stretched across to that of America, with the intention of exploring it between the latitudes 68° and 69°. In this attempt, however, the explorers were disappointed, being stopped on the 7th by a large and compact field of ice connected with the land. They therefore altered their course to the westward in the hopes of finding some opening, and thus being able to get round to the north of the ice. They continued sailing in that direction till the 9th, for nearly forty leagues, without discovering an opening. Still their dying chief persevered in his efforts till the 27th, although unable to penetrate farther north than 70° 33′, which was five leagues short of the point which had been gained the previous year. In the attempt the *Discovery* was nearly lost, and received very severe damage. She became so entangled by several large pieces of ice that her way was stopped, and immediately dropping bodily to leeward, she fell broadside on to the edge of a considerable mass. At the same time, there being an open sea to windward, the surf made her strike violently on it. The mass of ice, however, at length either so far removed or broke as to set the ship at liberty, when another attempt to escape was made; but, unfortunately, before she gathered sufficient way to be under command she again fell to leeward on another fragment. The swell now making it unsafe to lie to windward of the ice, and there being no prospect of getting clear, the ship was pushed into a small opening, the sails were furled, and she was made fast with ice-hooks. In this dangerous position she was seen at noon by her consort, a fresh gale driving more ice towards her. It is easy to conceive the anxiety felt on board the *Resolution*, which was kept in the neighbourhood, firing a gun every half-hour. At last, towards evening, there was a shift of wind, and by nine o'clock the *Discovery* appeared, having, by setting all sail, forced her way out of the ice. She had, however, lost a considerable amount of sheathing from the bows, and had become very leaky from the blows received.

While in these latitudes several sea-horses were killed, which the seamen were persuaded without much difficulty to eat in preference to their salt provisions. Two white bears were also killed, which, though having a somewhat fishy taste, were considered dainties. Finding that all prospect of carrying the ships through any passage which might exist to the eastward was utterly hopeless, Captain Clerke announced his intention of returning to Awatska Bay to repair damages, and thence to continue the voyage in the direction of Japan. Joy brightened every countenance as soon as these resolutions were made known. All were heartily tired of a navigation full of danger, in which the utmost perseverance had not been repaid with the slightest prospect of success. Notwithstanding the tedious voyage to be made and the

AMONG THE ICEBERGS.

immense distance to be run, every one seemed to feel and speak as though they were once again approaching the shores of Old England.

There was one, however—the gallant commander of the expedition, Captain Clerke—who was destined never again to see his native land. On the 17th he was too weak to get out of bed, and therefore gave directions that all orders should be received from Mr. King. On the morning of the 22nd of August he breathed his last, to the deep regret of all who served under him. He had spent the whole of his life at sea from his earliest boyhood. He had been in several actions, and in one, between the *Bellona* and *Courageux*, having been stationed in the mizen-top, he was carried overboard with the mast, but was taken up unhurt. He was a midshipman in the *Dolphin*, commanded by Commodore Byron on his first voyage round the world, and afterwards served on the American station. In 1768 he made his second voyage round the world, in the *Endeavour*, under Captain Cook, and returned a lieutenant. His third voyage of circumnavigation was in the *Resolution*, and on her return, in 1775, he was promoted to the rank of master and commander. When Captain Cook's third expedition was determined on he was appointed to command under him.

On the 23rd the ships again anchored in the harbour of St. Peter and St. Paul. No sooner had they brought up than their old friend the sergeant came on board, and all were greatly affected when he announced that he had brought some fruit for their captain.

The charge of the expedition now devolved on Captain Gore, who took command of the *Resolution*, while Captain King was appointed to the *Discovery*. Captain Gore immediately sent off an express to Bolcheretsk, requesting to be supplied with sixteen head of cattle. The stores from the *Discovery* being landed, attempts were made to repair the damages she had received. On stripping off the sheathing, three feet of the third strake under the wale were found to be stove in, and the timbers within started. The farther they proceeded in removing the sheathing, the more they discovered the decayed state of the ship's hull. The chief damage was repaired with a birch tree which had been cut down when they were there before, and was the only one in the neighbourhood large enough for the purpose; but Captain King gave orders that no more sheathing should be ripped off, being apprehensive that further decayed planks might be met with which it would be impossible to replace. This condition of his ship could not have been a pleasant subject of contemplation to the commander, when he considered that he had yet more than half the circuit of the world to make before he could reach home.

Large quantities of salmon were now caught with the seine, and salted for sea stores, and the sea-horse blubber was also boiled down for oil, all the candles having been long expended.

On Sunday the 29th, the remains of Captain Clerke were interred with all the solemnity possible, under a tree in a spot which the Russian Papa, or priest, of the settlement said he believed would form the centre of a new church it was proposed shortly to build. The officers and men of both ships walked in procession to the grave, attended by the Russian garrison, while the ships fired minute guns, and the service being ended, the marines fired three volleys.

The remainder of the time in the harbour was spent in waiting for stores, in further repairing the ships, in two or three bear-hunting expeditions, in entertaining the garrison and natives in return for the hospitality which had been received, and in receiving a visit from the acting governor and other Russian officers.

On the 9th of October, the ships having cleared the entrance of Awatska Bay, steered to the southward for the purpose of examining the islands to the north of Japan, and then proceeding on to Macao. The condition of the ships' hulls and rigging rendered it dangerous to make any more prolonged explorations. Even the larger part of this plan it was found impossible to follow, for strong westerly winds blowing they were driven off the land, and after passing Japan they anchored at Macao. Here, not without some delay and difficulty, they procured the stores they required; Captain King having to make an excursion to Canton for the purpose. He here sold about twenty sea otter and other skins, belonging chiefly to their deceased commanders, for the sum of eight hundred dollars. On returning, he found that the larger portion of those on board had been sold and had realized not much less than two thousand pounds. The large profits on the skins, which had been looked upon as of little value beforehand, had so excited the minds of the men that two of them made off with a six-oared cutter for the purpose of returning to North America; and as they were not overtaken, they probably very soon perished.

The reports brought home by the expedition probably set on foot that trade in furs with the west coast of North America which afterwards became of considerable importance. In consequence of hearing at Macao of the war which had broken out between England and France, the ships mounted all their guns; but Captain Gore being informed at the same time that the French had issued orders to their cruisers that the ships under the command of Captain Cook should be treated as belonging to neutral or friendly powers, resolved himself to preserve throughout the remainder of the voyage the strictest neutrality.

The expedition left Macao on the 12th of January, 1780, and on the 20th, anchored in a harbour of Pulo Condore. Here a supply of buffaloes was obtained. They were large animals, and very wild. Two were kept on board the *Discovery* by Captain King, who intended to take them to England. They soon became perfectly tame, but, unfortunately, one of them suffered a severe injury, and both were killed.

On leaving Pulo Condore, the ships passed through the Straits of Banca, in sight of the island of Sumatra. The *Resolution* brought up off the island of Cracatoa, in the Straits of Sunda, and filled up her casks with water, which the *Discovery* was unable to do, in consequence of being becalmed. On reaching Cape Town, the English were treated with the same kindness and attention which they had received on their former visits. Here they obtained confirmation of the intelligence that the French had given directions to their cruisers not to molest them. Having taken their stores on board, they sailed out of Table Bay on the 9th of May, and on the 12th of June, passed the equator for the fourth time during their voyage. The ships made the coast of Ireland on the 12th of August, but southerly winds compelled them to run to the north. On the 4th October, the ships arrived at the Nore, after an absence of four years, two months, and twenty-two days. During that time the *Resolution* had lost but five men by sickness, three of whom were in a precarious state of health when leaving England, while the *Discovery* did not lose a man. It is remarkable that during the whole time they were at sea the ships never lost sight of each other for a day together, except twice; the first time owing to an accident which happened to the *Discovery* off the coast of Owhyhee; and the second, to the fogs that were met with at the entrance of Awatska Bay—a stronger proof cannot be given of the skill and vigilance of the subaltern officers, to whom the merit of this entirely belonged.

The death of Captain Cook was already known in England by means of the despatches sent home through Major Behm. All that a nation could do was done to testify respect for his memory. His widow received a pension of 200*l.* a year, and each of his children had 25*l.* a year settled on them. Other sums were granted to his widow, and medals were struck to commemorate his achievements, while a coat of arms was granted to his family.

Of his six children, three died in their infancy, and the other three were cut off in their early manhood. The second, Nathaniel, a promising youth, was lost when a midshipman on board the *Thunderer*, in a hurricane off Jamaica, on the 3rd of October, 1780. The youngest, Hugh, was intended for the ministry, and died at Oxford, in the 17th year of his age. The eldest, James, who was in the navy, commanded the *Spitfire* sloop-of-war. He was drowned in 1794, at the age of thirty, when attempting to push off from Poole during a gale of wind to rejoin his ship.

It is said the bereaved mother, on receiving tidings of the death of her last surviving son, destroyed all the letters she had received from her husband, in the vain hope of banishing recollection of the past. She survived, however, to the year 1835, when she died at the age of ninety-three.

A handsome piece of plate was presented to Major Behm, in acknowledgment of the attention and liberality with which he treated the English in Siberia; while gold medals were offered to the French king for his generous orders with regard to the ships of the expedition, as also to the empress of Russia, as it was in her dominions, and by one of her officers, they had been so liberally treated.

CHAPTER V.

SUBSEQUENT HISTORY OF POLYNESIA.

IN the concluding pages of this work it is proposed to give a brief sketch of the progress of Christianity and civilization in the islands of the Pacific visited by Captain Cook.*

The accounts brought home by the discoverers of the degraded moral condition of the islanders stirred up the hearts of Christians in England; and when, in 1795, the London Missionary Society was formed, one of its first proceedings was to send to those distant lands the gospel of Christ's salvation.

They began their labours upon an extensive scale. They purchased a ship, and sent out twenty-five labourers to commence missions simultaneously at the Marquesan, Tahitian, and Friendly Islands.

The following is the account given of the reception of this band of Christian evangelists:—

"On the 7th of March, 1797, the first missionaries from the *Duff* went on shore, and were met on the beach by the king, Pomare, and his queen. By them they were kindly welcomed, as well as by Paitia, an aged chief of the district. They were conducted to a large, oval-shaped native house, which had been but

---

* Australia, Tasmania, and New Zealand, having become parts of the British empire, and colonized by British subjects, are not included in this sketch; their history belongs to that of the mother country. The wonderful progress they have made is due to the influx of European settlers, not to the elevation of the native races.

recently finished for Captain Bligh, whom they expected to return. Their dwelling was pleasantly situated on the western side of the river, near the extremity of Point Venus. The islanders were delighted to behold foreigners coming to take up their permanent residence among them; as those they had heretofore seen had been transient visitors.

"The inhabitants of Tahiti having never seen any European females or children, were filled with amazement and delight when the wives and children of the missionaries landed. Several times during the first days of their residence on shore large parties arrived from different places, in front of the house, requesting that the white women and children would come to the door and show themselves. The chiefs and people were not satisfied with giving them the large and commodious " Fare Beritani" (British house), as they called the one they had built for Captain Bligh, but readily and cheerfully ceded to Captain Wilson and the missionaries, in an official and formal manner, the district of Matavai, in which their habitation was situated. The king and queen, with other branches of the royal family, and the most influential persons in the nation were present; and Haamanemane, an aged chief of Raiatea, and chief priest of Tahiti, was the principal agent for the natives on this occasion.

"Whatever advantages the king or chiefs might expect to derive from this settlement on the island, it must not be supposed that any desire to receive moral or religious instruction formed a part. A desire to possess European property, and to receive the assistance of the Europeans in the exercise of the mechanical arts, or in their wars, was probably the motive by which the natives were most strongly influenced.

"Having landed ten missionaries at Tongataboo, in the Friendly Islands, Captain Wilson visited and surveyed several of the Marquesan Islands, and left Mr. Crook, a missionary, there. He then returned to Tahiti; and on the 6th of July the *Duff* again anchored in Matavai Bay. The health of the missionaries had not been affected by the climate. The conduct of the natives had been friendly and respectful; and supplies in abundance had been furnished during his absence. On the 4th of August, 1797, the *Duff* finally sailed from the bay. The missionaries returning from the ship, as well as those on shore, watched her course as she slowly receded from their view under no ordinary sensations. They now felt that they were cut off from all but Divine guidance, protection, and support, and had parted with those by whose counsels and presence they had been assisted in entering upon their labours, but whom on earth they did not expect to meet again.

"Their acquaintance with the most useful of the mechanic arts not only delighted the natives, but raised the missionaries in their estimation, and led them to desire their friendship. This was strikingly evinced on several occasions, when they beheld them use their carpenters' tools, cut with a saw a number of boards out of a tree, which they had never thought it possible to split into more than two, and make with these chests and articles of furniture. When they beheld a boat built, upwards of twenty feet long, and six tons burden, they were pleased and surprised; but when the blacksmith's shop was erected, and the forge and anvil were first employed on their shores, they were filled with astonishment. When the heated iron was hammered on the anvil, and the sparks flew among them, they fancied it was spitting at them, and were frightened, as they also were with the hissing occasioned by immersing it in water; yet they were delighted to see the facility with which a bar of iron was thus converted into hatchets, adzes, fish-spears, fish-hooks, and other things. Pomare, entering one day when the blacksmith was employed, after gazing a few minutes at the work, was so transported at what he saw, that he caught up the smith in his arms, and, unmindful of the dirt and perspiration inseparable from his occupation, most cordially embraced him, and saluted him, according to the custom of his country, by touching noses." *

It is not to be wondered at that the favourable reports sent home by these missionaries encouraged those who received them to believe that almost all difficulties had already been, or were in a fair way of being speedily overcome, and that these distant islands were, to use the figurative language of Scripture, "stretch-out their hands unto God." They did not know—it was wisely and mercifully hidden from them—that a long night of toil had yet to be passed before the dawn of that better day they longed to see, and for which they prayed and strove.

"Decisive and extensive as the change has since become," says the writer just quoted, "it was long before any salutary effects appeared as the result of their endeavours; and although the scene is now one of loveliness and quietude, cheerful, yet placid as the smooth waters of the bay, it has often worn a very different aspect. Here the first missionaries frequently heard the song accompanying the licentious areois dance, the deafening noise of the worship, and saw the human victim carried by for sacrifice. Here, too they often heard the startling cry of war, and saw their frightened neighbours fly before the murderous spear and plundering hand of lawless power. The invader's torch reduced the native hut to ashes, while the lurid flame seared the green foliage of the trees, and clouds of smoke, rising up among their groves, darkened for a time surrounding objects. On such occasions, and they were not infrequent, the contrast between the country and the inhabitants must have been most affecting; appearing as if the demons of darkness had lighted up infernal fires in the bowers of paradise."

* Abridged from "Polynesian Researches," by the Rev. W. Ellis.

These representations probably did not reach England until after the missionaries had been some time in the islands; and meanwhile the ship *Duff* was sent out a second time with a strong reinforcement of thirty additional labourers.

"God, however, for a time appeared to disappoint all their expectations; for this hitherto favoured ship was captured by the *Buonaparte* privateer. The property was entirely lost; and the missionaries, with their families, after suffering many difficulties and privations, returned to England." In addition to this trial, "the Marquesan mission failed. At Tongataboo some of the missionaries lost their lives, and that mission was, in consequence of a series of disastrous circumstances, abandoned." More discouragements were in store, for "those settled at Tahiti under such favourable auspices had, from fear of their lives, nearly all fled to New South Wales; so that, after a few years, very little remained of this splendid embassy of Christian mercy to the South Seas. A few of the brethren, however, never abandoned their posts; and others returned after having been a short time absent."

In addition to all other disappointments, these returned missionaries and their brethren appeared to be labouring in vain, and spending their strength for nought. "For sixteen years," we are told, "notwithstanding the untiring zeal, the incessant journeys, the faithful exhortations of these devoted men, no spirit of interest or inquiry appeared, no solitary instance of conversion took place; the wars of the natives continued frequent and desolating, and their idolatries abominable and cruel. The heavens above seemed to be as brass, and the earth as iron.

"At length," continues the Christian historian, "two native servants, formerly in the families of the missionaries, had received, unknown to them, some favourable impressions, and had united together for prayer. To these many other persons had attached themselves, so that, on the return of the missionaries to Tahiti, at the termination of the war, they found a great number of 'pure Atua,' or 'praying people;' and they had little else to do but to help forward the work which God had so unexpectedly and wonderfully commenced.

"Another circumstance demanding special observation in reference to the commencement of the great work at Tahiti is that, discouraged by so many years of fruitless toil, the directors of the Society entertained serious thoughts of abandoning the mission altogether. A few undeviating friends of that field of missionary enterprise, however, opposed the measure." Their persuasions prevailed; and after special and earnest prayer to God, instead of a recal, "letters of encouragement were written to the missionaries. And while the vessel which carried these letters was on her passage to Tahiti, another ship was conveying to England not only the news of the entire overthrow of idolatry, but also the rejected idols of the people. Thus was fulfilled the gracious promise, 'Before they call I will answer, and while they are yet speaking I will hear.'" *

Among the converts of Tahiti was the king, Pomare, who having been severely tried by the rebellion of some part of his subjects, became deeply impressed with the insufficiency of his idol gods to help him, and, after having recalled the banished missionaries, listened to their instructions, and embraced the faith of Christianity. His example being followed by the majority of his people, the idols were renounced, as already mentioned; and, as soon as he was firmly re-established on his throne, he built a Christian church, which was opened in the year 1819; and the first baptism of a native Tahitian was administered within its walls, in the presence of upwards of four thousand spectators, the king himself being the subject of the rite.

* Williams's "Missionary Enterprises in the South Sea Islands."

Thus inaugurating a new era in his reign, Pomare introduced a code of useful laws, and brought about many much-needed reforms in his kingdom. He not only proved himself a warm friend of the missionaries, but gave them valuable assistance in the important work of translating the Scriptures into the Tahitian tongue—a fact which proves Pomare to have been a man of no ordinary natural abilities. He did not live long enough, however, to see the completion of this design, but, dying in 1821, he left it to his daughter, who succeeded him in his sovereignty, taking her father's name, Pomare.

Among the laws passed in Tahiti at this time was one prohibiting the importation and sale of ardent spirits, which had been so great a bane to the people; and the law was found to be beneficial to the prosperity and moral character of the country, though the foreign traders who had made a large profit by its importation were enraged when this source of gain was cut off.

In 1835 the translation of the Bible was completed, and its publication was attended and followed by happy accompaniments and results. At this time the number of natives in communion with the Christian churches throughout the island numbered over two thousand; and among the candidates for Church fellowship were the queen herself, her husband, and her mother.

And now arose a dark cloud which, for a time, brought great distress upon the faithful followers of Christ in Tahiti, and was permitted to try their constancy, while at the same time the freedom and liberty and prosperity of the island were grievously threatened. It may be stated, in few words, that Louis-Philippe, at that time king of the French, had set his eyes on Tahiti, and had introduced his agents into the country that an excuse might be found for taking possession of the island. First the consuls insisted that as the law prohibiting the introduction of liquor interfered with trade, it should be rescinded. This was firmly refused. Then two

French Roman Catholic priests were landed, but were ordered by the queen to quit the country. They complied; but one shortly returned with a companion, and the French admiral, appearing directly afterwards, insisted, with his guns bearing on the town, that they should be allowed to remain, and demanded 400*l.* for the injury they had been supposed to suffer when compelled to quit the island.

French ships continued to be sent at frequent intervals, and French troops were landed; the queen fled to a neighbouring island; the people fought bravely, but were defeated; the mission houses and stations were destroyed; the missionaries were driven out of the country, and Mr. Pritchard, who had been a missionary, and was now British consul, was imprisoned and otherwise ill-treated.

The Protestant missionary societies throughout Europe and America were indignant at this conduct of a civilized nation. In consequence of the representations of England, France desisted from her attacks on the other islands, but Tahiti fell into her power in 1846. The French, however, could not turn the people from the simple faith they had learned from the English missionaries. They chose ministers from their own people, and continued to meet and worship God with the simple forms to which they had been accustomed, and it is a remarkable fact that Romanism, notwithstanding its gorgeous ceremonies and corrupt practices, did not captivate them.

One only of their beloved missionaries was allowed to remain, the Rev. William Howe, as chaplain to the British consul, and who was ever ready to give the native pastors the benefit of his advice and assistance, though opposed by the Romish bishop and the priests. At length, through his earnest representations to the French Protestant missionary societies, an appeal was made to the Emperor Napoleon, who permitted French Protestant missionaries to go out. They were cordially received by Mr. Howe and the native preachers, and the greater part of the Romish priests were subsequently withdrawn.

In the words of a recent report of the British and Foreign Bible Society,* "The Bible still continues to supply the inhabitants of the Tahitian group of islands with a safe guide amidst all the errors to which they are exposed, and a sure ground of hope in the prospect of eternity. The sale and distribution of the Scriptures progresses steadily, and the strong attachment of the people to the truths of the Gospel remains unabated, and forms a security against the seductions of popery, which it is not easy to over-estimate. Games and sports and feasts are all alike tried to seduce the natives from their allegiance to Him whom they have learnt to love and to serve; and though, through the weakness of the flesh, some are attracted and drawn aside, yet for the most part they soon become convinced of the emptiness and folly of these things, and return to the sound and wholesome food which they had been tempted to forsake."

After leaving Tahiti, the first place at which Captain Cook touched was the lovely and fertile island of Huaheine. This became the refuge of the first party of missionaries when, in 1808, they were driven from Tahiti; and it was afterwards visited by John Williams, Ellis, and others, accompanied by some chiefs from Eimeo, who purposed forming a mission there. As this place became, in a certain degree, the centre of operations, that particular missionary enterprise in the Society Islands is generally known as the Huaheine mission.

While Mr. Williams was residing at Huaheine, Tamatoa, the king of Raiatea, who had, while visiting Eimeo and Tahiti, learned

* That of 1868.

something of the principles of Christianity, arrived with several chiefs, entreating that missionaries might be sent to instruct their people in the truth. Messrs. Williams and Threlkeld promptly responded to the call, and accompanied the king back to Raiatea. The population of the island was at that time only thirteen hundred, though the island is the largest of the group, and, from its reputed sanctity, and from being the centre and head quarters of all the idolatries and abominations of the neighbouring islands, its chiefs exercised great authority over them.

Tamatoa, instructed by the Holy Spirit, and aided by others who had learnt something of the truths of Christianity, had for some time been labouring among his fellow islanders. He had himself been converted by what might well be considered a providential circumstance. Two years before, a small vessel, having on board the king Pomare, Mr. Wilson the missionary, and several Tahitians, had been driven by a storm from her anchorage at Eimeo down to Raiatea. Here they were hospitably received, and continued three months, the whole of which time was employed by Mr. Wilson and the king in preaching the Gospel to the inhabitants. The chief Tamatoa was among their principal converts.

After their teachers had departed, Tamatoa and his fellow inquirers felt an earnest desire to learn more of the truth. They built a place of worship; met together for mutual instruction; kept holy the sabbath, and put away their idols and heathen practices. Several times the heathens laid plots to destroy them, but were each time signally foiled in their wicked plans.

At length Tamatoa paid that memorable visit to Huaheine which resulted in Messrs. Williams and Threlkeld taking up their abode at Raiatea. Having collected the hitherto scattered inhabitants into villages, he built a substantial missionary house as a model, which was readily imitated. Places of worship and school-houses were also built; and though many years elapsed before the abominations of heathenism were eradicated, the great mass of the people became not only well educated and moral, but earnest and enlightened Christians. The satisfactory progress made by the inhabitants of the islands where Mr. Williams resided was owing, humanly speaking, to the wonderful rapidity with which he had acquired their language and was able to preach to them, in it, the Gospel of Jesus Christ.

Soon after the mission at Huaheine was established, Mr. Ellis set up a printing press, from which quickly issued the Gospel by Luke, 800 copies of which were sent to Raiatea. Small schoolbooks were also printed in the native language. The desire for instruction became general wherever missionary stations were established. Not only the children, but adults became scholars. During the hours of instruction other engagements were suspended, and the various scenes of busy occupation throughout the settlements forsaken.

Such was the picture to be seen at that time in several islands of the Society group. Borabora, or Bolabola, whose inhabitants in Cook's time had been the fiercest warriors of the neighbouring islands, yielded to the benign influence of the Gospel. The history of the last island visited by the great navigator before he left the eastern side of the Pacific for New Zealand, called by him Oheteroah, but known generally as Rurutu, is of great interest. It is situated about 250 miles to the south of Raiatea. A destructive pestilence having visited the island, two chiefs, one named Auura, built two canoes, and, with as many of the people as they could convey, left their native shores in search of a happier land, and to escape from their infuriated deities.

After touching at Tubuai, they were cast on the reef surrounding Maurua. Here, instead of being murdered, as might once have been their fate, the starving voyagers were received with all kindness and charity. How was this? Through the agency of native teachers the people had learned the blessed truths of the Gospel, and were trying to obey its precepts. Auura and his companions, hearing that the white men who had brought to their seas that beautiful religion, the practical fruits of which they had just experienced, were living in the islands the summits of whose mountains they could see, set sail once more, with the desire of hearing from their own lips a fuller account of the religion they taught. They missed Borabora, but reached Raiatea. Here they remained rather more than three months. When they were landed, they were ignorant savages, wild in appearance and habits. Before they left Auura could read the Gospel of Matthew, had learned the greater part of the catechism drawn up for the natives, and could write correctly. Several others could do nearly as well, though previously ignorant that such an art as writing existed.

But these earnest men were not content to go back to their people alone; they entreated that some missionaries would accompany them. Two native deacons at once offered themselves, and were accepted. Auura's great fear was that many of his countrymen would have been carried off by the pestilence before the glad tidings of salvation could be preached to them. At that time a vessel belonging to a friend of the mission touched at Raiatea, and the captain agreed to carry Auura and his companions, with the missionaries, to their home.

Within fifteen months after this, Rurutu was visited by Dr. Tyerman and G. Bennet, Esq., who had been sent out by the directors of the London Missionary Society to visit their stations in the Pacific. When they reached it they were not certain what island it was, but were greatly surprised at seeing several neat-looking white houses at the head of the bay. A pier, a quarter of a mile in length, had been constructed of vast coral blocks, affording a convenient landing place. Besides the two comfortable missionary houses, there was a large place of worship, eighty feet by thirty-six, wattled, plastered, well floored and seated, built within a twelvemonth under the direction of the two native missionaries, who performed much of the work with their own hands. Many of the chiefs were dressed in European clothing, and all were attired in the most decent and becoming manner. Not a vestige of idolatry was to be seen, not an idol was to be found in the island.

Mr. Turnbull, in his account of a voyage he made to the Pacific in 1804, describes the way in which the then savage inhabitants of Raiatea attempted to cut off the ship in which he sailed. See the contrast in the conduct of the people of Rurutu shortly after they had embraced Christianity. Captain Chase commanded the *Falcon*, an American trader, which was cast away on a reef off their island. He says, "The natives have given us all the assistance in their power from the time the ship struck to the present moment. The first day, while landing the things from the ship, they were put into the hands of the natives, and carried up to the native mission house, a distance of half a mile, and not a single article of clothing was taken from any man belonging to the ship, though they had it in their power to have plundered us of everything that was landed. Since I have lived on shore, I and my officers and people have received the kindest treatment from the natives that can be imagined, for which I shall ever be thankful."

Aitutaki, one of the Hervey group, was another of the islands discovered by Captain Cook. It contained about two thousand inhabitants, described as especially wild and savage. Mr. Williams heard of it from Auura, and on a voyage to Sydney which he was compelled to take on account of the health of his wife, he landed on its shores two native missionaries, Papeiha and Vahapata. On first landing they were led by the people to the marae and given up to the gods; but their lives were spared and they were left at liberty.

Wars broke out in the island, and all their property was stolen; but they persevered in preaching the Gospel, and by degrees gained converts. The king, Tamatoa, became a Christian; but his old grandfather refused to give up his gods. While holding a high festival in their honour, a beloved daughter was taken ill. In vain he besought his gods to restore her to health; she died. In his rage, he ordered his son to set fire to his marae and to destroy it with his idols; two others caught fire near it, and the son was proceeding to burn others, when the people dragged him away, expecting to see him struck down by the vengeance of the outraged gods. As no evil consequences followed, the idolaters began to call in question the power of their deities.

Shortly after, a vessel arrived from Raiatea, bringing another missionary, with many books, and several pigs and goats, which Papeiha and his companion had promised the people. This raised the missionaries in their estimation, and they with one accord threw away all their idols, and resolved to listen to the teaching of the Gospel. On his return from Sydney, Mr. Williams, calling at Aitutaki, found that all the inhabitants had nominally embraced Christianity, while a chapel two hundred feet long had been built for the worship of the true God. They have now the entire Scriptures in their own language, and their desire after and reverence for the word of God is very remarkable.

The description given of the inhabitants of Aitutaki applies equally to numerous other islands of the Pacific, which have been for some time under missionary instruction, provided there are no ports where the crews of foreign vessels remain for any length of time, and set a bad example to the surrounding population.

Rarotonga, one of the Hervey group, about seven hundred miles south of Tahiti, and discovered by Williams in 1823, when the people were in the most savage condition, is now the chief missionary station in the Pacific. In 1839 a missionary college was established, the buildings consisting of a number of separate neat stone cottages, in which the married students and their wives could reside, a lecture-room, and a room for female classes. Up to 1844 thirty-three native missionaries, male and female, had received instruction, and six of the young men had gone forth as pioneers to Western Polynesia. Up to 1860 two hundred students had been admitted, a considerable number of whom were married, and the institution had been greatly enlarged in many respects. The course of instruction embraces theology, Church history, Biblical exposition, biography, geography, grammar, and composition of essays and sermons. The students are also taught several mechanical arts, and for two or three hours every day are employed in the workshop. At the printing establishment on the island a variety of works have been translated, printed, and bound. In three months, ending March, 1859, *Bogue's Lectures*, the *Pilgrim's Progress*, 1200 copies of *Voyages of Mission Ship*, hymn-books, Scripture lessons, and several other works were turned out of hand. The press-work of these various books, comprising nearly 300,000 sheets a-year, had all been performed by young men, the first fruits of missionary labours before their fathers had any written language.

We must now describe the present state of other solitary islands and groups discovered by Captain Cook. In the course of his second voyage (1774) he fell in with a low solitary island which, from the ferocity of the inhabitants, he called Savage Island. The inhabitants, numbering between 3000 and 4000, for very many years remained in the condition in which Cook found them. The first attempt to leave native missionaries was made by the Rev. John Williams in 1830. But the natives refused to receive them. In 1840, and in 1842, other attempts were made. In the latter year the Rev. A. Buzacott nearly lost his life.

TITIKAVEKA CHAPEL, RAROTONGA.

Still these visits had a good effect on the younger part of the population, who desired to see more of the strangers. Several found their way to Samoa, where they embraced the Gospel, and two of them, after a course of instruction at the training college in Samoa, were found well fitted to return and to spread its glad tidings among their benighted countrymen. They were accordingly conveyed to Savage Island in the *John Williams*, missionary ship, but were received with a good deal of suspicion by the natives, and only one remained. He narrowly escaped being put to death, but undauntedly persevered, and by degrees gathered converts around him. When visited in 1852 by the Rev. A. W. Murray, he had upwards of two hundred sincere believers gathered into a church, and many heathen practices had been abandoned by others.

In 1861 the *John Williams* conveyed Mr. and Mrs. Lawes to Savage Island. They were the first European missionaries appointed to labour there. Hundreds of men and women, all well clothed, were assembled on the shore to receive them. Outwardly not a vestige of heathenism remained among them. There were five good chapels in the island, one of which held eleven hundred, but it was too small for the congregation. Prayer meetings were frequently held, at which all the people in the district attended. On each occasion when they were held by Mr. Lawes, not less than eight hundred were present. The whole of the inhabitants are now professing Christians, and a very large proportion are earnest and enlightened believers.

The reader will call to mind the incidents of Captain Cook's visit to the Tonga, or Friendly group, the high state of cultivation in which he found the islands, the apparently friendly reception he met with from the chiefs, and their treacherous purposes to cut off the ship, as they shortly afterwards did a merchantman which visited their shores,—murdering most of the crew.

In consequence of Captain Cook's too favourable report, a number of missionaries were sent out by the London Missionary Society in the ship *Duff*, already mentioned, under the command of Captain Wilson. These pious men landed on the islands in 1797, but they made no apparent progress, and, war breaking out, three of them lost their lives, and the rest escaped to Sydney. This was in the year 1800.

In 1802, Mr. Lawry, of the Wesleyan Missionary Society, commenced a mission at Nukualofa in Tongataboo. Though compelled for a time to abandon it, he returned in 1826, and, through his instrumentality, Tubou, the king, and many of his chiefs and people, embraced Christianity. It is worthy of remark that, just before this time, the London Missionary Society had commenced a mission on the island; but they yielded up the field to the Wesleyans, while the latter retired from Samoa, where they had commenced a mission. The Wesleyans have since then laboured exclusively, and with most encouraging success, in the Friendly and Fiji Islands and New Zealand, leaving to the London Missionary Society the wide scope of the Pacific.

In 1827, the Revs. Nathaniel Turner and William Cross took up their residence at Nukualofa. At that time Josiah Tubou was king in Tonga. Taufaahau, now King George, was king only of Haabai, and Feenau was king of Vavou. The first became a Christian, as did his queen, and was baptized on the 10th of January, 1830. He died in 1845, Feenau having previously died; thus George became king in chief, and reigns over the three groups, Tonga, Haabai, and Vavou, or the whole of the Friendly Islands. The labours of the two zealous missionaries just mentioned were largely blessed, and when Tubou was baptized the congregation amounted to six hundred professing Christians.

King Josiah's reign was not altogether free from difficulties.

MISSIONARY CHURCH IN THE FIJI ISLANDS.

The heathen party was strong, and took up arms against him, being supported by some French Roman Catholic priests who had settled in the islands. They tried to embroil him, as they had already done Queen Pomare of Tahiti, with their own government, but were unsuccessful; and with the assistance of King George the rebels were put down.

King George had himself become a Christian, and a preacher, and contributed greatly to the spread of the gospel among his countrymen. He is thus described by Mr. Lawry after he had become sovereign of the whole group. It was in the large chapel at Nukualofa: "The king was in the pulpit. The attention of his audience was riveted while he expounded the words of our Lord, 'I am come that ye might have life.' The king is a tall graceful person; in the pulpit he was dressed in a black coat, and his manner was solemn and earnest. He held in his hand a small bound manuscript book, in which his sermon was written, but he seldom looked at it. His action was dignified; his delivery fluent and graceful, and not without majesty. His hearers hung upon his lips with earnest and increasing interest. Much of what he said was put interrogatively, a mode of address which is very acceptable among the Tongans. It was affecting to see this dignified man stretching out his hand over his people, and to observe that one of his little fingers had been cut off: this was formerly done as an offering to a heathen god, a custom among his people before they became Christians. But while he bore this mark of Pagan origin, he clearly showed that to him was grace given to preach among the Gentiles the unsearchable riches of Christ."

The Tongans have been especially blessed in having had several missionaries of high character, abilities, and zeal sent among them. There are schools sufficient for the wants of the whole population, under native teachers, and overlooked by the missionaries, whose duties are somewhat arduous. There is a training institution at Nukualofa, for missionaries, and for masters and mistresses of schools. There are also schools, or colleges, for the upper classes; indeed, many of the wants of a civilized and intelligent community are supplied in the Tonga Islands. The population of the whole group is supposed to amount to between thirty and forty thousand.

The islands of Western Polynesia—New Hebrides, Loyalty, and Britannia, were little known, or, at all events, little thought of, till the year 1839, when they were brought into melancholy prominence by the distressing tragedy which occurred in one of them, the island of Erromanga.

The Rev. John Williams, after his return from England in the previous year, sailed in the *Camden* missionary vessel, resolved to convey the Gospel message to the inhabitants of these remote islands, hitherto sunk in the deepest heathen darkness. It is not too much to say that there was no species of wickedness practised by heathens in any part of the world which could not have found its parallel in those countries. Barbarous rites, nameless abominations, and cannibalism in its most fearful forms, characterized the whole population. Mr. Williams was accompanied by several European, and a considerable number of native missionaries, who were to be landed as opportunities might offer, to preach the Gospel.

Having landed missionaries at the island of Tanna and elsewhere with every prospect of success, the *Camden* proceeded to Erromanga, off which island she arrived on the 20th of November, 1839. Here Mr. Williams, Mr. Harris, Mr. Cunningham, and Captain Morgan landed, and while the two former were at a distance from their companions, the natives attacked and killed them. The murder had been provoked, not by the crew of the *Camden*, but by that of some other ship, who had ruthlessly shot down several of the natives and carried off their provisions. Thus the innocent suffered for the guilty, and while the life of one eminent missionary was sacrificed, that of another was cut off at the commencement of what might have been a course of similar usefulness. Let it be added as an interesting fact that the murderer of John Williams was afterwards converted to God, and lived as a sincere and consistent Christian.

Notwithstanding the sad commencement of this missionary enterprise, it was resolved to pursue it with vigour. At Aneiteum, the first island of the New Hebrides visited by the missionary ship in 1841, two Samoan missionaries were landed. These devoted men had much to endure, and it was not till after years of toil that they saw any really satisfactory results from their labours. By degrees many came to seek instruction, some of whom abandoned their heathen practices; and subsequently other native teachers were introduced; but when, in 1848, the Rev. J. Geddie arrived at Aneiteum, he still found the great mass of the people fearfully degraded, and addicted to the most horrible cruelties. Soon after his arrival eight women were strangled:—one, an interesting young woman whose husband he had been attending till he died, he attempted to save, and was very nearly clubbed to death by her relatives in consequence.

A wonderful change is now evident. In 1858 there were sixty villages on the island, each of which had a school-house or a chapel, with a resident teacher. Nearly the whole of the New Testament, and some books of the Old, had been translated; and a large number of these lately degraded heathens could both read and write.

Fatuna is a small island, containing about a thousand inhabitants. Here Williams touched just before his death; but no teachers were left there. A couple of years afterwards, however, two Samoan evangelists, Samuela and Apela, were landed, the former accompanied by his wife. They laboured for four years with some success, when, a severe epidemic breaking out among the inhabitants, they were accused of being its cause, and were killed and eaten. Samuela's faithful wife was offered her life if she would become one of the wives of the chief. She replied, "I came to teach you what is right, not to sin amongst you." No sooner had she uttered the words, than she fell beneath the club of a savage. Notwithstanding this tragedy, missionaries from the lately heathen Aneiteum have gone to Fatuna, and many of the savages have been converted.

At Tanna, supposed to possess fifteen thousand inhabitants, Mr. Williams left three missionaries the day before he was murdered at Erromanga; but two of them soon died, the climate being more injurious to the natives of Eastern Polynesia than to Europeans. In 1842, Messrs Turner and Nisbet were sent to occupy the island; but were driven away by the savages, and sought shelter in Samoa. Native teachers from Aneiteum, however, took their places, and met with some success; and in 1858 several European missionaries landed on the island; and the larger part of the people have come to the truth.

With Erromanga the name of Williams will always be associated. After his death, native evangelists from Samoa and Rarotonga landed on its shores, but died, or were compelled to leave, from the effects of the climate. In 1857, the Rev. G. N. Gordon, and his wife, took up their residence on the island. They laboured on with considerable success, Oviladon, the chief of the district, being among the first-fruits of their toils. The greater number of the inhabitants of his district also became Christians.

An epidemic however broke out in 1860, and the heathen inhabitants of another district, believing that it was caused by the Christians, attacked the settlement, and killed Mr. and Mrs. Gordon. The day after, they were buried, amidst the tears and lamentations of the people; the native teacher, who had escaped, stood beside the grave, and delivered an address which powerfully affected the bystanders.

In the large island of Faté or Vaté, Christian teachers have been landed at different times, but some have been killed and eaten, and others have died of disease. In 1858, however, three teachers with their wives were landed under encouraging circumstances. From Nina, a small island near Tanna, several of the natives hearing of the wonderful things taking place on the latter island, proceeded thither to procure a teacher. In consequence of their application in 1858, the *John Williams* took them two from Aneiteum, who are now labouring successfully among them.

The Loyalty group must be briefly noticed. Native teachers were landed in 1841, and after they had induced many natives to abandon heathenism, the Messrs. Jones and Creagh arrived in the island in 1854. Their labours have been blessed; the Gospels and other parts of the Scriptures have been printed in the Nengonese language, and upwards of three thousand of the inhabitants are under Christian instruction, although a large number of the natives still follow their heathen customs.

The mission in Lifu was not commenced till 1843, when native evangelists were landed, and in 1858, two European missionaries arrived to take charge of the work. The inhabitants amount to about ten thousand, and of these very few, if any, now remain heathens, though it is to be feared the great mass of the converts can only be looked on as nominal Christians.

The small Britannia group near New Caledonia has been occupied by teachers from Rarotonga and Marè since 1837, but Roman Catholic priests have arrived on the principal island, sent, they say, by the French governor of New Caledonia. They have built a capital, called Port de France; but it is a penal colony, and free emigrants have not been attracted to its shores.

The last islands visited by Captain Cook were those to which he gave the name of the Sandwich Islands, and which now form the small but independent kingdom of Hawaii, having a capital called Honolulu, with a population of eleven thousand, not less than a thousand of whom are white foreigners. With its well-paved, lighted streets, its king's palace, its houses of parliament, its cathedral church, its numerous hotels, its police, and other accompaniments of high civilization, it is difficult to imagine that a hundred years ago this was the home of tattooed savages. To Englishmen in advanced years, indeed, the murder of Captain Cook at Owhyhee seems like an event that happened in their own childhood. And in truth, not fifty years ago the natives of Hawaii were ignorant and idolatrous heathens, while it is but as yesterday that a refined, elegant, and well-educated lady, the queen of those islands, was visiting England.

When Cook was killed Kalampupua was king. He was succeeded by his nephew Kamehamea I., who made himself sovereign of the entire group. When visited by Captain Vancouver in 1793, it is said that he requested that Christian missionaries might be sent to him. Whether Captain Vancouver delivered the message to the English government or not, no attention was paid to it. Captain Vancouver, however, returned the next year with some horned cattle and sheep, which he presented to the king, obtaining a promise that none should be killed for the space of ten years. This promise was faithfully kept; but so rapidly did the animals increase that they became exceedingly troublesome to the natives by injuring their fences and taro plantations. They were accordingly driven into the mountains, where they now form a source of considerable wealth to the nation.

Ramehamea was about to abolish the taboo system when he died in 1819, and was succeeded by his son Liholiho, who took the name of Kamehamea II. He carried into effect his father's intentions, and also destroyed his temples and gods.

In that very year the American Board of Missions resolved to send to the Sandwich Islands an efficient band of missionaries with three native youths who had been educated in the States. Joyful and totally unexpected news awaited them on their arrival. Idolatry was overthrown, and the king and most of his chiefs were ready to afford them protection and support. They had, however, an arduous task before them in their efforts to impart instruction to a population numbering at least 100,000, dwelling in eight islands, with a superficial area of 7000 square miles. Owhyhee alone, now written Hawaii, being 415 miles in circumference.

In 1824, there were 50 native teachers, and 2000 scholars, and so rapidly did education advance, that in 1831 there were 1100 schools, in which fully 1700 scholars had obtained the branches of a common education, and were able to read, write, and sum up simple accounts. The prime minister, seven leading chiefs, and the regent were members of the Christian church; and a very decided change was manifest in the general population.

Within a few years the language was reduced to a written form, and two printing presses were at work at Honolulu. A large edition of the Gospels in the Hawaii language, printed in the United States, was in circulation, and there were no less than 900 schools and 45,000 scholars. In 1853, after a great awakening, there were above 22,000 church members, and there were chapels at all the stations. One at Lahaina could hold 3000 persons.

In 1853, the mission of the American Board was dissolved, their object having been fully realized in Christianizing the people, planting churches, and making them self-supporting. Kamehamea III. the brother and successor of the king who died in England, reigned well and wisely till 1854. On his death, Prince Alexander Liholiho, a well educated and religiously disposed young man, became king. His wife is the Queen Emma who lately visited England. They lost their only son in 1862. This so affected the king that he never recovered from the shock.

At the present time a brother of the late king reigns over the kingdom under the title of Kamehamea v. His uncle had established a too democratic constitution; he has given the people one more suited to their ideas and the state of the country. The chamber of nobles and that of the representatives of the people are convoked every two years. It is their duty to make the laws and to vote supplies. Several foreigners are employed in the government, and the foreign population of English, Americans, French, and Germans is increasing rapidly.

The Hawaiians own a considerable number of vessels, which trade to China, California, British Columbia, and other parts of the Pacific. The national flag is composed of coloured stripes with the Union Jack of old England quartered in the corner. The independence of the island kingdom is guaranteed by England, France, and America, and it will probably continue, as it is at present, in advance of all the other states which may arise in the Pacific. With these signs of prosperity, it is no wonder that Romish priests are doing all in their power to spread their tenets through the Sandwich Islands. But the Bible and a free press will, it is devoutly to be hoped, triumph.

Among other publications constantly issuing from the Hawaiian press are several newspapers, both in English and the native language, which have a wide circulation. That there is a steady increase in the commerce of the country is shown by the exports of sugar, coffee, and other produce, while several manufactures have been introduced to give employment especially to the women. The port of Honolulu has long been the chief resort of whale ships in the Pacific, and now many others, trading between the coasts of America and Asia, call there for supplies.

Other islands and shores visited by Cook remain in much the same condition as in his day. The sorrowful history of the attempt to convey the Gospel to the inhabitants of Terra del Fuego, by Captain Allen Gardener, is too well known to require further mention. Java has been restored to its original masters, the Dutch; and the Cape of Good Hope is now a British colony. The great southern land of which Cook went in search has been found to exist, though its approach is guarded by immense barriers of ice; and the great problem of a north-west passage has been solved by the sacrifice of some of England's bravest sons.

Not much need be added in the closing paragraphs of this volume. In following the interesting narrative of the voyages of the eminent discoverer whose name is a household word in English biography, the reader, while he sees some things to regret, will award to him a well-deserved tribute of admiration for his courage and skill, his perseverance and enterprising spirit. One thing was set before him, and that one thing he did. His main object was scientific; his first voyage was undertaken to observe the transit of the planet Venus, the Royal Society having represented that important service would be rendered to the interests of astronomical science by the appointment of properly qualified individuals to observe that phenomenon. The second was in search of a southern continent, which at that time was a favourite object of geographical speculation. The third and last was to endeavour to find a passage from the Pacific into the Atlantic Ocean. These objects were praiseworthy: yet they were not the highest aims of the truest and purest ambition. To be a martyr for science was earthly glory: but to be a willing martyr for God is glory, honour, immortality, and eternal life.

The discoveries made by Captain Cook were barren of any results beyond those which are necessarily doomed to perish when the world and all that is in it shall be dissolved, until God was pleased in His own good time, and by the influence of His gracious Spirit operating on the minds of His servants, to make them show forth His praise. Then was made manifest His almighty power, His infinite wisdom, and His amazing love in the triumphs of the Gospel of the Lord Jesus Christ in the very strongholds of Satan and sin; conveying to His waiting people the assurance also that He had listened, and still listens to their aspirations and prayers.

HOUSE AT RAROTONGA, OCCUPIED BY THE MISSIONARY WILLIAMS.

EASTERN and WESTERN POLYNESIA, or the ISLANDS of the PACIFIC.

EASTERN POLYNESIA.*

Name of Group. Character. Number of Islands. Inhabitants.	Name of Islands. Native.	English.	Size and Character.	Christian or Heathen.	No. of Inhabitants.	Missionary Agencies.	Remarks.
SANDWICH ISLANDS. Volcanic. Lofty mountains. 10 islands. 130,000 inhabitants. 8 inhabited.	Hawaii Maui Ranai Moro Kai Oahu Tauai Nihau Tahurawe	Owhyhee Mowee Lanai	Miles. 97 lg 78 w 48 lg 29 w ·· 40 lg 7 w ·· 46 lg 23 w ·· ··	Christian	85,000 20,000 2,000 3,000 20,000 10,000 2,000	American Board of Foreign Missions. An English Bishop of Honolulu.	A Christian king, with a constitution. Many foreigners are settled in the group.
MARQUESAS. Volcanic. Mountainous. 50,000 inhabitants.	Noutahiva Ouahonga Ohtvaoa Taowatte	Washington Island	200 sq. miles.	Heathen and very barbarous	·· ·· ·· ··	The London Missionary Society attempted a Mission, but abandoned it.	Taken possession of by the French.
GEORGIAN ISLANDS, or WINDWARD. Volcanic. Mountainous.	Otaheiti Eimeo	Tahiti Moorea	600 sq. miles.	Christian	9,000	London Missionary Society. Their first efforts in the South Seas.	Taken possession of by the French in 1842. Under certain restrictions, the English missionary and also French Protestant missionaries are allowed to preach to the natives.
SOCIETY ISLANDS, or LEEWARD. 18,000 to 19,000 inhabitants.	Huaheine Ulitea Bolabola Tahaa	Huahine Raiatea Borabora Tahaa	·· ·· ·· ··	·· ·· ·· ··	1,700 1,100 800 700	Nearly all the inhabitants are Christian by profession.	English missionaries in the Society group are quite unfettered in their ministrations.
AUSTRAL GROUP.	Rimatara Oheteroa Toobouai Vivatoa	Rimatara Rurutu Tupuai Ravaval Rapa	··	Christian	4,000	Native missionaries from Tahiti and Rarotonga.	

* All in Eastern Polynesia are of the fair or brown race.

Eastern and Western Polynesia, or the Islands of the Pacific.

EASTERN POLYNESIA—continued.

Name of Group. Character. Number of Islands. Inhabitants.	Name of Islands. Native.	Name of Islands. English.	Size and Character.	Christian or Heathen.	No. of Inhabitants.	Missionary Agencies.	Remarks.
THE LOW ARCHIPELAGO, or PAUMOTU GROUP. Low coral islands, some with lagoons, 8,000 inhabitants, 200 islands nearly, many uninhabited.	Aana	Chain Island	Miles.	Christian partly	5,000	Native missionaries from Tahiti; fruits of the labours of the early missionaries of the London Missionary Society.	The inhabitants of four or five small islands round Aana have been converted partially, but the larger number of the inhabitants of the group are still heathens. These islands extend in a long line e st of the Society group.
	Manihi Aratica Mairsa Metia	... Dean's Island Aurora Island King George's	...	...	100 60 70 350		
	Kawahe Raraka Wytohee Otooho	Rurick Vincennes ... Bow Isle Searle Island Clermont de Tonnere	...	Christian	200 700 30 40 70 40 60		
GAMBIER ISLAND. High. Volcanic.					2,000		
PITCAIRN'S ISLAND. Volcanic. High. Fertile.			2¼ long 1 broad			Adams, mutineer of the *Bounty*.	Most of the inhabitants conveyed to Norfolk Island in 1855.
EASTER ISLAND. Volcanic. Lofty hills. Inhabitants very few.			40 in circumference		600		Contains some curious stone monuments.
HERVEY GROUP. Known also as COOK'S ISLANDS. Lofty, Volcanic. Small. 14,000 Inhabitants.	Rarotonga		30 in circumference Low coral lagoon	Christian	6,000	London Missionary Society.	
	Mangaia Aitutaki Atiu Mauke Mitiaro				8,000 2,500 940 240 130	Christianity introduced in 1821 by Davida and Tiera, members of the Church in Tahaa.	

Eastern and Western Polynesia.

PENRHYN ISLANDS. Large, low coral islands. They are numerous, but little known.	Manihiki Tongareva Rakaanga Fou Tokeran Puka Puka	Humphrey's Penrhyn's ... ... Danger Island	... ...	Christian Christian Christian Heathen Heathen Christian	463 390 403 500	Native teachers from Aitutaki. Many of the inhabitants have been converted by these means, but others remain heathens. There are eight resident teachers.	Four islands are occupied as sub-stations to the Rarotonga Mission.
SAVAGE ISLAND. Not 100 feet high.	Niué	Savage Island	40 in circumference	Christian	5,000	London Missionary Society.	
FRIENDLY ISLANDS, or TONGA ARCHIPELAGO. Some are high and volcanic, others low and of coral. Consist of three groups, viz.:— Tongataboo—south. Hapai—middle. Vavau—north. 40,000 inhabitants. 150 islands in all.	South group. Tongataboo Eoa Anamookn Middle group. Hapai Lifuka Tofua Kao Nomuca North group. Vavau	Amsterdam Middleburg Rotterdam	20 long 10 wide 9 lg 4 brd Volcano ... ... 36 in circumference	Christian Christian Christian Christian Christian	10,000	Wesleyan Missionary Society, began in 1822. The entire population has become Christian. The Mission is now self-supporting.	Tongataboo is the sacred Tonga. Trade and Native productions have greatly increased under the influences of Christianity.
SAMOA, or NAVIGATOR'S ISLANDS. Volcanic. Moderate height; beautiful scenery. They run from east to west in order given. Consist of eight islands and some islets. Area, 1,700 sq. miles. 40,000 inhabitants.	Tau Olosenga Ofu Tutuila Upolu Manono Apolima Savaii	Tau Olosenga Ofu Tutuila Upolu Manono Apolima Savaii	... 60 in circumference 130 in circumference 150 in circumference	Christian, and more advanced than any of the other groups	34,700	London Missionary Society, Rev. J. Williams landed here with native teachers in 1830. Christianity had been introduced into Tau by some natives of Savavai, one of the Austral group, 2,000 miles distant, who had been driven out of their course after wandering about for four months. The Wesleyan Missionary Society has also a few stations.	
BOWDITCH AND PHŒNIX ISLANDS. Low coral reefs. Population uncertain — not very great. Very fertile.	... Oatafu Fakaafo	Enderbury's Birnie's Duke of York Duke of Clarence Bowditch Swain's	3 lg 2½ w 8 lg 5 w 8 lg 4 w	Heathen		The inhabitant's appear well disposed; friendly to the officers of the U.S. exploring expedition.	

There are numerous other islands scattered throughout Eastern Polynesia, mostly of coral formation, and generally small, the inhabitants of which remain sunk in heathenism.

EASTERN and WESTERN POLYNESIA, or the ISLANDS of the PACIFIC.
WESTERN POLYNESIA.*

Name of Geogr. Character. Number of Islands. Inhabitants.	Name of Islands.		Size and Character.	Christian or Heathen.	No. of Inhabitants.	Missionary Agencies.	Remarks.
	Native.	English					
FIJI GROUP, known also as VITI. Volcanic, containing 225 islands and islets. Lofty mountains; rich and fertile, grand and beautiful scenery. From 200,000 to 250,000 inhabitants. The black race.	Viti Levu	Great Fiji	Miles. 90 long 50 wide	Christian	..	Wesleyan Missionary Society. Began in 1835. Have of late years made wonderful progress. Half the population are church attendants, and cannibalism has been extensively abandoned. Few professed heathens remain.	They were the very worst cannibals and the most horrible monsters in the Pacific. Upwards of 2000 native teachers are employed, besides many English missionaries.
	Vanua Levu	...	100 long 25 wide				
	Yalhata Vatuvara Vulgana Mothe Lakemba Mbau Matukee Taviuni						
	Totoya	Somosomo		..	..	No mission at first appeared more hopeless. None has been more especially blessed in the extent and rapidity of its progress.	Very lovely. The third in size, and lovely. More southern.
	Kandavu Moala Koro Ngau Mbungga			..	..		
ELLICE'S GROUP and surrounding Islands. All low coral reefs, but fertile.	Nukulaelae Vaitupu Funafuti Nukufetau Nui Otafu Akaafo Mikanono		..	Christian	..	Visited by United States' exploring expedition. Inhabitants seemed well disposed, and since by missionaries of the London Missionary Society.	
KINGSMILL GROUP. 15 Islands, on either side Equator. Coral formation, with a fertile black soil. 60,000 population.	Morakl	Matthew's	..	Heathen	10,000	Visited by United States' expedition. The inhabitants of this island are fairer, better-looking, and less barbarous. They have had no wars for 100 years.	The inhabitants of all the Islands, with the exception of Maktu, are savage, treacherous, and cannibals.
	Maktu and Taritari	Pitt's	6 long 1 wide	..	..		
	Apia	Charlotte's	16 lg 1 w				
	Tarawa	Knox's	20 long				

* The natives throughout Western Polynesia are generally black or very dark.

Eastern and Western Polynesia.

There are several other islands belonging to the group.	Maiana Apamama Kuria Nanouki	Hall's Hopher's Woodle's Henderville's		United population, 28,000		A king governs these 3 islands. Kirby, an Irishman, found living on Kuria. There are many towns thickly peopled. One of the crew murdered. The Americans fired on the people, killed many, and burnt the town.
	Nanouti	Sydenham				
	Taputeonea	Drummond's				
	Peru	Francis Island				

The following Islands are visited by the vessel of the Melanesian Mission, from New Zealand, and nearly two hundred natives from them are under instruction at the Missionary College, at Auckland, New Zealand, to fit them for becoming teachers to their brethren.

NORFOLK ISLAND. Very fertile and beautiful.	Norfolk			Christian		Now peopled by the former inhabitants of Pitcairn's Island.
SUNDAY ISLAND.						The figures below show the number of scholars from each island at the Auckland College belonging to the Melanesian Mission.
NEW CALEDONIA. Very fertile. Negro race.	New Caledonia		300 long 80 broad	Heathen	Mission attempted. Missionaries driven away.	Now occupied by the French, several Romish priests being employed. 1 scholar.
ISLE OF PINES.	Korie	Isle of Pines	40 in circumference	Heathen	Mission attempted. Missionaries murdered.	
LOYALTY ISLANDS. Mission commenced in 1841.	Nengone	Maré	60 in circumference	More than half Christian.	London Missionary Society.	6,000
	Toka			Christian	ditto.	
	Lifu	Lifu	80 in circumference	Christian	ditto.	
	Uea	Uea		Heathen	ditto.	
NEW HEBRIDES. Consists of 6 islands. Teachers landed in 1839.	Aneiteum			Mostly Christian.	Presbyterian Missions.	1 scholar.
	Taua		90 in circumference	Christian	Presbyterian Mission; Native Teachers from Samoa.	
	Fotuna			Many Christian.	Native Missionaries.	2 scholars.
	Nina					

EASTERN and WESTERN POLYNESIA, or the ISLANDS of the PACIFIC.
WESTERN POLYNESIA—*continued*.

NAME OF GROUP. Character. Number of Islands. Inhabitants.	NAME OF ISLANDS.		Size and Character.	Christian or Heathen.	No. of Inhabitants.	Missionary Agencies.	Remarks.
	Native.	English.					
NEW HEBRIDES—*continued*.	Erromanga	...	Miles, 100 in circumference.	Part Christian.	...	Presbyterian Mission and native teachers, supplied by London Missionary Society.	5 scholars. The Rev. J. Williams and Mr. Harris were here murdered.
	Faté	Sandwich Isle	...	A few Christian.	...	Missions commenced by London Missionary Society, but missionaries murdered.	1 scholar.
NORTHERN NEW HEBRIDES.	Mau Sakelaia Nguna Mataso Makura	Hinchinbroke Montague Two Hills	...	...	...	Now under charge of the Melanesian Mission. The ship visits once every year and places or takes off native teachers.	
	Mai Tasiko or Apee Lupirvi Paama or Paum Malicolo or Sesok Ambrym	Three Hills.	...	...	...	In nearly all, natives with some knowledge of Christianity, if not advanced Christians, are to be found, and soon native teachers instructed in New Zealand will be placed on each.	10 scholars.
	Opa Maiwo	Whitsuntide Leper's Island Aurora Espirito Santo	...	...	...		2 scholars.
SHEPHERD'S ISLES. Consist of 7 Islands, north of Faté.			...	...	...	...	1 scholar.
BANKES' ISLANDS. Consist of 18 Islands, north of Espirito Santo.	Gaua Vanua Lavu Vahia Ureparapara Vani Koro	Santa Maria Great Bank Isle Saddle Bligh Perouse Island Torres Island	...	...	...	...	9 scholars. 6 scholars. 1 scholar.

Eastern and Western Polynesia.

SANTA CRUZ ARCHIPELAGO. Consists of 10 Islands.	Minanga Bakarimo Icli Someni Nideni Tenacula Analogo Nupani	Swallow Isle Santa Cruz Volcano	..	Mostly Heathen.
SOLOMON ISLANDS. Consist of 18 Islands.	Ourl Oaraha Bauro Alaua Ugi Bio Gera Masu Mara	Santa Catalina Santa Anna St. Christovel Contrarieté Gulf Islands Guadacianas Malautu	.. ..	Occupied by a few Wesleyan native teachers. 19 scholars, 3 scholars. 22 scholars. 7 scholars.
STEWART'S ISLANDS. 4 small Islands.	Sikaiana Mongava Nongiki	Stewart's or Hogan's Isle. Kennell Belloua	..	Shore visited by the Bishop of New Zealand. Dutch claim authority on S.W. shores. A black race, superior to Aborigines of Australia.
PAPUA, or NEW GUINEA.	..	..	400 wide	Heathen
		No attempts have been made to carry the Gospel to any of these islands.		
NEW BRITAIN.	..	..	..	Heathen
NEW IRELAND.	..	..	..	Heathen
CAROLINE GROUP OF ISLANDS.	Foderby's Gilbert Pelew Isles Radack Ralick	.. ..	.. ..	Heathen Heathen Heathen Heathen Heathen
LOUISIADE ARCHIPELAGO. 80 Islands in all. Scantily inhabited.	..	..	..	Heathen

EASTERN and WESTERN POLYNESIA, or the ISLANDS of the PACIFIC.
WESTERN POLYNESIA—continued.

Name of Group. Character. Number of Islands. Inhabitants.	Name of Islands.		Size and Character.	Christian or Heathen.	No. of Inhabitants.	Missionary Agencies.	Remarks.
	Native.	English.					
AWRU, or AROO ISLANDS. A large group, belonging to the Dutch. The natives are called Araperas.	…	…	…	Heathen			
LADRONE, or MARIANNE ISLANDS. Belong to Spain. Almost depopulated. Numerous small islands. Volcanic. Very fertile.	Guahan Rota Tinian Saypan						
BONIN ISLES. Belong to England. Well timbered.	Peel Island		…	Christian nominally.	…	Means of instruction unknown.	Valuable as a coaling station.
VOLCANO ISLANDS. To the south of the Bonin.							
NEW ZEALAND. Consists of three islands.	Many of the natives have been brought to a knowledge of Christianity, chiefly through the agency of Church Missionary Society and Wesleyan Mission. Here native missionaries are being instructed under the care of the Bishop of Melanesia, and hence they are sent forth to the numberless islands of Western Polynesia. Some, since the war began, have returned to heathenism.						
THE AUCKLAND ISLANDS.	Under the New Zealand government. Used as a station for whalers. No natives found on them.						
THE CHATHAM ISLANDS.	Dependencies of New Zealand. The native race was nearly exterminated by the New Zealanders.						

LONDON: PRINTED BY WILLIAM CLOWES AND SONS, STAMFORD STREET AND CHARING CROSS.

www.ingramcontent.com/pod-product-compliance
Lightning Source LLC
Chambersburg PA
CBHW032355230426
43672CB00007B/714